**FROM ABDULLAH I
TO ABDULLAH II**

Copyrights Reserved
2017

THE HASHEMITE KINGDOM OF JORDAN

FROM ABDULLAH I TO ABDULLAH II

By
Mohamed Mahmoud Al-Tawara

THE HASHEMITE KINGDOM OF JORDAN
FROM ABDULLAH I TO ABDULLAH II

THE HASHEMITE KINGDOM OF JORDAN
FROM ABDULLAH I TO ABDULLAH II

His Royal Majesty, The Venerable King Abdullah II Bin Al Hussein

THE HASHEMITE KINGDOM OF JORDAN
FROM ABDULLAH I TO ABDULLAH II

THE HASHEMITE KINGDOM OF JORDAN
FROM ABDULLAH I TO ABDULLAH II

**His Royal Highness The Venerable Crown Prince
Al Hussein Bin Abdullah II**

THE HASHEMITE KINGDOM OF JORDAN
FROM ABDULLAH I TO ABDULLAH II

In the name of Allah, The All-Merciful, The Ever-Merciful

DEDICATION

To the head of the virtuous Aal al-Bayt
(People of the Prophet's Household)
MY LORD HIS HASHEMITE MAJESTY
KING ABDULLAH II BIN AL HUSSEIN
The King of hearts
The staunch supporter of innovation
The source of happiness for souls and minds
Looking forward to elevation

After greetings,

Our modest effort is shrinking in comparison with your endless tender and your rational deeds. It is an expression of my thanks to your Majesty, the king who works day and night and sets his sights to the interest of the country and the sublimity of the Jordanian man.

My few lines look incapable of describing the virtues of the blessed Aal al-Bayt (People of the Prophet's Household), who are destined to be the cresset which lightens the horizons of darkness of our nation and the entire humanity, and identify people with the runways of sublimity, sovereignty and achievement.

My master and lord

I have been inspired by your great feats, confident vision, enlightened thought, distinctive personality, strong will and honorable achievements.

My book is merely a whit of your love which resides in

souls and guides those who seek hope, joy and liveliness.

Thank you very much sir! Thank you for what you have been doing to exalt Jordan and boost it as a free country thanks to its human element, its granting and its ability to innovate and contribute in the entire human civilization.

May Allah bless and perpetuate your life. May Allah sustain your efforts on the righteous path and help you to fulfill this noble human Mustafawy mission. He who does not thank people, does not thank Allah.

«Allah intends only to remove from you the impurity [of sin], O people of the [Prophet's] household, and to purify you with [extensive] purification.»

DEDICATION

I dedicate this modest work to the reason of my coming to life, my dear father, who taught me patience and success and gave me everything. It is also dedicated to my dear mother who instilled in me the true meaning of homeland which grows within our hearts.

The dedication is extended to my life-long companion, my wife Um Muhannad, who bestows me in every look with a pleasure-giving face with its beautiful smile that radiates love, tenderness, kindness and faith. She is the person who endured the life conditions with me and helped me overcome all the difficulties in my way. She made God›s satisfaction her wish, and building her family is her ultimate and consistent goal in life.

To my soul mates, my sons Muhannad and Muayyad, may Allah bless them with good health, as well as my daughter Madlin, may Allah grant her success, my brother «Jamal» and my dear sisters.

To everyone who taught me something that enlightens my path. To my relatives, the people of Shobak, and my dear kindred Al-Tawara. To my professors and my colleagues in the embassy.

To all these, I dedicate the letters of homeland that I weaved from the depths of my heart, pray for Allah to grant it with success and approval.

- **Mohamed Mahmoud Al-Tawara**

JORDAN: WISE LEADERSHIP AND ENLIGHTENED PEOPLE

INTRODUCTION

The historical Jordanian gain, the cultural heritage and the notable development witnessed by our country are a real model for generations and a source of boasting for the Jordanian citizens while they read through the bright pages in which the Jordanian awareness was one of the crucial elements of maximizing efforts and recognizing achievements.

Providing a fertile soil for this national achievement in interrelated areas honestly attracts the young people›s attention to what their ancestors have established and laid its foundations over the phases of political development that Jordan successfully passed. Despite the difficult challenges and extremely hard conditions, God enabled Jordan to overcome them, thanks to its wise Hashemite Leadership that served as a source of convergence and justice for people who were totally convinced that the mission of the Hashemites is one of good, construction, development, and peace for all humanity.

Hence, I highly appreciate the efforts exerted by the cultured well-read researcher Mr. Muhammad Mahmoud Al-Tawara while he documents the journey of construction and achievement in a book that is worthy to be possessed by all families; to be a song on the lips of school and university students; and a chant for our good kin in their fields, factories, offices and all areas of serving this lofty country.

Documentation is the starting point in further research and a true nucleus for specialized studies. So, I see this book as a reliable reference and an important contribution in the broader journey, the journey of immortal nation. God bestowed our country with a political, legal and legislative environment that qualify it to study the success stories and benefit from our past for a bright future that is full of success where we will be just like one body. When one of the limbs suffers, the whole body responds to it with wakefulness and fever. This makes the Jordanian achievement and the confidence in it a starting point for discussing various phenomena through a comparison between the past and the current conditions that the wise Hashemite Leadership paid attention to and took care of in the form of legislations, laws and realistic accompaniment in which the people and the leader were one hand in building the glory of Jordan, assure its prosperity and protect it from all the turmoil that take place in the surrounding area, so that our country can be an oasis of safety and security and an example of the freedom of expression that unleashes imagination towards worlds of creativity that contribute to the benefit of Jordan, the successor of the Great Arab Revolt and its true mission that is commemorated after one hundred years in the sky of the Arab Nation in order to make a glory, identity and a true initiative for Arabs in building their modern Renaissance model.

From time to time, the Jordanian citizen, whatever his position, needs to read through the book of home, benefit from the leaders› wisdom and be armed with patriotism and belonging to protect and defend this authentic home. Thus, the book written by the dear friend, Al-Tawara, opens a room for all to be acquainted with exciting details while they are reading the chapters of the success story since the foundation of the emirate till now. It is important to study the details of this period and explore this huge legacy.

He who reads through this book will find honest and documented information about national unity from the era of the Great Grandfather and founder of modern Jordan His Majesty King Abdullah I bin Al Hussein , followed by King Talal, the constitution-maker, and His

Majesty the Constructor King Al Hussein bin Talal, God bless their souls. The final stage is the efforts of His Majesty the Supportive King Abdullah II bin Al Hussein who works day and night so that the bright Jordanian flag can continue to be a source of inspiration for countries and peoples in building and construction.

The readers of this book will find patriotic concepts that represent a source of national commemoration while recounting the glamorous success story that the Hashemites have achieved since the stage of foundation and independence. This is accompanied with an explanation of the details of the Jordanian policy, the parliamentary life and political parties of Jordan in addition to the external Jordanian relations, society factions, the Jordanian economy and its tributaries, media, press, the conscious and smart Jordanian treatment with what is called «the Arab Spring» represented in the comprehensive insight of His Majesty King Abdullah II bin Al Hussein in understanding the new inputs, and continuing the reformist effort, building the Jordanian mind and opening its horizons, interest in the creative powers of young people whom he have called, in the pre-Arab Spring period, Change Knights.

It is a good biography and rich vocabulary compiled by Mr. Al-Tawara, who has been brought up on the Jordanian success story that has inspired him in his success through his work in our embassy in London and Washington. He was, as everybody knows, an amiable and a really cultivated person carrying the Message of Amman which has been deeply-rooted in his mind and sentiment and translated into real deeds in all the countries he served in.

If I am to speak about the legislative parliamentary development in Jordan, I can say that it is a long and honorable journey that started with the Basic Law of the Emirate of East Jordan in the late twenties of the last century till 2016. This began with the election of the first legislative council, followed by the Parliament of Jordan (Bicameral National Assembly) with its two chambers: the Senate and the Chamber of Deputies. This is followed by the new era of democratic life in 1989 and the subsequent councils that brought development, transparency and achievement; the tributes that have always been dreamt of by His Majesty, May Allah prolong his life, in order to boost Jordan and keep its stability.

To conclude, people should use this book, with its simple language, smart chapterization and coherent sequence, to expand their political, legal, parliamentary, economic and cultural terminology. Actually, it is a book that allows the reader to grasp information in a patriotic sense whose reliability is apparent in its bright pages enriched with the history of Jordan, the leadership wisdom and the Jordanians› awareness.

ENG. ATEF TARAWNEH
The Speaker of the of the Chamber of Deputies

ACKNOWLEDGEMENTS

I MAY BE GRATEFUL TO ALLAH THE ALL-SUBLIME, THE ALL-POWERFUL WHO GRANTED ME WITH THE BLESSING OF REASON AND RELIGION.

In this regard, it is my pleasure to extend my sincere thanks and appreciation to HE.Mr. Fayez Altarawneh, Chief of the Royal Hashemite Court, His Excellency Mr. Amer Al-Fayez, Chief of the Royal Protocol, and all the employees of the Royal Court of the Majestic King for their good efforts that assured for everyone that the Royal Hashemite Court is truly the house of all Jordanians, the habitat for the liberal and the honorable, support of the weak and the relief for the poor, the homeless and the needy over the past decades and years. It still defends the values of truth, justice, freedom and human rights, and wipes the tears in the eyes of the sad, the orphan, the homeless and the destitute.

I would also like to thank His Excellency Brother Nasser Judeh, the Deputy Prime Minister, the Minister of Foreign Affairs and Emigrants and the artful politician, who takes over the accomplishment of His Majesty King Abdullah's political and diplomatic visions in the international forums. I also extend my thanks to my colleagues in our embassies in London and Washington for their support and assistance especially Her Excellency the Venerable Dr. Alia Bouran who represented Jordan politically and diplomatically in many important countries of the world, His Excellency Prof. Dr. Albert Boutros who combined science with politics as well as His Excellency Mr. Fouad Ayoub, who was close to Al Hussein, May Allah rest his soul in peace, and the current Ambassador of the Hashemite Kingdom of Jordan in London His Excellency Mr. Mazen Kemal Al-Homoud who works day and night to serve the cherished homeland ably and efficiently, in addition to all the brothers and sisters, either diplomats or administrative, with whom I have had the honor to work in the Jordanian embassies.

As an acknowledgement of the favor, I express my thanks and gratitude to the faithful people who exerted a great effort to help me from the beginning of preparation to write this book, each in his/ her own way, especially the educationalist and media man Mr. Muhammad Rafea Khidr Al-Beshtawy. I would also like to thank the journalist in Al-Rai Newspaper Mr. Ibrahim Al-Sawaeer who proofread this book and reviewed it linguistically as well as the creative Lady Kifah Fadel Al-Shebib, who provided me with this excellent design of this book. I hope that this book achieve the ends and goals for which I spent days and hours so that this book can be worthy of its content and embrace the history of our beloved Kingdom from the time of the foundation till the present day.

I cannot forget to thank everyone who supported and sustained me in the days of work which preceded the issuance of this book.

- **THE AUTHOR**

PREFACE

This book is written in commemoration of the Jordanian political and economic achievement and the united society that is mutually reinforcing intimacy and constructive cooperative work. To collect the material of this book, I have cooperated with many people, each according to his specialty. This required a big deal of information. It took me a long time and uninterrupted effort to obtain the accurate information for which I have spent many months searching for my sources. My sources varied between my long experiences in public work, reading what has been written and published in all the scientific references inside and outside the country, and sometimes the translation of some global references and texts which exist in libraries and contain trusted information about the kingdom, people, history and civilization of Jordan.

As a habit of our good people, they have an inherit welcome to those who ask for information and search for the history, heritage and the gold-embellished anecdotes of our home. They gave me the needed information and provided me with a plentiful supply that helped me to go through this book with its varied chapters and vocabulary in order to put it between the hands of the dear reader so that they can be acquainted with the biography of a unique Hashemite leader and the journey of a dignified Jordanian homeland.

This book about the biography of the Hashemite kings, our leaders, especially His Majesty King Abdullah II bin Al Hussein , and about our homeland is but a modest effort in a life full of tender for a national, Arab, Islamic and global character that is rare in today's world. Such a book is not enough for a figure like my Master His Majesty King Abdullah II bin Al Hussein . No author can gather all the dimensions of this figure, and no eloquent person, whatever his eloquence and figurative language is, can write down and record his vision and achievements.

This book is intended to highlight this lofty human figure of our beloved Kingdom. I hope that I have been granted success in it, and reimbursed a historical debt in my neck and the neck of every Jordanian citizen loyal to a beloved homeland and a great man who managed, with the strength of his faith and the purity of his soul, to open new paths in the history of the nation, the Arabs and the world, and won the respect of the world and its leaders by virtue of his honesty and situations, and establish, thanks to his purity and deep insight, a set of sublime principles that call for dialogue and peaceful coexistence between peoples.

I also hoped that I have been granted success in the chapterization of this book based on my practical vision that reflects my personal vision, knowledge and experience derived from my previous jobs as an employee in the Jordanian Ministry of Interior, chair of the Jordanian Embassy Office in Washington and London and Director of Protocol and Ceremony.

All these positions gave me the chance to meet His Majesty King Abdullah II bin Al Hussein and the members of the Hashemite Royal Family in addition to the high Jordanian officials during their visits to the United States of America and the United Kingdom. This gave me an unique chance to deal with all of them closely, especially the human situations of His Majesty King Abdullah II bin Al Hussein through his words, attitudes, views, talks and his scientific journey that I read and searched for: beginning with his service in the Armed Forces, being the crown prince and finally the king of our cherished kingdom.

Writing about King Abdullah II bin Al Hussein, may Allah protect him, is writing about a nation embodied in one person and a world represented in one humane leader whose actions speak of his words, a leader who feels as a citizen and the homeland at the same time. He is concerned with the sublimity of his people in the face of global challenges and the consolidation of the process of comprehensive development and construction and the reformist efforts, both on the internal and external level. It is His Majesty My master and lord whom we all love. History will stand up for him as an acknowledgement, loyalty and recognition of all this giving.

INTRODUCTION

Historical writing is very important in the course of countries development and progress, because a nation with no history is a nation with no origin. Also, a country with no past can never be a country of a future.

The definition of history differs according to cultures, knowledge and levels. The definition of Arabs may be different from that of all other nations, and the contemporary definition may differ from the one of ancestors.

When we come to the definition of history, we can say that it is related to time. It means the clarification of something related to the past. It may be the past of an individual, institution, a party or a kingdom.

So, my dear readers want to know the past of one of hadith narrators, by studying his biography and news based on his masters and followers. In other words, you are studying his history. On this basis, the books of hadith narrators were written, such as the history of Al-Imam Al-Bukhari and the books of narrators and renowned figures.

You may be talking about a nation or a kingdom. Here, the definition of history is wider and deeper such as the kingdom of Persians and Romans or the history of a well-known Islamic kingdom.

However, history may be more comprehensive, especially when it is about a certain period of time such as the Medieval history. Here, it is not a discussion of a certain kingdom; it is rather a discussion of a certain era.

Based on the above, we can say that history comprises two types: public and private. Public history is represented in the researcher's induction of a certain kingdom's news in order to extract public concepts and overall rules. Private history is a narration and description of previous news of peace and war, for example. Here, there is no room for thought or opinion.

The importance of history for nations and peoples lies in the manuscripts, legacies and folk stories that the ancestors have kept in order to play an essential role in the formation of the young generations› sentiment in order to follow on the elderly path.

History held a great position for Muslims; it has been mentioned in some verses of the holy Quran. Allah, the Exalted, said «There was certainly in their stories a lesson for those of understanding». Allah also said «Have they not traveled through the land and observed how the end of those who were before them was?» On this basis, we know the importance of studying and writing history as well as its importance in people's knowledge of their past and building their future. This book searches in the history of the Hashemite Kingdom of Jordan, its kings and citizens with the aim of identifying and enlightening the Jordanian citizen, especially young people, with the history of their country in addition to instilling pride and hope in their hearts concurrently with some Arab peoples overlooking and forgetfulness of their history because of the hard circumstances they are living.

I will also try to give a true image of the history and present of the

Hashemite Kingdom of Jordan through all the monarchs who came in power and the methods of the transition of power. I will benefit from the culture of this beautiful country. So, it can be said that this book will try to attract more cultured and interested people inside and outside Jordan to know about the ancient and modern history of Jordan.

This work can be of a very great benefit for students and scholars in the documentation of their researches, studies and theses. So, I will exert my best effort to make this work one of the references of the history and academic research about Hashemite Kingdom of Jordan. I also dedicate a section of this book for the Jordanian economy and the kingdom's public policy as well as other topics about the kingdom and the citizens.

The reader of this book may ask about the word «Jordan», what is its origin?

Actually, many researchers assure that the word «Jordan» is related to the sacred river, Jordan (or Sharia) River which springs from Jabal El-Sheikh, South Lebanon and flows into Lake Tiberias, Sea of Galilee, which is the capital of Jordanian soldiers. After the Lake, the river receives water from further tributaries including Yarmouk River and Jalud River, as well as many valleys. The name «Jordan» results from the meeting of Jur River and Dan River. So, the name becomes «Jordan» or «yordan» in some languages. It is a linguistically and geographically correct naming. With the passage of time, it became (as transliterated from Arabic: Urdan or Urdun). The Arabs gave it its current name «Jordan» (Al-Urdun, as transliterated from Arabic).

Writing about a country like Jordan is not a comfy task. Its history is as great and long as the civilizations, cultures, kingdoms and the bodies that lived in Jordan, as well as all the events that took place in Jordan since the dawn of history till the modern state founded by the Hashemites, which represents a model and a symbol of civilization and freedom, independence and humanity in today's world.

In this context, it is noteworthy to say that Jordan has never been a desolate place. On the contrary, it has always been over-populated thanks to the succession of many civilizations and the stability of many emigrants in it. The country's varied climate and its strategic location, that links the continents of the Ancient World, and acts as a channel for trade and human travel between the different countries of the Middle East, helped to establish civilized and prosperous communities in all fields.

Consequently, the Hashemite Kingdom of Jordan witnessed the rise of many kingdoms; the most notable of them are the Kingdom of Moab led by King Yusha and the Nabataean Kingdom that held a wide-spread reputation thanks to its control over the area extending from Bosra Sham to Mada'in Saleh. Moreover, the present-day North of Jordan was the main pillar in the Decapolis (the League of the Ten Greek Cities).

Dear Guest Reader:

As soon as you enter the Hashemite Kingdom of Jordan, you feel the civilizations and kingdoms that lived in this country in light of the mountains and archaeological sites that you can watch in all the corners of Jordan. From the first glance, these sites and mountains speak of their deep-rooted history.

In addition, Jordan also witnessed a period of the Roman rule which gave Jordan a distinctive dimension in the region's civilization as a part of the strong Roman Empire.

With the spread of Islam, the special strategic location of Jordan, as the gate of sham, gave it a special importance. The Battles of Yarmouk, Mu›tah and Ofra which took place on the Jordanian land are from the most important features of Islamic rule in Jordan, besides some crucial and decisive events such as the arbitration between the supporters of Ali bin Abi Talib And Muawiya bin Abi Sufyan, May Allah be pleased with them, which took place in Tall al-Ash›ari, near the Jordanian Ma›an.

Jordan had also played an important role in the Umayyad and Abbasid Eras. This role was represented in the effective participation of Jordan in the Crusades to support Islam and the Muslims as the link between Egypt and Sham. In Jordan, there are shrines of an array of the famous Muslim leaders such as Abu Ubaidah Ibn Al-Jarrah (Custodian of Ummah), Sharhabil Bin Hassneh, Dhiraar Bin Al-Azwar, Jaafar Bin Abi Talib and other companions of the Prophet, peace be upon him. This is a big pride for Jordan because it is an archaeological and historical evidence of the effective participation of Jordan in a very important period of the Islamic rule.

On the other hand, Jordan played a big role in the development of the economy of the Ottoman reign; it was a passage of their convoys and a necessary and indispensible area for supporting the existence of the Ottoman state. That is why there are many Ottoman monuments in Jordan till the present day. the palaces, castles and monuments where you can wander to set back in history and live a glimpse of the Ottoman history in Jordan and have more knowledge of the important role of the Jordanian state at this time constitute clear evidence. .

In the early Twentieth Century and concurrently with the then growing Arab Nationalism, the people and leadership of Jordan played an undeniable role. The squares and places of Jordan witnessed huge liberation revolts such as the Karak Revolt, Bani Hamida Revolt, AlKaraan Revolt in Ofra as well as the hostile attitude of Arab nationalism towards pan-turanism.

April 11th, 1921 was a very important date for Jordanians. It witnessed the establishment of the first Jordanian government presided by Rashid Tali'a. In this concern, researchers say that the

Jordanian government was more Arab than Jordanian. This is due to the Arab nationalist policies and approaches that Emir Abdullah believed in, as the first King of Jordan. He crowned his efforts by the establishment of the Jordanian army which was called «the Arab army» at that time.

While speaking about the history of Jordan, we cannot forget the struggle and fight of Jordanians against occupation and their independence on May 25th, 1946. This was the time when the Hashemite Kingdom of Jordan was being established by Emir Abdullah I, who was the first king of Jordan. Then, Jordan began to step into the constitutional and parliamentary life.

Notably, Jordan provided many sacrifices for the Palestinian case represented in his participation in the 1948 War in spite of its modest capabilities then. It contributed to maintain Jerusalem and the West Bank. The Jordanian Arab Army recorded the best epic and heroic deeds in the history of Arab armies. Furthermore, Jordan received thousands of Palestinian refugees as a support of the Palestinian case.

In the context of Jordan›s support of Palestine, the Jordanian-Palestinian Unity was established to help in the confrontation to the Israeli aggression. This led to the assassination of King Abdullah I. He was succeeded by his son, King Tala, who passed away after a short time because of illness. He was followed by the constructor King Al Hussein who could confront many grave events that took place in his reign, and helped Jordan to pass them peacefully. None can deny Jordan's heroic support of Egypt to face The Tripartite Aggression against Egypt, and many other brave decisions of King Al Hussein . From his last decisions was the objection to the «War of Aggression against Iraq» following the Iraqi invasion of Kuwait in 1990.

In addition, Jordan participated in defending the Palestinians in the 1967 War and the Six-Day War. Furthermore, the Arab Jordanian army showed a great courage in the immortal Battle of Karameh against the Israeli aggression in 1968 when it invaded Eastern Highlands. In 1973, the Jordanian role was not restricted to wars and military operations; it went further to include crucial and effective decisions on all levels as a contribution to solve many crucial issues that concern Jordan and Arab states. Jordan was one of the first countries to recognize the PLO (Palestine Liberation Organization) as the only legitimate representative of the Palestinian people in the Rabat Arab Summit Conference in 1974.

In the post-eighties years, Jordan continued his support of the Arab issues, especially the Palestinian issue in light of the Arab weakness that prevailed in that period. It embraced two important Arab summits: the first was in 1980 which was the nucleus of the Joint Arab Economic Action, and the second was in 1987 which stressed the necessity of the Arab strap reunion.

The nineties of the last century witnessed great contributions from the Kingdom, especially in the Palestinian-Israeli negotiations. This was represented in Madrid Conference 1991, in which the Palestinian delegation entered within the Jordanian delegation. This period also witnessed the illness of King Al Hussein and his decease in 1999. His son His Majesty King Abdullah II succeeded him and was a contemporary of The Second Palestinian Intifada in 2000, and exerted every possible effort to quell sedition and cool things down.

Jordan hosted the 13th Ordinary Session of the League of Arab States (Amman, Jordan, March 27th, 2001) as a trial to strengthen, mobilize and reunite the Arab strap as His Majesty made it clear in his speech to the Opening Session « Jordan holds nothing dearer than its pride in belonging to the Arab Nation.

It cherishes its commitment to serve Arab causes and to mobilize its resources towards building a future that is suitable for the nation's history and contributions to humanity and world civilization.»

«It is time to turn that page and overcome our differences. It is time to open a new page in joint Arab action with open hearts and clear consciences. This new chapter should reflect our brotherhood, sacred bonds and common interests. Our nation is facing enormous challenges. We have to confront those challenges and meet the expectations and aspirations of our people. »

«Let this summit be the beginning of a new era in joint Arab action. Let it be a new starting ground towards solidarity and integration in all fields; political, economic or relating to national security. From this moment on, let our work be institutional and comprehensive in vision; let it not be reactive or emotionally driven that fades with the change of emotions and motifs.»

This is always the case of Jordan that incarnates its belonging to the Arab nation and its consistent concern about the political and economic integration between brothers. It took the responsibility laid on its shoulders to promote the standard of the Arab countries, raise the status of our Arab and Islamic nation and restore its prestige in the international forums, and improve the economic and living standard of the Arab citizen who holds a great priority among Jordan›s interests.

This is always Jordan's attitude in terms of the achievement of a comprehensive vision to promote our Arab nation to its natural position between nations. So, it is consistently interested in its superiority in the near future, God Willing.

Currently, Jordan is suffering from some economic problems, almost like all Arab countries. The state is trying to recover from these problems by all the possible means which include adjustment of government expenditure, rescheduling of external debt, attracting investment and obtaining grants and financial aids.

This was an introduction and a historical tour in the history of Jordan on its basis. I tried to build the ideas that helped me write and edit this book.

Finally, I pray to Allah to grant the Hashemite Kingdom of Jordan success with its wise leadership. I also hope it rises along with this nation to the highest ranks between nations. Perhaps, it can achieve what other countries cannot.

I would also like to thank everyone who advised, guided and helped me in this work. I wish them good luck.

And the last of their call will be, «Praise to Allah, Lord of the worlds!»

- **Mohamed Mahmoud Al-Tawara**

JORDAN'S NATIONAL UNITY FROM KING ABDULLAH I, THE FOUNDER TO KING ABDULLAH II, THE REINFORCE

Jordanian citizens of all stripes recognize the national unity as a historical fact throughout the Jordanian history that teems with challenges and central situations nationally and Islamically since the foundation till the present day. National unity is still unarguable basis around which Jordanians gather together and aspire to a fixed goal. The crucible of national unity combines all the sects and spectrums and components of society which takes in various cultural, social and ethnic spectrums.

In all international occasions, the Jordanian citizens of all spectrums, officials, academicians, and intellectuals assure that the awareness of the Jordanian citizen and his avoidance of the suspicious calls to upset the national security signify that the efforts exerted by the governments of His Majesty King Abdullah II Bin Al Hussein to raise the citizen's standard of living have positive echoes represented in the opposition to sedition and all forms of anarchy.

They also refer to the cohesion between the Hashemite leadership and the Jordanian people which has been made clear in the awareness of Jordanians in the Arab Spring period and their opposition to the media campaigns calling for protests and demonstrations, sending a message to the whole world that reform and the development of society should be peaceful and gradual and that the open door policy has closed the door before troublemakers. The Jordanian citizen proved to be worthy of the responsibility and is not affected with troublemakers inside and outside the country. They also refer to the role of the clerics in clarifying the reality of things and explaining that claiming rights has its legal methods that are completely away from anarchy, especially when the doors of officials are open to receive the citizens demands. This led to the failure of these fishy calls which received no response and Jordan avoided the trouble and anarchy that prevailed in the neighboring countries.

The faithful Jordanian people proved that the strength of any people is represented in the level of its cohesion, being home-centered and national consensus on some basic concept such as all people are one front in building their society and the participation in building, defending and developing it; the cohesion and understanding with the rulers of the country making home the notable banner in our actions; and avoidance of all forms of classification, either geographical, ideological, tribal or intellectual.

Also, the Jordanian people proved his recognition and gratitude to the favor of the wise leadership through its opposition to the devastating calls. Home has many favors; we grow in it, benefit from its riches, eat from its soil, drink its water and breathe its air. Sharia imposes many rights towards home in respecting its Arab and Islamic culture and defending its land exactly as the Jordanians do true to the saying of Imam Ali bin Abi Talib «a people invaded is a people humiliated».

Invasion is not only the external conquest, it is also the internal conflict which results from the grudge and hatred to this nation and its citizens from our enemies who make trouble and arouse sedition which is tougher than murder and its victims are the sons of the nation who in order not to find security for himself, his properties and his honor. So, we have to live peacefully in this country with our rulers and form an impenetrable fortress against our vengeful and envious enemies. All Jordanians agreed that there is nothing that requires anarchy, absurdity and demonstration in streets, because the Kingdom enjoys many good tributes, security and justice that rarely exist in the region and the world. Everybody realizes the dangers of intervention in the internal affairs of countries. So, he who calls for our country's sedition and trouble is either an ignorant or a malicious person.

On the other hand, the Kingdom, with its leadership and people, is praised for its vision and prediction of the future. The naivety of troublemakers blinded them from realizing the volume of our society commemorations and our pleasure with our national occasions and special days which proved the benign relationship between the leadership and the people. Everybody is convinced that the Jordanian society, in all its corners, frustrates any suspicious attempt. Home is for all; whether an ordinary citizen or an employee, we are all involved in defending this society by our words and our actions and frustrate the vicious plots of our society enviers. The Jordanian citizen lives safely and peacefully. He is not worried about his property or honor. So, he cannot protest against his rulers, sell his home or follow the troublemakers. He should rather aspire to maintain his, his children's and his homeland's security. Security and stability are the most important things in life. If we neglect this aspect of our life and let things run out of our hands, this will complicate our lives and raise the status of trouble and stress.

All we need is a closer look on what is going on outside. Then, we will observe things clearly. Without unity and cohesion, there will be destruction and mess which can affect our brothers, sisters, our parents and our kin. Society is an interconnected association exactly as if it is one family.

Allah the Exalted says «obey Allah and obey the Messenger and those in authority among you». This is the doctrine of the sober-minded faithful Jordanian people which is cautious to troubles and seditions, and assures that sedition is the pathway to destruction and rationality is the righteous way. The state applies the open-door policy; the doors, from the door of His Majesty to the smallest official, are open for citizens. Security is an unapproachable red line, and everybody should realize that insecurity is a real disaster. Therefore, everyone should take the responsibility, abide by law and pay no attention to intruders. We are a different country that God bestowed with a Hashemite King, a descendant of the Prophet, peace be upon him.

The people›s support and lining up behind the king notably influences the political and economic stability of the country. It is also a positive indicator of the country's safety and security. The people's loyalty and belonging to their leaders and rulers is honest and comes from the bottom of their hearts in recognition of the efforts exerted to raise the standard of living and achieve their pride in all life aspects under the current conditions experienced by the international society.

The Jordanian people, with all its categories, realize, since the beginning of the Arab Spring, that the tendentious calls that swept some of the Arab World corners and aroused troubles and anarchy are peculiar to these countries and peoples for special and relevant reasons, which are not necessarily applicable to other countries and peoples. The faithful and intellectual citizens warn to respond to these calls, because of their disastrous effects on the peoples of these countries. This is not contrary to calling for reform and development. Most of Arab countries are developing and are in a dire need for overall development and proper political reforms that uproot tyranny and corruption. No one doubts the necessity for reform and development, but it should be gradual and in the proper ways void of chaos and seditions.

The people of our loyal Kingdom proved his rejection to these improper ways and the refusal of anarchy and seditions. There wasn›t any response to these tendentious calls, as a clear evidence of the Jordanian people›s awareness and refusal to these methods.

The citizens in all the regions and governorates of the country stress the importance of national unity as well as the cohesion and communication between the people and the leadership with all its levels. They also reject the disunion and dissipation of the citizens of the nation, and call for their unity. Officials always state that national unity is an authentic and a serious demand for all the loyal sons of this nation. It can be achieved through programs, especially the initiatives of His Majesty to reinforce the national dialogue between all the spectrums of society, and to confront those who disperse the sons of the nation.

This experience should be maintained by focusing on the partnership, unity and the Jordanian national identity and treating all the causes of dispersion. They see that the tendentious calls that erupted and soon died in their cradle are mainly sick calls for chaos which cannot be accepted by the Jordanian society. That is because our Kingdom is one of reform, freedom of expression and tolerance. Whatever happens in the surrounding countries, it will not affect its self-strength and the bond between its people and the leadership.

Clerics do not differentiate between belonging to this blessed country and belonging to its leaders and working with them as one arm to consolidate its unity, raise its position and maintain its security, stability and prosperity. Even Christian clerics assure that all the society components are one hand; because they are witnessing a peerless religious freedom in the Hashemite Kingdom. It is a secure and peaceful life that reassures peoples fears and shelters the weak. This is due to three reasons: it is the country of the Hashemits that God bestows with peace and security. The second reason is the Jordanian governments that implement the King›s visions and mobilize all their efforts to provide rest and stability for the citizen and the refugees who live on the Kingdom's land, and spread security through a highly aware and experienced security system that is run by highly experienced and professional people. The third reason is the cohesion between the spectrums of society. All people live in the country as one hand. They live in an atmosphere of love and cooperation to build their society glories united by one noble national goal and one destiny under the rule of His Majesty King Abdullah II Bin Al Hussein , may Allah protect him.

All Jordanians agreed that demonstrations do not coincide with the country›s principles, policies or constants.

They point out that the only way for claiming demands is the national dialogue which gives the leadership the opportunity to listen to the opinions and proposals. Jordanians considered the street protests in the street as a revolt against Sharia and law. They asked them to put patriotism and the country's interest above all.

How wonderful is this cohesion between the people and leadership in all corners of the dear nation!

How beautiful is the spirit of belonging and loyalty to home and its leader His Majesty King Abdullah II Bin Al Hussein who devoted all his effort and thought to the benefit of the citizen and providing him with good life!

Congratulations to the nation of pride, virtues, leading achievements and humanitarian initiatives!

We pray to God to protect the builder of our renaissance, our leader

His Majesty King Abdullah II Bin Al Hussein and grant him health and well-being. We also pray to Allah to perpetuate the blessing of security and stability; protect our country from the enemies of the nation and religion; and repeat our eids (Islamic celebrations), pleasures and national days with security and prosperity under the rational and wise Hashemite leadership.

THE HASHEMITE KINGDOM OF JORDAN

JORDAN:
A FASCINATING SUCCESS AND NOTABLE DEVELOPMENT
SINCE THE ESTABLISHMENT AND INDEPENDENCE TILL THE PRESENT DAY

JORDAN: A FASCINATING SUCCESS AND NOTABLE DEVELOPMENT SINCE THE ESTABLISHMENT AND INDEPENDENCE TILL THE PRESENT DAY

The development, modernity and growth that Jordan witnessed since the foundation and the subsequent years of the Kingdom's independence, despite the challenge related to its geographic nature, and the political, economic and human resources make this country the focus of attention and an example to be followed in the entire world.

Building, developing and modernizing the Jordanian state is a step that reflects the strength of this country that could combine modernity with the inherited traditions that distinguish the people as well as the leadership of this country such as tolerance, generosity, justice and commitment to all international norms and charters.

Jordan defeated all the challenges of various kinds, political, economic and security, by virtue of some integrated elements that shaped the modern Jordan.

Our Hashemite leadership's realization of the importance of Jordan's stubbornness to address challenges through establishing a democratic legitimacy was the only support that enabled it to surpass these challenges.

The stages of Jordan's development and progress, since the reign of His Majesty the late King Abdullah I Bin Al Hussein, the founder of the Hashemite Kingdom of Jordan, reflect an important period that remarkably and confidently continues till now. With the endeavors of Jordanians and the Hashemite leadership, Jordan surpassed the challenges that faced this journey.

The investigator of these stages finds crucial phases that take him from the foundation period to the stage of growth up to the stage of development and modernity.

- **The stage of foundation:**

The pages of history will always speak about His Majesty the late King Abdullah I Bin Al Hussein, the founder of the Hashemite Kingdom of Jordan, as a unique character that emerged along with the contemporary Arab world.

His Majesty the late King Abdullah I Bin Al Hussein was the guide of his grandson His Majesty the late King Al Hussein, may Allah bless his soul. His character was a mixture of authenticity and modernity. Also, in the journey of his life, he was generally modern and always looked forward.

This is shown in the adoption of the constitutional royal system in the subsequent years of the foundation of his country to be one of the leading Arab leaders to do so. This is also represented in his realistic experience and interaction with his people.

His Majesty the late King Abdullah I Bin Al Hussein , the founder, led the Arab forces under the Hashemite banner during the Great Arab Revolt. He was also inspired by his father's ideas with his brothers Ali, Faisal and Zaid. With the end of World War I, the Great Arab Revolt freed Damascus, Modern Jordan and most of the Arab Peninsula.

His Majesty King Faisal took the throne of Syria. After the Battle of Maysalun, the rhythm of things got faster, and King Abdullah headed to Jordan to establish the state. Then, King Faisal took the throne of Iraq.

His Majesty the late King Abdullah I established the Emirate of Transjordan on April, 1921 ,21 after the establishment of the first centralized governmental system in a society of Bedouin tribes. Through the three decades, the late King set his head to consolidate and establish the modern Jordan.

Armed with determination and forward-looking vision, he began to take steps to autonomy and independence by establishing a democratic legitimacy. In 1928, he promulgated the first constitution of Jordan, which provided for a parliament known as the Legislative Council, and elections were held for the first time in 1929.

Also, during these three decades, the King negotiated many treaties with Britain. The last of these treaties was called the Anglo-Transjordanian Treaty on March 22nd, 1946 which ended the British mandate over Transjordan which gained its full independence and its name officially changed into the Hashemite Kingdom of Jordan on May, 25th, 1946.

Gaining its full independence, Jordan maximized its role on both the Arab and international levels, besides attending conferences. The first of these conferences was the Anshas Summit on May 28th, 1946, only a few days following the independence. This enabled Jordan to intensify its role in serving the Palestinian case.

During the Arab-Israeli War, 1948, the Arab Legion effectively defended Jerusalem and other parts of Palestine. The Jordanian Army demonstrated fabulous courage and he was known for his professionalism, stability and courage against a superior power in the machinery and number.

The Arab Legion defeated the Jewish forces in Bab Al-Wad, Latrun and Jerusalem, and could maintain the East Jordan despite the severe Israeli attacks that tried to snatch it from the Jordanian Army, but it was of no avail. The war ended by Mid-July, 1948, and a number of armistice agreements were held between Arab parties and Israel in Rhodes Conference, under which the border lines between the East Jordan and Palestine were demarcated.

On July 20th, 1951, King Abdullah I headed to Jerusalem to attend Friday prayers in the company of his grandson, Prince Al Hussein, later to be King Al Hussein. He was shot at the steps of Al-Aqsa Mosque near the shrine of his father, Al Hussein, who paid his life for all Arabs.

King Al Hussein, the crown-prince then, was in the company of his grandfather. He received a bullet at his chest, but the bullet ricocheted off a medal on his chest. Thus, these moments were very crucial and decisive in his entire life; he realized the inevitability of death and the importance of his responsibility in the subsequent years.

In his autobiography book «Uneasy Lies the Head» written in English, King Al Hussein narrated that his grandfather told him in

Jerusalem, three days before that ominous day, «my son, I hope that you recognize that you are going to take over this responsibility one day. I wish that you exert your best effort to make sure that my efforts do not go with the wind. I look forward to you to continue to serve our people.»

The prince, later to be King Al Hussein warmly and seriously promised his grandfather that he would do all his best to achieve his mission, not aware that they had little time to spend together.

- **The modern constitution stage:**

His Majesty King Talal Bin Abdullah took power immediately after the martyrdom of his father His Majesty the late King Abdullah I in Jerusalem on July 20th, 1951.

But, he could not continue in office and abdicated in less than a year due to health reasons on August 11th, 1952. During his tenure, King Talal achieved a notable progress in the improvement of the relations between Jordan on one hand and Egypt and Saudi Arabia on the other hand.

He was also responsible for the development of a new modern constitution which made the government collectively and the ministers individually responsible before the parliament. It was ratified on January 1st, 1952.

- **The reconstruction stage:**

His Majesty the late King Al Hussein Bin Talal will remain in our memory and hearts as a leader who led his country through conflicts and disorders until Jordan became the oasis of peace, stability and justice in the Middle East.

Jordanians commemorate him with all love and appreciation as the source of inspiration for the climate of openness, tolerance and sympathy that Jordan enjoys. His Majesty the late King Al Hussein laid a prosperous heritage that paid off a promising history through the long years to come. He was one of the longest-serving leaders in international politics. He also held a great position among Muslims in all parts of the globe because he belonged to the 42nd generation of the descendants of the Prophet, peace be upon him.

King Al Hussein was born in Amman on November 14th, 1935, the eldest son of King Talal bin Abdullah and Princess Zein al-Sharaf bint Jamil. After completing his elementary education in Amman, he was educated at Victoria College in Alexandria, Egypt. He proceeded to Harrow School in England, and then pursued his military study at the Royal Military Academy Sandhurst in England.

On September 1st, 1951, King Talal, the eldest son of King Abdullah, came in power. He was soon succeeded by his eldest son, Al Hussein , who was proclaimed King of the Hashemite Kingdom of Jordan on August 11th 1952; he was under 18 lunar years old. So, a Regency Council was appointed until he came of age according to the constitutional eligibility requirement. He was enthroned on May 2nd 1953 according to the Jordan Constitution.

Early on, King Al Hussein concentrated on building an economic and industrial infrastructure that would improve the quality of life of Jordanians. During the 1960s, Jordan's main industries – including phosphate, potash and cement – were developed, and a network of highways was built throughout the kingdom.

Social indicators reflected King Al Hussein successes on the human area. While in 1950, water, sanitation and electricity were available to only %10 of Jordanians, today these reach %99 of the population. In 1960 only %33 of Jordanians were literate, while by 1996, this number had climbed to %85.5.

UNICEF statistics show that between 1981 and 1991, Jordan achieved the world's fastest annual rate of decline in infant mortality – from 70 deaths per 1000 births in 1981 to 37 per 1000 in 1991, a fall of over %47. King Al Hussein always believed that nothing was dearer for Jordan than the Jordanian people. During his reign, he encouraged all citizens, including the disabled, the orphans and the less fortunate citizens, to achieve more and more to help themselves and the country.

Throughout his -47year reign, King Al Hussein struggled to establish peace in the Middle East; he played a central role in the crystallization of UN Security Council Resolution 242 after the 1967 Arab-Israeli War. According to this resolution, Israel withdrew from the territories occupied after the 1967 War for the establishment of peace. This resolution acted as the backbone of the subsequent peace talks. He also played a prominent role in Madrid Peace Conference 1991; he helped the Palestinians to negotiate their future as a part of a joint Jordanian-Palestinian delegation.

The Israel-Jordan Treaty of Peace 1994 was a basic step in the achievement of a just and lasting peace in the Middle East.

King Al Hussein also sought to settle the conflicts between Arab countries. He exerted grave efforts during the 1991-1990 Gulf Crisis to guarantee that Iraq withdraw peacefully and Kuwait regain its sovereignty, and issued the White Paper indicating the truth of the rational attitude of the Jordanian leadership towards this crisis.

His efforts to achieve true Arab conciliation were the spark of mediation in Yemen Civil War. In most of his speeches His Majesty called for providing international humanitarian aid to mitigate the daily suffering of the Iraqi people.

His Majesty King Al Hussein commitment to democracy, civil freedoms and human rights made Jordan a model for the countries in the region. Internationally The Kingdom has always been recognized for its human rights policies in the Middle East concurrently with the latest reforms that opened the way in front of Jordan to resume its irreversible democratic journey.

King Al Hussein ordered the establishment of a Royal Commission representing all the spectrums of society and charged it with the task of drawing up a National Charter. Today, along with the constitution, this charter establishes general guidelines on the exercise of political pluralism and democratic institutionalization in the country.

In 1993 ,1989 and 1997, Jordan witnessed parliamentary elections which were internationally recognized to be peerless in the Middle East in terms of freedom, fairness and honesty.

Since its inception, Jordan performs its national role. Since its birth as a nation, it supported Syrians in their struggle against occupation and colonization.

The period (1946-1923) was eventful; the most notable of them is Britain›s warning to King Abdullah to invalidate the Ashair department that was incepted in the government, and Britain unconditionally imposed full control over financial affairs. After negotiations with the British, the King reached fair solutions that guaranteed Jordan›s sovereignty and high position.

- **The stage of development:**

On June 9th 1999, Jordan commemorated the ascension of His Majesty King Abdullah II Bin Al Hussein to the throne after the passing away of his father His Majesty the constructor King Al Hussein , may Allah bless his soul, after building the institutions of the country.

On February 7th 1999, His Majesty King Abdullah II Bin Al Hussein started his reign with the oath to uphold the constitution and to be faithful to the nation, the oath sworn by every Jordanian to be faithful to the King and the nation, to uphold the constitution and set his heart to achievement.

Early on, His Majesty began a new stage that is a comprehensive revolution in the method of work and administration and the involvement of all the society spectrums in the process of development. He made continuous initiatives calling everyone to be creative and outdo themselves for the sake of improving the quality of life. This came as a result of his recognition that global development does not stop or wait for any one, and Jordan has to cope with the time in order to indulge itself into the stage of the modern and global country with open thought, justice and knowledge in order to benefit from the change that has become a realistic will. He succeeded to consolidate the will of change that it became a national Jordanian action in all areas of development.

His Majesty King Abdullah II Bin Al Hussein saw that the new stage requires the openness to the world and introducing Jordan to it as well as upholding the deeply-rooted constants and values of the Islamic Arab Jordanian society with its firm Arab identity. His Majesty was thoroughly interested in the Jordanian citizen in the first place. The training, education and qualification of the Jordanian citizen were the axis of all development plans. His Majesty called for the investment in the Jordanian human resources and the qualification of the Jordanian citizen as the basis for the success of investment in its overall meaning. With the awareness and productivity of the citizen, development infiltrates to the economy, education, tourism, agriculture, and all areas of society.

His Majesty›s interest in the Jordanian citizen is represented in the attention to young people who represent %60 of Jordan›s population. Almost all His Majesty›s speeches address young people and assure the importance of their role in the development and construction of society. Moreover, His Majesty is keen to participate in their conferences and forums to speak with and listen to them. He also visits them in schools and universities and gives them the chance to take part in global meetings in the company of His Majesty. The third World Economic Forum Meeting at the Dead Sea witnessed a notable presence of the Jordanian youth through all its sessions.

In all international occasions, His Majesty asserts that« we must pay great attention to our youth, take care of them and activate their role in the process of development, making change and building the future according to a comprehensive and clear vision and working with the spirit of one team that belongs to and believes in his mission, vision and ability to reach achievements».

Jordan boosts its youth institutions that grow every day and expand their comprehensiveness to take in all young people in order to be suitable for the application of youth strategies and plans that aspire to merge them in the sustainable development.

«In Jordan, we think about future and the generation of youth and how to achieve their dreams. We aspire to beat the odds in their way and provide them with good education because this contributes to the reduction of poverty and unemployment and helps to support our initiative to develop Jordan and elevate the standard of living of our people».

Youth are the pillar of the educational process. So, His Majesty's directives always stress the development of education. He released Jordan Education Initiative by supporting the educational system to qualify Jordan as one of the global sources of providing the experiences relevant to the electronic system and knowledge economy. Now, Jordan has the institutes that qualify trainers to prepare the trainees of technological education. According to UNESCO, Jordan is in the 18th place between 94 countries in the standard of education.

Jordanians pay a special attention to the generalization of technological education. This development helped in the computerization of the education system in thousands of schools in addition to the completion of building the fiber-optic network to adopt information technology to include schools, universities and community colleges in partnership with the private sector. All Jordanian universities must contain a faculty of information technology or specialized courses making this aspect of knowledge an essential pathway to all sciences.

In the field of education, the royal initiatives provide education services and help students through King Abdullah II Center for Excellence with its various branches in the different universities. The center is based on the concept that education is a right for all people and the economic conditions of some students should not prevent them from the education opportunities and showing their abilities.

Also, His Majesty ratified directives to insure proper housing in many of the remote areas which became model villages in addition to establishing projects in the same areas to provide job opportunities for the residents of these areas.

In the fields of economy, industry and trade, Jordan is witnessing a progressive growth represented in the increase in the coming capital for investment because of the facilities, decisive legislations, security and stability. Businesses and projects are varied in Jordan and His Majesty personally supervises and takes care of some of them such as the Jordan Gate project, in addition to the projects of Aqaba Special Economic Zone in the integrated cities that will change the front of Aqaba and increase investment for more than 1 billion JD as well as the infrastructure projects in the Jordanian governorates and the launching of developmental zones in these governorates.

The Arab free-trade became active especially after signing the Arab Free-Trade Agreement which Jordan joined. The statistical indicators refer to a marked growth in the Jordanian national economy.

The foreign trade volume indicates a wide trade activity through the public-private sector partnership. Jordan also pays a special attention to debt and deals with it credibly and transparently.

Since His Majesty King Abdullah II Bin Al Hussein reigned, he has given a special attention to the development of human resources, reinforcement of the basic government services, the acceleration of the implementation of the national projects of water, energy and infrastructure and the participation of the national capital in these projects, in addition to the implementation of poverty-control programs, providing job opportunities to fight unemployment through the governorate development programs and the development and support of small businesses.

To support the development of governorates, the King has granted governors wide authorities of supervising the implementation of the developmental blueprints. His Majesty King Abdullah II achieves a success after another in his global tours explaining the reality of the Jordanian economy and the ambitions of Jordan which is acting according to a comprehensive economic plan that seeks to attract external investments that allow many job opportunities for Jordanians.

Focusing on the development of governorates and the distribution of the development gains was one of the priorities of the development plans. So, His Majesty created an initiative of dividing the country into three development zones with elected development councils and elected municipalities along with one political parliament for the country in achievement of interaction and concentration in the implementation of the development plans. He also asserted the decentralization and regions in order to expand the space of public participation in decision-making and the arrangement of the priorities of setting the plans and programs concerning our development process. His Majesty said:" Our vision is represented in reaching a modern Jordan that meets the ambitions of the Jordanian citizen in terms of development and prosperity and uniting the efforts in the public and private sectors, the National Assembly and the civil society institutions in media and press in order to establish a comprehensive agenda that combines all the national goals that incarnate the society vision and determine the strategic programs and the national policies that form a burden on the successive governments.

His Majesty asserts the need for reform. A deep look at the near and far past of the nation tells us that the country needs more interventions that free it from confusion, muddling and narrow vision.

The national agenda answers the question of how the Jordanians can unite their efforts; it is an agenda that accepts nothing but the honest national vision that needs no explanation of who the Jordanian is, accepts no definition of the homeland away from its pure Jordanian one and accepts no meaning of identity other than the united national Jordanian identity.

This agenda is set to meet the challenges that will face the Kingdom throughout the following ten years in all the political and developmental sectors.

It is a consensual integrated vision that predicts the future and prepares the nation to confront changes and surprises.

The Royal is extended to include media and assure its independence and the necessity of having a national media that supports the freedom of the press. So, His Majesty gave his directives that support the media institutions in order to be run by a new philosophy and vision that aims to build a new media model while asserting the freedom of the press and assuring this by legislations and laws that give an enough space for expression in order to reach a media that expresses the conscience of the nation, expresses its identity and realizes the true meaning of Jordan, the implication of the national agenda and the visions of comprehensive reform that springs from the our souls.

The Amman Message which explains the curriculum of Islam that is based on the respect of human values and rejection of violence and extremism and calling for dialogue, and shows the true image of Islam that is based on goodness, justice, tolerance and moderation is a message that is approved by the global community. This message carries the great teachings of Islam including mercy, honor of humanity, and mutual affection between people, in addition to respecting charters and covenants and urging the religious scholars to do their best to show the reality of Islam and its sublime values.

Jordan could prove its presence in the region as well as the world especially in its defense of the issues of its nation particularly the Palestinian case which is considered its central case in addition to its support for all Arabs and their cases.

The policy of transparency and openness and moderation that has been made firm by the Hashemite leadership is one of the main factors that made Jordan the focus of attention internationally and globally to meet the challenges and obstructions that the region faces.

Regionally, Jordan has a distinctive position concerning its legislative and legal development according to the constitutional provisions as an inevitable result of the Hashemite leadership's commitment to the constitution and upholding its sovereignty as well as the constitutional amendments that Jordan witnessed since its establishment and aimed to reinforce the aspects of life in terms of the political, economic and social development.

Commemorating the 70th anniversary of independence, Jordanians boost their legal and legislative achievements since the dawn of establishment when they launched the first constitution of the state that represented the first Arab constitutional system and made Jordan the first Arab country that establishes its own constitution.

The journey of Jordan since the establishment and independence till now reflects the Jordanian success. It is the journey launched by the wise and unequaled Hashemite leadership who paid dearly for it.

THE HASHEMITE KINGDOM OF JORDAN

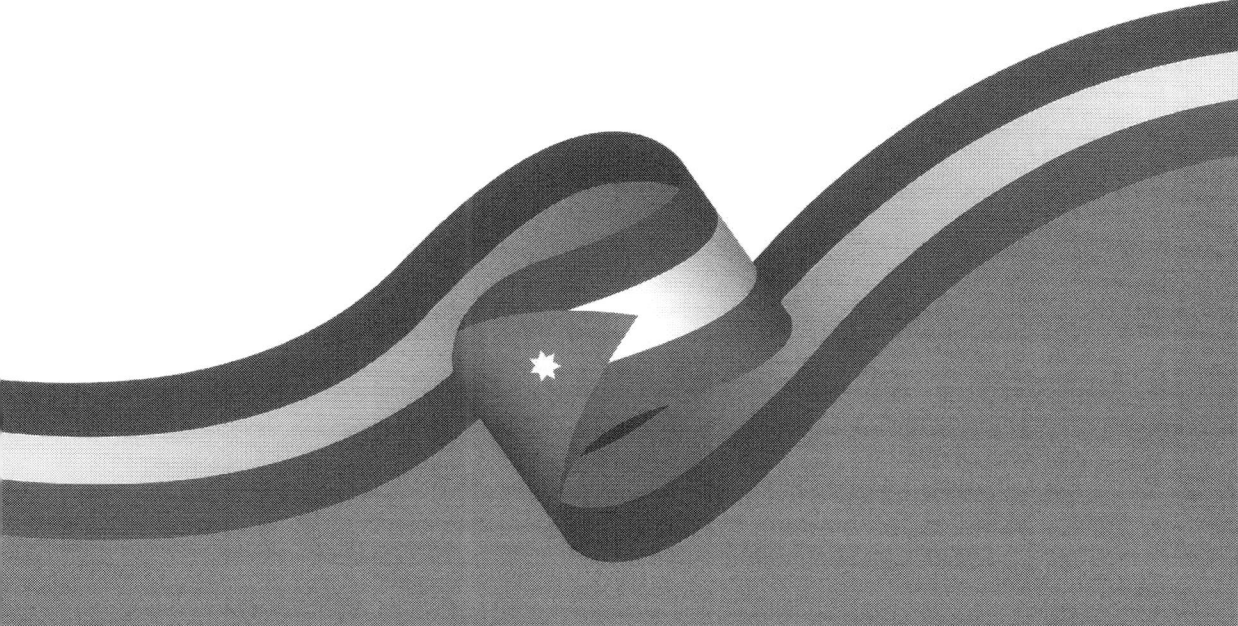

CHAPTER ONE

THE HASHEMITES AND BUILDING THE MODERN STATE

CHAPTER ONE
THE HASHEMITES AND BUILDING THE MODERN STATE

The Great Arab Revolt started the march towards freedom and a true awakening began anew. After a resounding defeat in the Caucasus campaign on 15 January 1915, the Ottoman state asked Sharif Hussein bin Ali to announce jihad in the name of Sultan Mehmed V Reşâd and to prepare volunteer Arab troops to send them to Syria. They also asked him to cooperate with Wali Wahib Bek in mobilizing, recruiting, arming and training Arabs to join the frontlines.

Sharif Hussein the Emir of Mecca responded in a telegram he sent to the Grand Vizier saying:

We will heed the demands of the high state if it meets the demands of Arabs, which are:

- Pardoning all Arab prisoners of conscience

Sharif Al Hussein bin Ali, the leader of national renaissance and the leader of the Great Arab Revolt with the Hashemite Kings

- Granting decentralized administration to Syria and Iraq

- Recognizing the prerogative of the Ashraf in Mecca as a hereditary right

This resulted in a political crisis that hastened the proclamation of the Revolt. Meanwhile, Britain was keen on establishing a coalition with the Arabs in Syria and Hijaz. In a letter to the Hashemite Sharif Hussein bin Ali in April 1915, British High Commissioner Sir Henry McMahon expressed Britain's readiness to help Arabs gain independence. Several letters followed in what has come to be known as the Hussein-McMahon Correspondence. Sharif Hussein agreed to enter into negotiations on the basis of the liberation and unity of Arabs as well as the proclamation of independence.

Sharif Hussein bin Ali was an Arab choice, with the free Arabs, who yearned for independence in the Levant, Iraq and other regions, looking up to him and seeing an embodiment of religious stature, political acumen and moral weight for all Muslims.

Britain agreed to Sharif Hussein's demands that stressed the importance of recognizing Palestine and coastal parts of Greater Syria as purely Arab lands, countering any British claims that sought to exclude them from the borders of the future Arab state. Meanwhile, Djemal Pasha was issuing arbitrary execution sentences that were implemented in Beirut and Damascus on 6 May 1916. In addition, many Arab nationalist figures were jailed. At the dawn of that bloody day, Prince Faisal, in Damascus, uttered his famous cry: "Oh Arabs, death is sweet!" And with that, the Great Arab Revolt's quest to liberate the land and the people began. The Arab armies — the Northern Army led by Prince Faisal, the Eastern Army led by Prince Abdullah and the Southern Army led by Prince Ali — fought on three fronts: Hijaz front in Mecca, Medina Munawara, Taif, Jeddah and along the Red Sea coast; the Jordan front in Aqaba, Tafila, Maan, Azraq, Shobak, Wadi Musa, Hassa and others; and the northern front of Syria starting with Daraa, onto Damascus and arriving at Homs, Aleppo and the northernmost point of Muslimiyeh.

The Army of the Great Arab Revolt during the march in 1916

With the end of World War I came the London Conference in 1918, followed by the Paris Peace Conference in 1919, where Prince Faisal represented the Arabs. But unexpected political developments and colonial ambitions came to the fore, pushing Arabs to fight a new kind of war to defend their independence and establish sovereign states.

Afterwards came the movement of Prince Abdullah bin Al Hussein from Hijaz to Maan and onto

Sharif Al Hussein bin Ali

Amman, so that the banner of the Revolt, Arabism and independence continues to flutter, symbolizing the principles of renaissance and statehood. Prince Abdullah — along with some leaders of the Arab independence movement, including Rashid Tlai, Ghaleb Shaalan and Awni Abdulhadi — held talks with the British officials on 29 March 1921, following some correspondence.

Prince Abdullah went through difficult negotiations, against the backdrop of previous decisions and secret agreements between France and Britain to carve up Arab lands, a British mandate endorsed by the League of Nations and the Balfour Declaration.

With political acumen and deep foresight, Prince Abdullah managed to secure Britain's recognition of the establishment of a state in Transjordan, amending the mandate to include identifying Transjordan as Arab land. This enabled Prince Abdullah and a group of national Arab leaders to embark on building the Jordanian state and its institutions, which eventually led to its independence as the government of Transjordan, developing later into the Hashemite Kingdom of Jordan.

- **Historical Roles:**

The Hashemites were the bedrock in the formation of the Arab identity in Syria, Iraq and Jordan. They could maintain Arab countries and protect them from many disasters, and stand against the division of Arab states. This is a continuation of their historical role that began in Dar Al-Nadwa up to the organization of pilgrimage affairs and serving the Holy House of God.

The Hashemites have a store of experience that enables them to handle great events, take in the global political movement and realize the nature of the negotiation criteria in the international issues. This was apparent in the negotiations of Sharif Al Hussein with Sir MCmahon Ami in 1915 and 1916 as well as the role of Prince Faisal in Paris Conference and his attitude to the resolutions of San Remo Conference. This was also apparent in the (Abdullah - Churchill) meeting in Jerusalem in 1921 when the Founding King Abdullah when he referred to the necessity of taking the opinion of the political parties concerning Churchill's offers and his refusal of Balfour Declaration.

- **The Hashemites and the State:**

Led by the Hashemites, the modern Arab Awakening sought liberation and sovereignty from more than four centuries of alienation and dispossession under Ottoman rule.

The firing of the first bullet, on 10 June 1916, marked the start of the Great Arab Revolt, ushering in a noble and arduous march towards the establishment of an independent Arab nation.

The Arab Awakening movement was inseparable from the Arab consciousness, which was deepening and expanding with the increasing activity of the free Arabs, who organized themselves into independence-seeking organizations and societies. At the centre of these various movements was Prince Faisal I, who served as a critical link between them and his father, Sharif Hussein bin Ali, who had been exiled to Istanbul in 1893 for his beliefs and activism, before returning to Mecca in 1908 to become its Emir. Sharif Hussein was sought as the leader of Arab renaissance and revolution because he embodied both religious and historical legitimacy as well as because he believed in the Arabs' right to freedom, unity and independence.

- ## The Founding King Abdullah Bin Al Hussein (1951-1882):

His Majesty King Abdullah I, may his soul rest in peace, was born in Mecca on 4 April 1882. Since early childhood, King Abdullah I showed interest in Arab history and was deeply acquainted with the customs and traditions of Arab tribes. These early cultural experiences had a profound effect on his character later on, with the Raghadan Palace built in Amman in 1927, becoming a destination for Arab intellectuals and poets, with whom he sparred in poetry and debates.

The Founding King Abdullah developed the political savvy and remarkable ability necessary to overcome crises and intervene decisively to resolve issues, making him one of the most important leaders of the Great Arab Revolt. After Faisal was proclaimed King of Syria, Prince Abdullah continued to play a leading role in the military operations in Hejaz. However, the end of the Arab government in Damascus, after the Battle of Maysaloun on 24 July 1920, necessitated his arrival to Transjordan in order to ensure that

King Abdullah bin Al Hussein signing the Declaration of Independence on May 25th 1946 at Raghadan Palace

the Great Arab Revolt's banner remains hoisted high and to establish a launching ground for supporting Arab independence advocates fighting the French occupation to liberate Syria.

Before the noon of March 2nd 1921, Prince Abdullah arrived in Amman coming from Ma'an and he was welcomed. Amman became a big center with a renewed renaissance that it became the destination of free people in the entire Arab world.

The arrival of Prince Abdullah marked the end of local governments and a new system and central government began to replace the old one.

Consequently, the Founding King Abdullah wanted to assure the Arab demand calling for the necessity of unity and the continuation of the Arab revolutionary approach which was the heart of the Great Arab Revolt. So, he had to face many problems and difficulties.

During his thirty-year reign (1951 - 1921), the Founding King Abdullah achieved important political achievements that include:

- The political recognition o f the Emirate of the Transjordan

- Ratifying the Basic Law as the first constitution of the Emirate of the Transjordan and signing an international treaty, namely the Jordanian - British Treaty

- The first legislative council in 1929

- Establishing the Arab Legion and paying attention to its development and empowerment

- Supporting the independence approaches in the Arab world by receiving its leaders in Amman and establishing the Independence Party opening the political horizons of political awareness for Jordanians to establish other parties

- Reinforcing the state prestige and building its institutions

- Declaring the Emirate of the Transjordan as an independent Kingdom in May 25th 1946

- Unifying the two banks as a real model for the Arab unity

He came to life as a fighter and passed away as a martyr

After gaining independence, Jordan had an independent decision. The beginning was in Anshas Summit May 28th 1948. The defeat of 1948 put Jordan in the spotlight. Jordan defended Jerusalem in Bab al-Wad and Latrun and in all parts of Palestine.

On May 18th, the sixth battalion in Jericho was ordered with its three families of ground forces to go to Jerusalem and spread in the important locations and gates of the town. They were well welcomed.

The courage soldiers could maintain Jerusalem and other parts of Palestine in what was later known as the West Bank.

After the defeat, the Jordanian situation's courage has been clear. So, the Arab brothers headed to Jordan as their only guarantee.

This also stressed the importance of the Jordanian – Palestinian unity leading to the first conference on October 1st 1948 presided by Sheikh Suleiman Al-Taji Al-Farouki who told King Abdullah that he is fully authorized by Palestinians to represent them. This paved the political climate to the Conference of Jericho on December 1st 1948 which attended by the nobles and leaders of Palestine who decided:

- To accept the Jordanian – Palestinian unity

- To pay allegiance for King Abdullah as King of Palestine

Early on, Jordan went ahead in the implementation of the unity decision and new elections were made on January 2nd 1950. The council contained representatives of Palestine and of Jordan. A new government has been formed in 1950 headed by Said Pasha Al-Mufti

On July 20th, 1951, King Abdullah I headed to Jerusalem to attend Friday prayers in the company of his grandson, Prince Al Hussein , later to be King Al Hussein . He was shot at the steps of Al-Aqsa Mosque near the shrine of his father, Al Hussein , who paid his life for all Arabs.

King Al Hussein , the crown-prince then, was in the company of his grandfather. He received a bullet at his chest, but the bullet ricocheted off a medal on his chest. Thus, these moments were very crucial and decisive in his entire life; he realized the inevitability of death and the importance of his responsibility in the subsequent years.

- **King Talal Bin Abdullah, Father of the Constitution (1972-1909)**

His Majesty the late
King Talal Bin Abdullah

His Majesty King Talal Bin Abdullah, may his soul rest in peace, continued to build Jordan, in line with the country's foundations of moderation, justice, equality, freedom and human rights.

During King Talal's reign, which lasted less than a year, the Jordanian Constitution of 1952 was completed adopted. It embodied the spirit of political development, based on the importance of the public's participation in decision-making. His Majesty King Talal's reign was also marked by endorsing the right of free education and the issuance of major legislation. He also bolstered ties with Saudi Arabia, Syria and Egypt.

Illness prevented King Talal from continuing to rule. As a result, a constitutional decision was taken to form a Regency Council on 11 August 1952, until his son, King Al Hussein , came of age. On this same day, Al Hussein was proclaimed King of the Hashemite Kingdom of Jordan.

• King Al Hussein Bin Talal, the constructor (1999-1935)

His Majesty the late
King Al Hussein bin Talal

Born in Amman on 14 November 1935, King Al Hussein received special attention from his grandfather, the Founding King. He completed his regular and military education at schools in Jordan and abroad, before being proclaimed King in 1952. He assumed full constitutional powers on 3 May 1953, amidst a delicate phase in Arab and international politics.

Despite all these challenges, King Al Hussein was able to achieve the high levels of development, especially in the political, economic and social fields. He became the builder of a moderate Jordan and succeeded in securing a decent life for his people. Under his leadership, Jordan continued to play its Arab, regional and international role ably and effectively, with keen prescience.

Under the -47year reign of His Majesty King Al Hussein Bin Talal, may his soul rest in peace, Jordan witnessed great progress in the political, economic and social sectors. With a focus on ensuring that their gains benefit all regions and all segments of society, His Majesty worked to enhance Jordanians' standard of living, in line with his motto: "The human being is our most precious asset," which was the main driver of the country's development plans.

King Al Hussein paid special attention to the Jordan Armed Forces-Arab Army, whose soldiers fought valiantly in the immortal Karama Battle, emerging victorious on 21 March 1968 and restoring faith back to Arabs after the 1967 Arab-Israeli war.

On the regional and Arab levels, Jordan was among the founders of the Arab League and has since remained committed to its decisions. His Majesty King Al Hussein also played a pivotal role in ensuring Arab unity, promoting joint Arab work, and supporting Arab causes, especially core ones, such as the Palestinian cause.

His attitude to the Iraqi issue was clear by assuring that the resolution should be an Arab one; otherwise, the whole region would witness endless disasters.

He also paid attention to political life evolution and established the National Chart and Shura Councils.

Since it was impossible to hold parliamentary elections in the West

Bank — which was part of the Hashemite Kingdom of Jordan — due to the Israeli occupation, advisory councils were created to fill the constitutional vacuum. Heeding the Palestinian brethren's will to take over their own affairs, Jordan took the decision in 1974 at the Rabat conference to recognize the Palestine Liberation Organization as the sole legitimate representative of the Palestinian people. This was followed  by Jordan's decision to disengage from the West Bank legally and administratively in 1988. The decision enabled the Kingdom to resume its constitutional democratic march in 1989, based on political pluralism, affirming the approach of shura and expanding the scope of political engagement to include women as voters and candidates.

His Majesty the late King Al Hussein , may Allah rest his soul in peace, a man of peace and war with courage and bright insight.

- **King Abdullah II bin Al Hussein "al-malik al-mu'azzaz" (1962 AD)**

When His Majesty King Abdullah II bin Al Hussein assumed his constitutional powers as King of the Hashemite Kingdom Jordan on February 7th 1999 AD, he announced with his oath before the National Assembly, the fourth covenant of the Kingdom which has been established on the hands of King Abdullah I bin Al Hussein bin Ali; whose constitution has been established by his grandfather King Talal; and built by his father King Al Hussein , may Allah rest their souls in peace.

His Majesty King Abdullah bin Al Hussein

At this time His Majesty took over the responsibility toward his people which he regarded as his family. He could harmonize between the zeal and vitality of youth armed with his knowledge and the deeply-rooted wisdom that has been built on objective foundations.

- **The Journey of Knowledge:**

The stages of His Majesty's life, since his birth on January 30th 1962, were a cognitive record that combined awareness, culture and knowledge that made his biography a model for those who seek knowledge from its sources. He realized the importance of cultural communication between peoples. He also has a determination to have a qualitative knowledge supported by civil and military learning at the same time.

His Majesty's journey began at the Islamic Educational College in Amman, enrolling in 1966; before attending Deerfield Academy in the United States and finally Georgetown University in Washington, DC.

Besides the academic studies, His Majesty added diverse military experiences in the USA, the UK and Germany. He began his military journey as a commander of a company in the 17th Royal Tank Battalion in the Arab Legion in 1989. He remained in the military service until he was promoted to Commander of the Royal Jordanian Special Forces with the rank of Brigadier General in 1949, and restructured these forces according to the latest international military standards.

This special type of education which His Majesty King Abdullah II received formed his strong motivation to empower his people to have an advanced and modern education. He expressed this saying "my

ambition is that every Jordanian receives the best education, since innovation is the tribute of our people. The journey of innovation begins with education. "

- **Investment in man:**

His Majesty King Abdullah II believes, exactly like his father the late King Al Hussein bin Talal, may Allah rest his soul in peace, that the real fortune of Jordan is its human being. The investment in the Jordanian man is the best investment for a country like Jordan with limited natural sources.

Starting from this belief, His Majesty, since the first day in office in 1999, began a new stage of the country's administration and the leadership of the overall development journey which requires taking many and big steps for the sake of development and change. Because man is the main factor of the process of development as well as its means and goal, His Majesty assured the necessity of the rehabilitation of the Jordanian citizen.

This can happen by reconsidering the programs and curricula of education in all its stages, setting qualification and training programs that qualify the citizen to indulge in the labor market and submit the experiences and technology that distinguish this element.

- **Politics:**

His Majesty King Abdullah believes that Jordan is the inheritor of the massage of the Great Arab Revolt. This is why Jordan should belong to the Arab Nation and be curious to fulfill the duties toward this nation and the ambitions of its people more than any other country. At the head of these issues is the Palestinian case which is the most important in the Arab world. So, His Majesty followed on the path of his father and ancestors in defending the Palestinian case and support Palestine with all Jordan's capabilities and relations with the whole world.

His Majesty continued to unite the Arab Nation and support his relations with the Arab brothers and all the friendly countries all over the world.

Internally, His Majesty gives a great priority to support the reform journey and democracy of Jordan in all fields, as well as protecting of the intellectual and political multiplicity, raising the standard of freedom and protecting it, encouraging the establishment of new parties and respecting the human dignity and freedom in thinking, belief, expression and political work.

- **Peace is the true meaning of Islam:**

His Majesty King Abdullah II is the successor of the religious

legitimacy in his reign and descent. His legitimacy depends on "Islam and achievement". In his opinion, Justice is the basis of reign that came to him as a result of the purified origin and the noble ancestry that goes back to the Hashemite Prophet Muhammad, peace be upon him.

He believes in the relationship between peace and the truthfulness of Islam. This is apparent in his constructive Islamic thought and his consistency in meeting the Islam scholars and achieving convergence in their points of view in order to generalize a just culture that aims to reinforce a moderate method that unites people and doesn't disperse them. In this context, he assures his commitment to defend Islam as one of his duties as a Hashemite Arab who is aware of the danger of what is aimed to hurt Islam, including hatred to and deformity of it because of the waves of sectarianism, extremism and closure which began to form a real danger on the whole world. In all international occasion, he stresses that "the Muslims of these days should bravely defend the justice of Islam which reinforces the sacredness of human life, defends the oppressed, serves man and woman equally, assures the brotherhood of the entire mankind. This is the real Islam to which our Prophet invited us. It is also the Islam that terrorists seek to destroy."

- **The simulation of young people:**

Nationally, King Abdullah II realizes his great responsibility and summarizes his national mission in the following slogan "sustainable development, the justice of planning and implementation and the empowerment of young people for a better future."

To consolidate these principles, the King instills these principles in the young people of Jordan who represent the biggest power of society in order to reinforce in their hearts and enable them politically, cognitively and economically because they are "the knights of

change" in Jordan as he described them in more than one occasion.

This relationship between the king and young people has a special nature that made the majority of young people simulate King Abdullah II in his activity and wisdom. They also take him as a model for them in his determination on achievement and work on all levels so that the final result is a scientific and cognitive revolution that balances modernity with authenticity and stand as a policy of work that respects the productive person.

His Majesty King Abdullah began his auspicious reign with the constitutional oath on February 7th 1999 in a good Hashemite journey that leads to the building of the modern contemporary state and progress in the fields of sustainable development as well as strengthening the relationships and reinforcing them with the Arab, Islamic and friendly countries, supporting the global peace process, claiming people's suffrage and paying attention to the issues of human rights and the development of societies.

THE HASHEMITE KINGDOM OF JORDAN

CHAPTER TWO

HIS MAJESTY KING ABDULLAH
AND
HIS ROYAL FAMILY

CHAPTER TWO
HIS MAJESTY KING ABDULLAH II AND HIS ROYAL FAMILY

- **From the speeches of His Majesty the venerable King Abdullah II bin Al Hussein**

- For Jordan, tolerance and moderation constitute a basis for our society and future. I'm proud that my country was the origin of Amman Message which expressed the true values of Islam, Muslims and others all over the world equally. This work is continuous and it should be, as long as the deformities and the conflicts between religious supporters continue to threaten our world.

- Improving the life standard of citizens, male or female, requires an interest in health care which is a right for all citizens, regardless their gender. The person who enjoys a good standard of health and feels endured for himself as well as his family is the

person who is able to work and produce.

- The government has taken actual steps in the expanding of the health insurance system to conclude all citizens and pay special care for infantry and maternity programs.

- We are going ahead in the journey of reform, modernization and overall development within the system of freedom, justice and equal opportunities. There is no delay or hesitation in dealing with the issues of reform, freedom and democracy.

- We are the offspring of one nation. We should defend its progress, sovereignty and democratic image. Our country is not new to reform and opposition, but it is the country of satisfaction and harmony between its people in all their affairs. Our constitutional democratic political system is our shield and firewall along with our heritage of freedom, justice, promising future and above all the love of home.

King Abdullah II bin Al Hussein bin Talal bin Al Hussein bin Ali Al-Hashmi was born in Amman on 30 January 1962.

He received elementary education at the Islamic Educational College in Amman, which he joined in 1966; and then he attended Saint Edmund's School in Surrey, Britain, before attending Eaglebrook School and Deerfield Academy in the USA. His university training was at Pembroke College, Oxford.

In 1980, he left Pembroke College and joined the Royal Military Academy Sandhurst in the United Kingdom as a beginner soldier in the Royal Hussars. After one year, he was commissioned as a second lieutenant. In 1987, he completed study in Edmund Lash School for Foreign Affairs at Georgetown University in the USA. In November 2009, he became Commander of the Royal Jordanian Special Forces with the rank of Brigadier General. Then, he restructured the Special Forces and other elite units under the leadership of the Jordanian Special Operations. After assuming power and according to his constitutional powers, he became the Supreme Commander of the Armed Forces. Now, he has the rank of Field Marshal in the Jordanian Army and the Jordanian Royal Air Force.

He ascended the throne on February 7th 1999 after the passing away of his father His Majesty the late King Al Hussein bin Talal, may his soul rest in peace. He was inaugurated on June 9th 1999 on the Royal Assent Day.

His Majesty King Abdullah believes that Jordan is the inheritor of the massage of the Great Arab Revolt. This is why Jordan should belong to the Arab Nation and be curious to fulfill the duties towards this nation and the ambitions of its people more than any other country. On top of this list of issues is the Palestinian case which is the most important in the Arab world.

So, His Majesty has followed on the path of his father and ancestors in defending the Palestinian case and has given support Palestine with all Jordan's capabilities and relations with the whole world.

His Majesty continued to unite the Arab Nation and support his relations with the Arab brothers and all the friendly countries all over the world.

Internally, His Majesty gives a great priority to support the reform endeavors and democracy of Jordan in all fields, as well as protecting of the intellectual and political multiplicity, raising the standard of freedom and protecting it, encouraging the establishment of new parties and respecting the human dignity and freedom in thinking, belief, expression and political work.

His legitimacy depends on «Islam and achievement». In his opinion, Justice is the basis of reign that came to him as a result of the purified origin and the noble ancestry that goes back to the Hashemite Prophet Muhammad, peace be upon him. He believes in the relationship between peace and the truthfulness of Islam. This is apparent in his constructive Islamic thought and his consistency in his meetings with the Islam scholars and achieving convergence in their points of view in order to generalize a just culture that aims to reinforce a moderate method that unites people and does not disperse them. In this context, he stresses his commitment to defending Islam as one of his duties as a Hashemite Arab who is aware of the danger of what is aimed to hurt Islam, including hatred to and deformity of it because of the waves of sectarianism, extremism and closure which began to form a real danger on the whole world. In all international occasion, he stresses that «the Muslims of these days should bravely defend the justice of Islam which reinforces the sacredness of human life, defends the oppressed, serves man and woman equally, assures the brotherhood of the entire mankind. This is the real Islam to which our Prophet invited us. It is also the Islam that terrorists seek to destroy.»

- **The Royal Initiatives:**

His Majesty has initiatives and contributions internally and externally, out of his desire to raise the nation's standard and improve its conditions and elevate the position of its people. He is working hard to raise and improve the conditions of his people who gave him their trust and love. If we want to speak about all his initiatives, it will take so long. So, we will mention some of them as follows:

- King Abdullah II Fund for Development

- Democratic Empowerment Program

- Fund for Support of scientific projects in the Middle East

- Hashemite Fund for the Development of Jordan Badia

- King Abdullah II Design and Development Bureau

- Youth Training and Employment

Inclusive Initiatives

- King Abdullah II Centre for Excellence

- His Majesty King Abdullah II Award for Excellence in Government Performance and Transparency

- King Abdullah II Award for Excellence for the Private Sector

- King Abdullah II Award for Excellence for Business Associations

- King Abdullah II Award for Physical Fitness

- Petra Conference of Nobel laureates

- 1st Petra Conference of Nobel laureates 19-18 May 2005

- 2nd Petra Conference of Nobel laureates 22-21 June 2006

- 3rd Petra Conference of Nobel laureates 16-15 May 2007

- 4th Petra Conference of Nobel laureates 19-17 June 2008

- The Eleven Group

- Economic Consultative Council

- 1st Economic Consultative Council

- 2nd Economic Consultative Council

- Third Economic Retreat in Aqaba

- Amman Message

- The National Agenda 2017 – 2007

- Jordan First

- A Common Word Initiative

- Kuluna al Urdun

- Kuluna al Urdun meeting

- Human Rights

- Justice

- Education

- Jordan Education Initiative

- Development of Education toward Knowledge Economy

- Other Education Initiatives

- Information Technology

- Rich Initiative

- National Information and Communication Technologies Strategy 2007

- E-government

- E-learning

- Knowledge Stations

- Information Technology Meeting

- Health Care

- Housing

- Housing for members of the Armed Forces and security bodies

- Low Income Housing

- Teacher Housing

- King Abdullah Bin Abdul Aziz Residential City in Zarqa

- Decent Housing for a Decent Living Initiative—known in Arabic as Sakan kareem la 'eish kareem

- Agriculture

- Energy

- Custodianship of Holy sites

- King Abdullah II and Jerusalem

- Reconstruction of the mosques and shrines of prophets and companions in Jordan

- Aqaba Special Economic Zone

We will speak briefly about some initiatives that had a great influence on the nation, the region in general and the international society in particular. This stems from His Majesty's interest to consolidate some concepts that had to be melted, clarified and be put in their proper context.

- **Amman Message Initiative:**

Amman Message has been launched on November 29th 2004/ the Night of Revelation in the month of Ramadan before Jordan's announcement to host the International Islamic Conference in 2005.

This message came to enlighten people with the core values and reality of Islam which presented to humanity the best examples of tolerance, moderation, justice, accepting the other and refusal of prejudice and closure.

The Message has been launched with the blessing of the King who personally undertook the mission of communication with the western communities in their language. He touched, like many others, the good influence of his speeches, which were a model in their modernity, honesty and truthfulness, on the political and media groups in these communities.

The Amman Message came in a critical time for the Muslim nation which needs something to reiterate its achievements, glories, civilization and glories over ages. On its shoulders, Amman Message burdened the mission of defending the values and moral principles of Islam in order to release the Islamic nation from the blockade and isolation and help it go back to the purposes of Sharia.

For scholars, they have been invited to contribute to the activation of the journey and the achievement of the priority that Muslims be the model and example in religion, morals, behavior and rational speech. They should provide the nation with the justice and simplicity of religion in its contemporary law which achieves its renaissance and happiness. They should also spread the values of good, peace and love between the members of the nation and the whole world.

Islam, according to the Message is the religion of means and goals. It seeks to achieve the benefit and good for people in this life and the hereafter. Defending Islam must be with moral means. In this religion, the end does not justify the means. The basis of the relationship between Muslims and others is peace. There is no fight or aggression. Instead, there is love, justice and charity.

- **King Abdullah II Fund for Development (KAFD):**

The King Abdullah II Fund for Development (KAFD) was established by a royal decree in 2001 as a non-governmental organization. It seeks to achieve an overall development in all the governorates and regions of the Kingdom. It also aims to contribute to supporting the social and educational developmental efforts in order to establish national developmental projects that guarantee the distribution of the gains of sustainable development through partnership between the private sector and civil society institutions with the aim of improving the citizen's conditions.

The fund actively seeks to push the wheel of sustainable development through the best employment of the citizens' capabilities, supporting their productivity, training and qualifying them, and supporting the programs of excellence and creativity in all its forms in order to reach a distinguished level of qualified human resources which is considered a main pillar of sustainable development witnessed by society.

It aims to qualify young people to enter the labor market by establishing 19 offices for career guidance in Jordanian universities.

It also established the Youth Association of Kuluna al-Urdun "We nare all Jordan" with 12 offices in the governorates of the Kingdom in addition to a media pulpit represented in the TV program Ihki Ilna "Talk to us".

The fund could achieve many things for young people qualification, and for some knowledge and creativity-based relevant institutions. It also presents technical and financial support for a number of projects in this concern.

- **Jordan First Initiative:**

In November 2002, His Majesty King Abdullah II launched the concept of "Jordan First" in order to reinforce the basics of the contemporary democracy. It is a plan of work which aims to consolidate the soul of belonging between the citizens; people are partners in the building and development of Jordan.

The concept of "Jordan First" assures that Jordan's benefit and interests are above any other things and benefits. It aims to spread the values of respect, tolerance and respect of supporting the concepts of parliamentary democracy, sovereignty of law, public freedom, accountability, transparency, justice and equality.

- **The Common Word Initiative:**

We will handle this initiative with more detail because of its local, regional and international importance. This initiative has been launched in 2007 and invited Muslim and Christian scholars to make a constructive dialogue on two main basic commandments: love of God and love of the neighbor, without touching any of the religious beliefs of them. These two commandments are in the essence of the three heavenly religions providing the most solid religious empowered ground.

The King sponsors the King Abdullah II Prize for the World Interfaith Harmony Week

Amman, 2014/4/27 (Department of Media and Communication- the Hashemite Royal Court)

King Abdullah II sponsored the Prize-giving ceremony for the World Interfaith Harmony Week.

During the ceremony held at Husseiniya Palace in the presence of Princes and high officials, His Majesty King Abdullah II delivered prizes to four winners in the prize derived from the World Interfaith Harmony Week which was initially proposed by His Majesty to the United Nations in its session No (56) and has been unanimously approved.

The Royal Aal al-Bayt Institute for Islamic Thought established the award in recognition of the best three events or texts that contribute to the spread and popularization of the World Interfaith Harmony Week established according to the UN resolution (34.A/65/PV). It is to be held in the first week of February every year.

The First Prize:

It is awarded to the United Nations Interfaith Harmony Partners in Philippines, in recognition of their week-long celebration of the 3rd World Interfaith Harmony Week in Zamboanga City, Philippines.

The Second Prize:

It is awarded to the Centre for Peace & Human Rights for their event 'An ordinary step for ensuring extraordinary peace' in Uttar-Pradesh, India.

The Third Prize:

It is split between Gamal Farghaly Sultan Secondary School for Boys, Asyut for their event 'Peace without Prejudice' in Egypt and Faiths Together Uganda for their gathering at the Goma Health Center III in Uganda.

The World Interfaith Harmony Week, established after the adoption of His Majesty King Abdullah's proposal by the UN in October 2010, is an annual platform for spreading understanding and awareness between the interfaith dialogue and goodwill groups through holding the events and activities that reinforce this purpose.

also avoids the repetition of the events held in this concern. The idea of this initiative concentrates on the leading work achieved by the Common Word Initiative launched in 2007 which invited Muslim and Christian scholars to make a constructive dialogue on two main basic commandments: love of God and love of the neighbor, without touching any of the religious beliefs of them. These two commandments are in the essence of the three heavenly religions providing the most solid religious empowered ground.

The president of Judges Committee, H.R.H. Princess Areej Ghazi, stated in her speech in the ceremony "It does give me the honor, on behalf of me and the rest of the judging committee of the World Interfaith Harmony Week's prize established by His Majesty King Abdullah II bin Al Hussein , to express my thanks and gratitude to be part of this noble project which is seen as an invitation to a new Hilf Al-Fudul (Alliance of Fudul)."

She added "Prophet Muhammad, peace be upon him appraised Hilf Al-Fudul (Alliance of Fudul) in the pre-Islam period and said that if he was invited to it in Islam, he would agree. You, sir, followed on the Prophet's path and invited the whole world and the followers of all religions to celebrate a global week which is built on the love of God and the love of Neighbor, or the love of Good and the love of Neighbor. The whole world accepted the invitation and all countries adopted and approved the idea."

She assured "this week became official in the United Nations in 2011. Your Majesty, Sir, accepted to name the prize after your noble name by the Royal Aal al-Bayt Institute for Islamic Thought in order that the whole world is encouraged to celebrate this week in their history according to the noble principles upon which it was established."

She also said "this is not strange for Your Majesty; your auspicious reign is full of initiatives in favor of Jordan, Muslims, peace and the whole world in spite of the rarity of our country's sources. However, our country has better and more expensive sources represented in its soul, people and history."

She added "the initiatives of the King in this concern are numerous. The most notable of them is the historical Islamic world consensus of the three fundamental principles of Amman Message defining who Muslims are; who has the right to declare apostasy (takfir between Muslims and the conditions of doing this; and finally who is eligible to issue fatwas and the conditions for doing this.) "

She stated "the Amman Message included the Great electronic Tafsir Project as the greatest tafsir (explanation of Quran) which was used by 25 million visitors last year providing more than one hundred tafsirs for the world every day."

She drew the attention to the Common Word Initiative which was established at the King's request and it has been described as the most successful initiative between Muslims and Christians throughout history.

She also said "God Willing, this prize will commemorate the ceremony of World Interfaith Harmony Week. Consequently, it will lead to eliminate religious tensions all over the world so that the whole world will become like our beloved Jordan which is the best model for interfaith harmony thanks to God's grace and the wisdom of its leadership and the smart and noble people of Jordan."

Dr. Minwer Al-Mheid – Director of the Royal Aal Al-Bayt Institute for Islamic Thought- said that after four years since the launch of the World Interfaith Harmony Week, it became a fact that witnesses more welcome and participation and attraction of all parties which love peace, good and blessing for all humanity regardless their religions, beliefs, their intellectual and thinking trends and their political backgrounds.

He added that the people who take over this noble initiative are united by one noble goal; that is to consolidate harmony between people and establish global peace and reinforce the mutual respect between the holders of different religions and beliefs.

He assured that countries, organizations, communities and individuals hold events and activities relevant to the World Interfaith Harmony Week on a voluntary basis. They also held sessions and lectures in schools and scientific institutes. They wrote books and articles in the same area. Your noble message reached the entire world. We hope that the numbers of participants as well as the events increase in the following years in order to reach the desired goal and spread peace all over the globe and humanity becomes void of hatred, animosity and grudge.

H.E. Sheikh Dr Ali Gomaa, the Chief Consultant of the Royal Aal al-Bayt Institute for Islamic Thought, said "we start this meeting which satisfies Allah and people, with peace and Allah's mercy and blessings be upon you; the greeting of Islam and a name of God and one of the names of Heaven and the name of the harmony, security and faith. This harmony week proposed by Your Majesty is the best representation of the content of this blessed greeting."

He added "the peace we aspire to reach in the World Interfaith Harmony Week can be achieved through the idea of participation; the participation and cooperation of man with his brother in the mutual work, living, principles and interests so that the earth is reconstructed. Allah said (He has produced you from the earth and settled you in it), Surah Hud 61."

He considered that the harmony week restores man's humanity, good nature and construction of earth through co-work which is mainly based on the youth from all nationalities and religions in order to take part in different works that melt differences between people.

He assured "you, Majestic King, are a descendant from the Prophetic origin, and your love is a must for all people and all hearts. Every family tree is cut in the Day of Judgment except for the tree of the Prophet to whom you belong."

H.B. Patriarch Theophilos III – Patriarch of the Jerusalem said that the celebration of the World Interfaith Harmony Week will bring with it a commitment to the goals and ideas of this week that should be spread all over the world. These goals and principles contribute to changing people's lives to better, especially in the societies that suffer from stress and tension.

He assured that the prize crowned the renewable commitment and efforts of the United Nations to build the culture of peace, rejection of violence and mutual understanding between the followers of different religions and highlight the commitment of the Hashemite Kingdom of Jordan in this important endeavor.

He added that these values are a great gift to the resolution of the United Nations and the Royal Aal al-Bayt Institute for Islamic Thought which the King Abdullah Prize established for the World Interfaith Harmony Week.

He stated that the award is not only an honor to the winners, it also sheds light on the values of the award around the world which reflects its vital role for all humanity "which we build together."

Patriarch Theophilos III congratulated the winners and said "we encourage others who cooperate with us so that peace prevails all over the world, especially we deliver to you the spiritual blessings from Jerusalem; the beloved city for all our hearts."

In the beginning of his speech, H.E. Bishop Munib Yunan – Bishop of the Evangelical Lutheran Church in Jordan and the Holy Land, and President of the World Federation of Evangelical Lutheran Churches, delivered the greetings of the people of Jerusalem to the

King and their prayers for peace and justice, expressing their thanks and recognition of the King's custodianship over the holy spots and all his efforts in favor of Jerusalem.

He added that in the time of global extremism, media presents a negative image about religion especially what is known as "Islamophobia". However, we find a fertile ground in most of societies to convert from extremism to justice and moderation.

He also assured that the influential powers will work not only to reinforce and empower those who spread the values of moderation and the Common Word which launched from Jordan in order to confirm the fact that the reality of religion is not just to love God but to love your neighbor as you love yourself.

He said "the winners are the champions who will change the world into a better place. They are also a main element for the achievement of our social progress when we find ourselves prisoners of prejudice and segregation". He called for enthusiastic action to continue dialogue between religions and man's education.

He added that our role, as religious leaders is represented in supporting all the initiatives that target the change of extremism into moderation, denial into acceptance.

Our role is represented in destroying the barriers of segregation, hatred, prejudice and fear. Also, we should find mutual acceptance between humanity. "Under your leadership, this is what we are committed to as Christians of Jordan. We are committed to work for peace and education to be a model that is followed all over the entire globe."

He also said "we promise you that Arabs and Christians will resume their role as the voice of Arab Muslims. We are brothers and neighbors in every place we go to. We promise to obey God's invitation for each one of us to be a voice of harmony and peace."

In his turn, Father Sebastiano Daomira said on behalf of the winners said: "It is our pleasure to be here today to express our gratitude to the King and to everyone who contributes to spreading World Interfaith Harmony Week" that is considered as a vital initiative that provides a platform for all those who work for peace between religions in the world.

He added "the Dialogue Series Movement that I represent began to work in Philippines between Muslims and Christians after the conflicts that left behind great losses and victims, in order to build the peace based on dialogue and love."

He confirmed the movement's welcome of any similar and new initiatives "because we believe in this path, and since the beginning, we confirmed the importance of peace that is based on the love of God and the neighbor."

In 2012, he said "We engaged many spectrums of citizens of Zamboanga to celebrate together in this special week and encouraged the Philippines Council of Scholars to take the lead of the initiative and devote the values of the World Interfaith Harmony Week.

He added that the winners here are from people who seriously aspire to spread the values of peace in their countries. Their presence is a chance for exchanging experiences and ideas and the global solidarity in the love of God and the neighbor.

Father Nabil Haddad – member of the judging committee- said that this is the second year of giving prizes. What distinguishes it for this year is that it is named after His Majesty King Abdullah, the source of the initiative, who presented it to the whole world to choose the best three events that transform the idea of the World Interfaith Harmony Week that is based on the love of God and love of the neighbor, or the love of Good and love of the neighbor in the atheist societies.

In a statement to the Jordan News Agency (Petra), he referred that the committee received a number of events from all over the world; the focus was not only one the dialogue between religions, but also on the personification of this dialogue and reaching to the young people and society.

He also said that World harmony interfaith is an idea that stemmed from Amman and presented to the whole world. From Amman, we present a model to the entire world for what our society witnesses according to a vision that is based on the Hashemite rule school that acts according to the love of God and love of the neighbor.

He said "what we find and boast of is being in the home of All Jordanians to present this model to the whole world and say to them: come and see."

The ceremony was attended by His Royal Highness Ghazi Muhammad, Chief Advisor to King Abdullah II for Religious and Cultural Affairs and Personal Envoy of King Abdullah II, Chief of the Hashemite Royal Court, the Director of the King's Office, Grand Mufti of the Kingdom and an array of high officials.

It is noteworthy that the number of events submitted to the World Interfaith Harmony Week since its inception in 2011 till this year is 213 events, 290 events, 363 events and 409 events for the current year 2014 respectively.

- **Fund for Support of scientific projects in the Middle East:**

In accordance with His Majesty King Abdullah II bin Al Hussein 's vision, the 3rd Petra Conference of Nobel laureates 16-15 May 2007 launched the Fund for Support of scientific projects in the Middle East which has been launched and inaugurated in the 4th conference with a constituent capital of 10 million Dollars (7 million Dinars). His Majesty contributed with two million Dollars and the fund started its work in spreading and strengthening scientific cooperation between academic institutions in the Arab Countries and the region.

The fund is devoted to the scientific research undergone by students in the Master of Science. This fund will encourage non-profit cooperation between countries. It will also facilitate cooperation between scientists in the Middle East universities. Moreover, it pays a special attention to the initiatives of scientific research directed to dealing with the urgent developmental challenges that surpass the borders of the one country such as energy, renewable sources of energy, water management, environment, health, technology, etc.

- **Human Rights:**

His Majesty King Abdullah II bin Al Hussein paid a great attention to the strengthening of human rights and public freedom. To achieve his vision in this context, he ordered to establish a royal authority that supports human rights in Jordan, leading to the establishment of the National Center of Human Rights in 2002 in order to achieve the royal vision to protect and strengthen human rights and public freedoms in Jordan based on the teachings of Islam, the Arabic and Islamic heritage, the relevant articles of the Constitution and the principles of international charters.

The strategy of the center included working to achieve a group of main goals centered on some axes that include:

- Education in order to merge the concepts of human rights in the educational curricula

- Reinforcing justice and developing legislations that protect human rights according to national legislations and international agreements

- Providing support and protection for the categories who are more apt to transgression so that they can be able to claim their rights

- Reinforcing the pillars of political and democratic development to widen the basis of public participation in decision-making and monitoring its implementation

- Devoting economic, social and cultural rights that enable the person to enjoy his/her economic, social and cultural rights according to international standards

Al Jafr prison has been closed and turned into a school and a training center.

The closure of Al Jafr prison completes the journey of the penal system reform in Jordan. This journey costs 24 million JDs. It aims to improve the infrastructure of the existing prisons and building new ones that reduce the crowdedness in prisons in addition to providing rehabilitation and reform programs for prisoners.

• Justice:

In the course of his application to the principle of "Justice is the basis for rule", a royal committee was established to develop the judiciary system in 2000. This committee began the development and improvement according to justice development strategy. This strategy seeks to surpass traditional thoughts and turns that disrupted its start and its indulgence in the world of modernity, legal and judicial reform that His majesty seeks. He is convinced that no political, administrative, educational or economic development can take place with radical reform in all the axes of the litigation process which devote security, stability and equilibrium and reinforce the investment gains in the country.

These reforms had international dimension, especially the reputation of any country and the extent of its progress or deterioration reflects the extent of the judicial system's commitment to monitoring systems and laws and guaranteeing their sovereignty according to the vision of institutions and sovereignty of law as an application of equality, transparency and equal opportunities between the members of society. Jordan is ranked 23 out of 102 countries in the independence of the judiciary system according to the Global Competitiveness Report 2005.

- **Aqaba Special Economic Zone:**

In the outset of 2002, His Majesty King Abdullah II launched an initiative to develop Aqaba to be a state-of-the-art business zone that provides local jobs and develops the skills of manpower, encourages foreign investment and becomes an economic power that pushes the country forward.

His Majesty King Abdullah II asked the concerned officials in 2002 to set a comprehensive plan to turn Aqaba into a special economic zone and assigned a temporary group of work with the setting of the legislative, executive and legal frame work of it.

This main and comprehensive plan was quickly accomplished. In 2001, the Authority of Aqaba Special Economic Zone was established.

Aqaba, which is full of vitality, will contain the Prince Hashim Bin Abdullah II Military Hospital, a branch of the University of Jordan, a Faculty of Hospitality in order to develop the tourism industry and help Jordanians find better jobs.

It will also contain the first faculty specialized in cinematic arts: the Red Sea Institute of Cinematic Arts which will be established

Aqaba Special Economic Zone

by the Royal Film Commission Jordan in partnership with one of the most famous and most important cinematic institutes, namely University of Southern California School of Cinematic Arts.

- **His Majesty King Abdullah II bin Al Hussein 's book "Our Last Best Chance" in its Arabic and foreign versions**

King Abdullah II bin Al Hussein 's book cover

In this book, King Abdullah speaks about his journey since the early childhood, the early and late study as well as his accompaniment of his father the late King Al Hussein till his assumption of power in a hard period and a region full of serious events. He also reviews the precise and sensitive issues that face the Middle East in addition to his own reformist vision which began with the assumption of his constitutional responsibilities. This includes his conviction that comprehensive reform is an inevitability imposed by the Kingdom of Jordan and the benefits of its people.

His Majesty assures that the Middle East will never witness stability as long as the Palestinian case is not settled and the Palestinian people get their rights of freedom and independence in terms of a comprehensive regional solution. He warns that the chance of achieving peace is vanishing and its gap is being narrowed in the face of the Israeli stubbornness. This puts the region on the verge of more states of war and conflicts that will be more disastrous than the former wars. He also says that Israel has to choose between being in an isolated castle surrounded by conflicts or peace which guarantees security and stability for all countries in the Middle East.

- **The Morals and Modesty of His Majesty King Abdullah II**

    The Independent Newspaper/ the UK say:

    "We all need the moral lesson and modesty shown by the Jordanian King"

Also, the newspaper stated that "the most people who need this are the presidents.

He is a person who removes dust from the grave of one of the citizens of his people and hides the tear in his eye to maintain the strength of his people whom he addresses as (my sons). He is an unrepeatable man. I wish I had been one of his people."

- International Council for. Human Rights, Arbitration Politics and Strategic Studies:

In 2013, the International Council for Human Rights, Arbitration Politics and Strategic Studies, under the supervision of Dr. Mohammed Mahmoud al-Jasmi, the Secretary-General of the council, launched a vote that included a big array of the famous world characters in the different fields which drew the attention of many sites.

After the end of the vote in July 2013, Dr. Al-Jasmi declared the names of the winners who are considered influential people in the course of action and the creation of a cultural and developmental climate. They are the people who influenced the history of humanity.

The list of presidents and political leaders included the elite of the people who played an important role in the political course of humanity. Those people were:

German Chancellor Angela Merkel, US President Barack Obama, Sheikh Hamad bin Khalifa al-Thani, British Prime Minister David Cameron, Brazilian President Dilma Rousseff, Turkish Prime Minister Recep Tayyip Erdogan, Jordanian King Abdullah II, Saudi King Abdullah bin Abdul Aziz Al Saud, French President François Hollande, Russian President Vladimir Putin, Sultan of Oman Qaboos bin Said, Moroccan King Mohammed VI, Sheikh Mohammed bin Rashid Al Maktoum, Dr. Saeb Erekat, Hillary Clinton

Kings Presidents and politicians

- **The Discussion Papers of His Majesty King Abdullah II:**

   Analytic reading in the Discussion Papers written by His Majesty King Abdullah II

   And a review of their most important elements

In a rare unprecedented method of Kings and leaders' communication with their people in the form of written messages, King Abdullah II issued five discussion papers to the sons of his nation.

The royal papers carried in their folds many of the concepts, meanings, implications, messages and political and social values that include the features of the King's reformist vision. They also assure that there is a deep insight supported by a serious and strong political leadership for the first decision-maker in the country in order to reinforce and deepen the democratic approach in practical and untraditional methods. This is a contribution from him to the journey of reform initiated by him which forces us to benefit from the historical moment that Jordan and the Arab world pass in order to strengthen and develop the building of the state so that it can able to meet the quick changes that sweep the Arab nation currently.

The vision is not less important than the political will. The vision develops or destroys; gives life or takes life. The will reflects the desire in achieving the desired change. Without the vision and the will, the hoped change can never take place and we cannot establish an integrated democratic system.

Since ascending the Throne in 1999, His Majesty King Abdullah II ibn Al Hussein has established a clear vision for comprehensive reform and the democratic future in Jordan.

In a series of discussion papers, King Abdullah II has sought to inspire a national dialogue on the reform endeavors and the democratic transformation process that Jordan is witnessing, with the aim of reaching a consensus, encouraging public participation in decision-making and sustaining the constructive momentum around the continuous reform process.

- **First Discussion Paper**

  Our Journey to Forge Our Path towards Democracy

- **Second Discussion Paper**

  Making Our Democratic System suitable for All Jordanians

- **Third Discussion Paper**

  New roles are awaiting us for the success for our new Democracy

- **Fourth Discussion Paper**

  Towards Democratic Empowerment and Active Citizenship

- **Fifth Discussion Paper**

  Deepening Our Democratic Transition: Goals, Achievements and Conventions

- **First Discussion Paper 2013/12/29**

  Our Journey to Forge Our Path towards Democracy

In its first part, the King addressed the timing of issuing the paper which was the launch of election campaigns for the 17th House of Representatives. These elections are still a source of debate for the Jordanian society despite the amendments that took place in the election process. It is not only the elections law which contains a space for the National List, what is equally important is the creation of an independent authority for elections that ends the domination of the executive power on the supervision on elections and sometimes on the results of the electoral process; this made the citizen lose faith and trust in the benefit of the process. Among the values that were stressed in this part is that representation is not an immunity or personal privileges or gains as it was practiced by many representatives in more than one term. It is rather a matter of serving people, representation of them and bearing a great national responsibility. He who meets this responsibility should put before his eyes the interests of the country in the beginning of his interests and considerations.

If the candidate is willing to achieve personal gains through the parliament, the citizen should bear a part of this responsibility through his electoral behavior and the criteria followed to choose a candidate. The citizen should give his vote according to political and democratic basis; to choose the candidate who is able to perform his mission and translate the expectations and hopes of people. They should not vote according to personal criteria; to choose his relative or the one who will perform a personal benefit for him. Getting this done, it will restore the trust which was lost in the parliamentary process making elections a chance for launching a comprehensive and direct national dialogue as well as a necessary reference for the national journey that all the concerns of the citizen and the country or both, away from compliments and compromising on the constants of home and its moral systems.

If this dialogue is our hoped path and our only choice in this stage, the participants of this dialogue should believe that none has got the ultimate truth and they should be sure that believing in the diversity and difference is one of the simplest requirements of the national dialogue that finally leads to the concord not consensus.

The paper warned against the monopoly of opinion or decision-making and blocking the way in the face of concord and compatibility, because this will lead to the regression of the democratic journey and what is more dangerous it leads to the foundation of the culture of marginalization, exclusion and tyranny and it may devote extremism and violence.

So, we should pass these ideas in order to restore freedom and democracy to its right path, because democracy is made complete only by the constructive initiative and accepting the other opinion as His Majesty said.

His Majesty thinks that there are four practices and principles that should be apparent in our social and political behavior in order to build the hoped democratic system. These four practices are shown in the following:

First: Respect for all fellow citizens' opinions is the essence of partnership between all.

Second: Citizenship and accountability go hand in hand.

Third: We may differ, but we should never get separated because dialogue and concord is a consistent national duty.

Fourth: We are all partners in gains and sacrifices.

In the final section, The King gave an answer to the following question: How can we know that we are on the right path?

He said that we make sure that we are on the right path as long as we apply the practices he mentioned till we achieve the following:

A shared sense of dignity and pride in what we are doing together as a nation;

A sense of achievement in overcoming the challenges and hurdles we confront together, through shared commitment and shared sacrifice, on our path to prosperity and greater security through a stronger democracy;

Active engagement in shaping the future of Jordan through voting in elections – a commitment to democracy as a national paradigm and a way of life;

Fruitful and respectful debates and discussions taking place in person and through social and digital networking;

Civility between citizens characterized by a strong volunteering culture and growing generosity and trust to, and from, people we do not personally know.

- **Second Discussion Paper 2013/1/16**

    Making Our Democratic System suitable for All Jordanians

His Majesty sees that democratic reform is not a mere amendment in the laws and systems, it rather requires a consistent development of the approach that controls the practices and relationship between citizens on one hand and the government and representatives who burden the responsibility of decision-making on behalf of the people who voted for them.

His Majesty says: In this paper, I want to discuss another critical aspect of our democratic development as a contribution in the national dialogue– the transition to parliamentary government.

The principles of our journey and reformist approach are clear.

We are committed to nurture and protect political pluralism and the rights of people. We will also continue to develop the censorship mechanisms and appropriate practical checks for the separation of and balances between powers for a properly functioning democracy. We will strengthen and enhance our civil society and ensure a level playing field for political competition. The rights of all citizens will be safeguarded as per our Constitution.

The essential question we must answer together is how our institutions and systems will continue to strengthen and protect these principles as we are making our transition?

Everybody should realize that we will meet some difficulties and challenges. There will be some setbacks, but more successes, and all of them will be subject to public scrutiny. But this is normal, for such developments are necessary to any emerging democracy and are a clear sign of its authenticity and credibility.

His Majesty spoke in some detail about the following:

- The democratic systems and the Jordanian model,

- Forming governments and the transition to transition to parliamentary governments,

- Working to achieve the comprehensive approach of parliamentary governments and the requirements of a successful democratic transition.

His Majesty also sees that reaching the comprehensive approach of parliamentary governments mainly depends on three basic requirements which rely on the cumulative experience and active performance; they are:

First: we will need to see the emergence of true national parties that aggregate specific and local interests into an applicable national platform.

Second: our Civil Service will need to further develop its abilities and work on the basis of professionalism and impartiality away from politicization to support and advise the Ministers of parliamentary governments.

Third: Changing the parliamentary conventions and the internal system of the House of Representatives in order to support parliamentary government. Opposition parties will similarly need to agree on conventions for how they cooperate in holding the Government to account and offer an alternative vision (as a shadow government). Their role is just as crucial for the success of parliamentary governments.

Looking ahead: Roles and Responsibilities:

The more quickly and successfully these three above conditions are fulfilled, the more successful our transition to parliamentary government can and will be. They are also the basis for the democratic transition in our political system. As we make that transition, it will be important that different groups and institutions in our political society take on new and changing roles and responsibilities.

- **Third Discussion Paper 2013/3/2**

    New roles are awaiting us for the success for our new Democracy

    His Majesty dedicated this paper for discussing the political development in Jordan and focusing on our mutual future and how to go ahead especially after the elections that took place on 23rd of last January.

The importance of these elections is that they were held in democratic and transparent atmospheres that were apparent in the unprecedented number of candidates who had been administered and supervised by an independent authority as well as Arab and Foreign observers for the first time. The produced House of Representatives is more representing society. Reaching active parliamentary governments requires the existence of parties with deep roots all over the country, strong programs which depend on the a general framework that is based on national democratic values incarnated as a democratic culture in our public institutions and our political life.

His Majesty says: in Jordan we realize the essential values of achieving the democratic transition and instilling the approach of parliamentary governments. The most important of these values are pluralism, tolerance, sovereignty of law and separation and balance of powers in addition to protecting the deeply rooted rights of citizens and insuring each spectrum that expresses a political opinion in a fair chance to compete through ballot box. The definition of parliamentary government is represented in the order of the relationship between the legislative and executive power as follows: the executive is accountable to the parliamentary majority through the vote of confidence as stipulated by the Jordanian Constitution.

General political practice in parliamentary governments worldwide allows for MPs to serve as ministers, and so does our Constitution, **but in parallel with a set of fundamental requirements:**

The first is an advanced set of checks-and-balances that preserves the separation of powers and stipulates monitoring tools.

The second is the gradual inclusion of MPs in the Cabinet should be gradual and in parallel to the evolvement of political parliamentary and political parties work.

The third is to develop government's work so that it becomes more professional, neutral and apolitical, so that it serves as a trusted reference and source of technical support for parliamentary government ministers in their decision-making.

His Majesty says: In the following sections, I would like to discuss the evolution of these roles, including my role as a King, and the responsibilities we all must assume as engaged and responsible citizens.

- The Role of Political Parties

- The Role of Parliament

- The Role of the Prime Minister and the Cabinet

- The Role of the Monarch

- The Role of the Citizen

The future ahead of us:

We will face real challenges along the way. Sometimes, this effort will feel unfamiliar and difficult. This is to be expected, because we are doing something truly different for the sake of a better future. I am sure we will confront and overcome these challenges together. Democracies do this better than any other system of governance, because everyone has a voice and a certain role to play.

- **Fourth Discussion Paper 2013/6/2**

    Towards Democratic Empowerment and Active Citizenship

    In light of these inputs, we are developing a uniquely Jordanian model of democracy, which reflects our distinct culture, aspirations and needs.

The vision is now clearer to many sectors of society, who began to vividly recognize that the essential reform goal is to enhance citizens' participation in decision making, by deepening our approach to parliamentary government through successive parliamentary cycles, in order to reach a state where political parties are able to achieve an effective presence in the Lower House of Parliament. This will allow the parliamentary majority to form a party-based and platform-based government, paralleled by a parliamentary minority that works as a shadow government and competes constructively with the ruling majority by providing alternative platforms and policies. These national parties will compete at the ballot box for the rotation of governments.

One of the most important requirements for democratization efforts is enhancing the role of civil society in observing and elevating the political performance of all institutions, by enhancing a democratic culture across society. This is the essence of this fourth discussion paper, which is concurrent with the launch of an additional civil society effort geared towards enhancing our democratic model by beginning to lay the building blocks for a democratic culture that guarantees a tangible and comprehensive change.

Consequently, and due to the vital role that civil society plays in enhancing our democratic model, I directed to the necessity to establish a Democracy Empowerment Program during my speech on December 2012, 10, in the University of Jordan's 50th anniversary.

Now, we witness the launch of this program under the umbrella of King Abdullah II Fund for Development.

This commitment and participation is the essence of what I have been referring to in my previous discussion papers as "active citizenship", which I also regard in this paper as an essential condition for democratization.

- Political Participation and Active Citizenship

Political participation has not got a positive influence unless it embraces the principle of "active citizenship", which is based on three pillars: The right to participate; the duty to participate; and the responsibility to participate peacefully and respectfully, and they go hand in hand with the following principles:

First, engaging in the political life is a right for all citizens. The space to freely express divergent political views must be protected.

Second, Political participation, in its essence, is a responsibility and a duty. Each citizen must share a part of the burden of deciding on the future we want to build for our next generations.

Third, active participation in political life also brings with it certain personal responsibilities about the engagement in political work.

- Let's go ahead in a democratic empowerment that provides the tools for active citizenship.

Going back to the democratic empowerment program, its official launch comes as an additional and a new station on the course of political development and participation reinforcement.

His Majesty says: I'd like to assure a group of principles for those who are responsible for the application of the program:

First: it should be neutral and non-partisan.

Second: the program should follow the rules of transparency in its providing of support.

I encourage all Jordanians with creative ideas, willingness to work hard to serve our country, and desire to lead this work of building our democratic political system to step forward and take advantage of this important new program.

Accepting this responsibility, you provide an example of leadership in political, social and civic work, and help in building a better and stronger Jordan for all citizens. You will make success stories for all the Arabs and the whole world that you are able to take the lead and achieve the success of our democracy.

- **Fifth Discussion Paper 2014/9/13**

    Deepening Our Democratic Transition: Goals, Achievements and Conventions

His Majesty says: according to the previously-mentioned, I will try through this 5th discussion paper to highlight the achievements fulfilled along three parallel tracks in addition to a review of the next achievement stations that must be achieved especially the system of values, practices, roles and conventions that we must continue to deepen and develop in order to retain our reformist journey and achieving its final goal successfully and in a way that meets the citizens' aspirations.

Here are the most important achievements fulfilled till now:

Legislative Achievements:

- Endorsing constitutional amendments through additional checks, thereby strengthening the separation of powers and freedoms,

- Achieving a new package of legislations that organize political life and came into force before the last parliamentary elections,

- A new State Security Court Law has been enacted that limits the Court's jurisdiction to treason, espionage, terrorism, drugs and currency counterfeiting and ensures that civilians stand trial only in front of a civilian court,

- Finally, the most notable progress made by the House of Representatives is represented in reforming its internal by-laws that help to improve its operations and effectiveness.

Institutional Achievements:

- Establishing a Constitutional Court that specializes in interpreting the Constitution and overseeing the constitutionality of the applied laws and regulations,

- Establishing a new Independent Elections Commission

- The House of Representatives has recently established a legislative research Centre to support the work of MPs and the specialized parliamentary committees, ensuring that their work and decisions are informed by facts and evidence,

- consistency to work to strengthen our Judiciary and enhance the national system for integrity, transparency and accountability,

- Supporting the National Centre for Human Rights (NCHR), along with a relevant network of institutions,

- Continue working on all public sector reform paths

- Finally, and consistent with our evolution towards a fully developed system of parliamentary government, many reforms are being applied in our national security agencies.

Milestones of Actors in Our Political System:

Our 'Jordanian Spring' must continue to adopt the following essential democratic practices: demonstrating respect for and embracing dialogue, even in the face of disagreement; accepting the reciprocity of rights and responsibilities as citizens; accepting that shared sacrifices lead to shared gains; turning disagreement into concords; and active and participation by all citizens.

Stakeholders in our political system – the Monarchy, MPs, government, political parties and citizens – must internalize and apply these values and practices in playing their national roles and exercising their responsibilities. These roles and responsibilities represent a major component of the third reform track:

- The Hashemite Monarchy is responsible for providing unifying leadership for all components that looks forward to ensuring the prosperity for all generations.

- Members of Parliament have the responsibility of serving as honest public servants. Their performance should reflect a balance of local and national interests and a balance between collaboration and constructive opposition to the government.

- Government, embodied in the Prime Minister, Ministers and Civil Servants, is responsible for developing and executing comprehensive programs for improving the economic opportunities and social well-being Jordanians deserve.

- Political parties have a responsibility to merge into a logical number of major nationally-based parties.

- Citizens have the responsibility to actively and constructively participate in all aspects of political life.

The democratic empowerment program will shortly launch an equally important new initiative, Akeed, the observatory of Jordanian media credibility, in partnership with the Jordan Media Institute. This initiative is designed to help citizens become fully and accurately informed about issues that matter to them by helping to check and verify news reports concerning government and elected politicians in popular media outlets from newspapers to websites. This is an important element of making our political system more transparent and accountable to the public.

Looking forward to the future:

His Majesty says: now, we have to consider the following stage of achievements that we have to pass as follows:

- Lawmakers must improve key political laws, assuring consensus and enhancing our parliamentary government experience. Furthermore, Parliament must enhance parliamentary blocs as they encourage political parties' action.

- Governments must continuously develop the public sector and the government system so that they can be highly professional, impartial, non-political and capable of producing evidence-based policy proposals advising future ministers of parliamentary governments.

- Political parties must continue to develop their internal systems and capabilities so that they evolve into programmatic, professional, nationally-recognized parties, capable of winning a majority of votes.

- Build our Judiciary's capacities should be an on-going process, because justice is the basis of government; in addition to developing the capacities of the Constitutional Court and the Independent Elections Commission.

- The Royal Committee for Evaluating the Progress of the National Integrity System's Executive Plan must continue overseeing the implementation of the National Integrity System's recommendations.

- Civil society organizations, including universities and think tanks, in addition to the private sector need to play a greater role in their contribution to produce ideas and researches that provide solutions to challenges facing the Kingdom.

- His Majesty goes on: Government, Parliament and the Civil Service must, therefore, develop further the conventions that already exist and build new ones in light of the arising changes and challenges.

- Areas in which enhancing existing conventions and building new ones are needed to ensure effective collaboration and coordination between our political actors include:

- The consultative mechanism for designating prime ministers as well as a mechanism for formulating the PM-designate and his Cabinet's four-year policy plan,

- Regulating question-and-answer sessions from Parliament to government ministers as well as identifying the roles of Ministers, MPs and the Civil Service,

His Majesty resumes: accordingly, we have a collective duty to embrace democratic values and practices and continue developing them in the years ahead. This can be achieved by enrooting them into our value system, education and laws through awareness campaigns, curricula and empowering national institutions to guarantee these values and practices.

I'd like to conclude this paper by reiterating that security, democracy and prosperity reinforce each other as the foundations for our future. They depend on each other. Current regional challenges represent an exceptionally pressing situation. However, Jordan is firmly following on the political development path. But our national economy, with the strains it is facing, requires our full attention.

Sayings and statements by His Majesty King Abdullah II bin Al Hussein :

- ### Security and Peace

    "Jordan could have never achieved these successes without the blessings of security and stability. Peace means development, the best future, economic growth and cooperation."

- ### The Palestinian Case

    "Jordan, the immune, safe and stable nation, will continue to support its Arab brothers in defending our Arab Islamic issues, above all is the Palestinian case."

- ### The Iraqi Case

    "I'm so optimistic about Iraq, because I believe in the Iraqi people and their vision of the elevation of their country."

- ### Islam and the Interfaith Dialogue

    "It is impossible to speak about interfaith harmony and coherence, especially between the East and the West without reaching the solutions to settle the conflicts in the Middle East."

- ### Attitude toward Terrorism

    "People realize the danger of terrorists on their security, stability and living. These terrorists don't differentiate between a civilian and military; a child or a woman. They have no case or reason to discuss or speak about with others, simply because their pretexts are invalid and find no echo in the streets."

- **Education and Health:**

"Improving the life standard of citizens, male or female, requires an interest in health care which is a right for all citizens, regardless their gender. The person who enjoys a good standard of health and feels endured for himself as well as his family is the person who is able to work and produce. The government took actual steps in the expanding of the health insurance system to conclude all citizens and pay special care for infantry and maternity programs."

- **Youth:**

"Young people, you are the future of this country. So, you should make this future; not only by participation but also by leading the journey of reform, change and building the desired future for your country and the generations to come."

- **Modernization and political and social reform:**

"Reform in Jordan is not restricted to someone in specific. Jordan has got a long walk to reform which has always been in the heart of our priorities."

- **Human Rights:**

"We want media to deliver a message of freedom and reform,

maximize the nation's achievements, and strengthen national unity and the interrelations between Jordanians and their relationship with the state on the basis of citizenship that is based on justice, respect of law, guarantee of public freedoms and human dignity."

- **Democracy:**

"We are the offspring of one nation. We should defend its progress, sovereignty and democratic image. Our country is not new to reform and opposition, but it is the country of satisfaction and harmony between its people in all their affairs. Our constitutional democratic political system is our shield and firewall along with our heritage of freedom, justice, promising future and above all the love of home."

"Finally, I'd like to say that democracy doesn't mean win or loss; it also doesn't mean that there are ultimately correct answers. Our strength lies in our treatment with variables around us. Be sure that we will all win as long as we continue to go ahead on the reform and overall development path on the basis that we are all partners in both gains and sacrifices."

- **Her Majesty Queen Rania Al-Abdullah**

Rania Al-Abdullah was born on August 31st, 1970. After earning her Bachelor's degree in Business Administration from the American University of Cairo in 1991, she began her career in the banking sector in Jordan and, later, in the information technology sector.

After marrying Prince Abdullah bin Al Hussein on June 10th, 1993, they had four children: Prince Hussein, Princess Iman, Princess Salma, and Prince Hashem.

Being a wife and mother, Queen Rania did not give up working hard to raise the standard of the lives of Jordanians by supporting their efforts and helping to create new opportunities for them.

Locally, she made great efforts in favor of the public education system development; empowering communities and women especially through microfinance initiatives; protecting children and families; and encouraging innovation, technology and entrepreneurship, especially among young people.

Internationally, Queen Rania is well-known for her support for tolerance, compassion and bridge building between people of all cultures and backgrounds. She has been globally recognized for her efforts to simultaneously challenge stereotypes of Arabs and Muslims, and promote greater understanding and acceptance between people of all faiths and cultures.

Her Majesty has got a great passion for education. She believes that every Jordanian girl and boy, and all children, should have access not only to stimulating classrooms and modern curricula, but also inspiring teachers and technology that can connect Jordan's children to the world and vice-versa. Her efforts in the education sector complement the work of the Ministry of Education through initiatives such as the Jordan Education Initiative, the Queen Rania Teachers Academy, Madrasati, Edraak and others. To realize these and so much more, Queen Rania has encouraged private sector partners to urge improvements and strengthen the foundations of Jordan's education system.

Queen Rania is also a global activist that guarantees the delivery of quality education for children around the world. In 2009, Her Majesty took part in the 1 Goal campaign for education; she is Honorary Chair of the UN Girl's Education Initiatives and has been defending the children's right to receive quality education in forums and gatherings around the world.

Her work and efforts to improve the learning opportunities for children have been recognized at the highest levels, nationally, regionally and internationally.

Additionally, through her position on the boards of the United Nations Fund and the World Economic Forum, Her Majesty can contribute to the support of their work. She is an eminent supporter for UNICEF; and was part of the UN appointed High Level Panel who advised on the shape and content of the Sustainable Development

Goals which aim to improve the lives of millions of people before 2030.

In recognition of her work, Her Majesty has received many awards, locally, regionally and globally. These include the Walther Rathenau Award from the Walther Rathenau Institute in Germany for her efforts in peace and understanding; the James C. Morgan Global Humanitarian Award from Tech Awards, USA; the Arab Knight of Giving Award from Arab Giving Forum, UAE; the North South Prize by the North South Prize, Portugal; as well as the YouTube Visionary Award.

Her Majesty has written several books primarily for children including Salma and Laila which was inspired by her own childhood experiences. She also has other stories such as "the Sandwich Swap" (Salma and Laila), the King's Gift and Lasting Beauty.

Initiatives of Her Majesty the venerable Queen Rania Al-Abdullah:

- **Queen Rania Foundation for Education and Development:**

Her Majesty Queen Rania Al-Abdullah has established this foundation to produce and store studies and events concerning the national, regional and global education issues that can contribute to making a positive change in the academic and practical attitudes and situations including education, its input, its outputs and motivation for innovation.

This can happen through the production and generalization of fliers, blogs, data and reports that facilitate the reader, the thinker and the researcher's access to the information and the updates of this field.

Mission:

> Support educational reform and policy development through specialized research and sustainable and influential initiatives.

Vision:

> QRF is the leading reference point in education for development in the region.

- **Jordan River Foundation:**

Her Majesty Queen Rania Al-Abdullah has established Jordan River Foundation, a non-governmental and non-profit foundation. This foundation chaired by Her Majesty Queen Rania Al-Abdullah is the leading foundation in the national developmental work in order to lead work in the areas of child protection and empowerment of societies and the women of Jordan.

Since its inception, the foundation took the initiative to establish various economic and social projects which aim to provide job opportunities for women that enable them to improve their standard of living. Concurrently, these businesses reinforce the skills of women in the traditional handcrafts as well as building their abilities in the field of businesses entrepreneurship and development.

Mission:

> Engaging Jordanians and empowering them to develop their own economic abilities and overcome the social barriers especially violence against children.

Vision:

> Jordan which can innovate the perfect solutions for the challenges which face it, and acts as a fertile ground for prosperity opportunities for all, whose future depends on the safety of its children.

- **Edraak:**

It is a non-profit Arabic platform for Massive Open Online Courses (MOOCs). It launched in May 2014.

Edraak makes quality education in Arabic available for all internet users and promotes lifelong learning, whether for higher education or professional development. Edraak provides a platform for a diverse range of free online courses, offered by top universities and entities. They do this by employing regional and global Arab talent to leverage technology developed by the Harvard- Massachusetts Institute of Technology (MIT) consortium, edX.

Mission:

> Providing high quality Arabic online education and bridging the gap between formal education outcomes and learners' needs in order to enable them to get the opportunities of their own and their societies' improvement.

Vision:

> Achieving a radical change in the process of providing quality education in Arabic with the aim of enabling the Arab society to fulfill its potential

- **The Children's Museum Jordan:**

It is a non-profit educational foundation established by Her Majesty Queen Rania Al-Abdullah in 2007.

The museum offers 150 interactive scientific models in the indoor and outdoor exhibits and the educational facilities including the Library, the Art Studio as well as the educational programs, the occasions and exhibits available all over the year.

Mission:

Reinforcing children's love of knowledge

Vision:

To be unforgettable experience in the bringing up of children

- **Royal Health Awareness Society:**

The Royal Health Awareness Society (RHAS) was established in 2005 according to the directions of Her Majesty Queen Rania Al-Abdullah to raise health and awareness and empower the local society to follow healthy behaviors. The society implements developmental programs to meet the needs of the local community in compatibility with the national healthy priorities.

Mission:

Increase the Jordanian society's healthy awareness through the implementation of preventative programs that seek the safety and health in accordance with the principles of health for all.

Vision:

A healthy and secure Jordanian society

- **Madrasati:**

The initiative of Madrasati has been launched since 2008 by Her Majesty Queen Rania Al-Abdullah with the aim of improving the educational environment in terms of the financial and educational aspects of the schools in Jordan.

To achieve this, the initiative gathered volunteers, private companies and institutions to support the most neglected public schools in Jordan.

The initiative serves Jordanian public schools run by the Ministry of Education identified as most underperforming and most in need of renovation and infrastructure maintenance.

Mission:

Providing a supportive and enabling school environment for both teaching and learning by building the abilities of the school staff and empowering students to master the fundamental skills of life, interactive citizenship and developing sustainable partnerships with all the relevant parties

Vision:

    A supportive and empowering educational environment that contributes to improve education outcomes

- **The Queen Rania Teacher Academy:**

Queen Rania Teacher Academy (QRTA) is an independent non-profit organization committed to the vision of Her Majesty Queen Rania Al Abdullah of empowering educators with the skills, recognition, and support necessary to excel in their classrooms.

QRTA was established in 2009 to raise the quality of teaching in Jordan by developing the skills of teachers through continuous training and professional development. QRTA draws on the expertise of their educational partners, Columbia University Teachers College and Columbia University Middle East Research Centre, to raise the quality of teaching in Jordan.

Vision:

    QRTA aims to lead the advancement in the quality of

teaching and the promotion of excellence in education in Jordan, and the region. QRTA simply believes that every educator should be given the skills, recognition and support to excel.

Mission:

QRTA's mission is to enable every educator to positively influence the future generation of Jordan and the Arab World by spearheading education policy reform and teacher professional development.

- **The Queen Rania Award for Excellence in Education:**

On October 2005, 5 AD, on the occasion of Teacher's Day, Her Majesty Queen Rania Al Abdullah and His Royal Highness Crown Prince Al Hussein bin Abdullah II initiated an annual teacher award, known as the Queen Rania Al-Abdullah Award for Excellence in Education.

QRAEE was initiated in recognition of the critical role education plays in developing a productive and informed society, to consolidate the role of educators in various positions in the upbringing of an intellectual and creative generation, leading the society towards excellence.

Mission:

Honoring educators, motivating the distinguished among them, disseminating the culture of excellence and creativity and contributing to knowledge creation.

Vision:

Creating new horizons in educational excellence to build future generations.

- **Al-Aman Fund for the Future of Orphans:**

Her Majesty Queen Rania Al-Abdullah launched Al-Aman campaign in 2003, that later was institutionalized as a charity non-for-profit organization under the name of Al-Aman Fund for the Future of Orphans, and is aimed at providing education to Boarding orphans who have resided in Orphan Care Centers for part of, or all their childhood and Non-boarding orphans supported by Orphan Support Organizations who live in poverty with a guardian or an immediate relative living below the poverty line to secure their future.

Mission:

To equip orphaned youth with the education and skills necessary to become self-reliant members of society, through the management of appropriate and effective support programs to meet their needs.

Vision:

Provide orphaned youth with a better future

- **The Jordan Education Initiative:**

The Jordan Education Initiative is one of Her Majesty's Queen Rania Al Abdullah not-for-profit organizations. It was initiated during the World Economic Forum in 2003 AD under the patronage

of His Majesty King Abdullah II and Jordan's Government. The Jordan Education Initiative (JEI) has emerged as the first model that manifests the true partnership between the public and private sectors on a local and global scale.

JEI was launched with the aim of supporting Jordan's efforts in improving the level of education, encouraging creativity, developing capabilities, and building a knowledge economy using modern technology means at (100) state school, later renamed (Discovery Schools); where the technological infrastructure in these schools was developed, through the provision of wireless networks and provide teachers with a laptop and projector.

Furthermore, it aims to the development of e-content consistent with the Jordanian curriculum and able to support it along with enabling the teachers to use these curricula in a manner that serves the educational process.

Mission:

> Accelerate education reform through innovation and integration of ICT in education to further add value to students, teachers and the education system and effectively contribute in building a knowledge economy.

Vision:

> A world class education innovation Center of Excellence that leverages public-private partnerships to leapfrog education transformation in Jordan and the region.

- **The National Council for Family Affairs:**

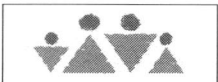 The National Council for Family Affairs (NCFA) was established by Law in July 2001 and is chaired by Her Majesty Queen Rania Al Abdullah. The NCFA is mandated to work as an 'umbrella' organization and as a coordinating body for relevant governmental, non-governmental, international and private agencies in the field of family affairs; in addition to its contributions to the development of policies, strategies and plans related to the family and its members and follow up its implementation to enhance and protect the family and secure its stability, in order to maintain its cohesion and identity to enhance its role, maintain its values and cultural heritage and to achieve a better future for the Jordanian family.

Mission:

> To contribute towards the formulation and steering of policies, and support efforts that enhance the status of the Jordanian family, optimize its role, and preserve its values and heritage.

Vision:

> To create an environment that is conducive to growth and enables the Jordanian family to achieve its stability and well-being.

- **His Royal Highness Crown Prince Al Hussein bin Abdullah II**

Prince Al Hussein bin Abdullah II: He was born in Amman on the 28th of June 1994 AD (Crown Prince of the Hashemite Kingdom of Jordan). The Crown Prince is the eldest son of Their Majesties King Abdullah II and Queen Rania Al Abdullah.

HRH Crown Prince Al Hussein was named Crown Prince by a Royal Decree on the 2nd of July 2009.

On May 2012, 29 AD, HRH Crown Prince graduated from King's Academy. Football and horse riding are some of his hobbies. He is studying Political and Economic Sciences at Georgetown University.

His Royal Highness Crown Prince's initiatives:

His Royal Highness has made the future of Jordan's youth, as their engagement in society and education and economic opportunity are among some of his primary concerns.

His belief that youth can excel if given the proper tools and means is evident in his initiatives, programs and activities seeking to connect with the youth. HRH advocates for a generation of youth which is committed to community service and volunteerism.

- **Cooperation with NASA:**

His Royal Highness Crown Prince Al Hussein has established contact with NASA Ames (affiliated to National Aeronautics and Space Administration "NASA"), Moffett Field, and California, to afford Jordanian youth with a rare opportunity to become interns at the prodigious agency.

The collaboration between Jordan and NASA encompasses

internships for Jordanians interested in pursuing a career in technology as well as a joint NASA/Jordanian team collaborating on building and programming a Nano satellite such as a Cubesat.

- **Global Forum on Youth, Peace and Security - August 2015:**

For the first gathering of this kind, young people, youth-led organizations, non-governmental organizations, governments and UN entities came together to agree on a common vision and roadmap to partner with young people to prevent conflict, counter violent extremism and build lasting peace.

- **Hearing Without Borders:**

"Through the [Hearing without Borders] initiative, we can make Jordan free of hearing disabilities. In Jordan, our strength is in our people. Each person has a voice and every voice is heard. This is the message upon which the Hashemites built this country".

- **Qusai Initiative:**

"As time passes by, I am more convinced of the necessity of having solutions placed at the service of our youth to protect them of any injury they might be exposed to, may God forbid. The passing away of

Qusai was a great loss to all of us. It motivated me to launch the (Qusai Initiative), which seeks to ameliorate the performance of sports paramedics and all those who treat injured athletes. It also aims to improve the quality of programs offered in sports therapy to ensure that sports therapists are equipped with the highest degree of knowledge in their field and are fully equipped and qualified so our youth will have a better chance to excel and innovate, being surrounded with a good care system, a right that is theirs."

- **Haqiq Initiative:**

An initiative initiated by HRH Crown Prince Al Hussein bin Abdullah II in 2013 AD in order to develop individual and community skills to reach the highest levels of professionalism in the cooperation and collaboration, through the planned organizational effort aiming to facilitate the acquisition of the skills, knowledge and voluntary work; in addition to the qualification of individuals through productive work, which helps to improve the performance and teamwork to build an integrated homogenous young generation, as well as creating an effective relationships between the youth based on respect, discipline and love.

HRH Crown Prince Hussein's "Haqiq" (achieve) initiative has won the 2016 annual award of the San Marino-Alexander Bodini Foundation, granted to the world's two best organizations or initiatives.

- **"The Role of Youth in Making Sustainable Peace" International Conference:**

HRH Crown Prince Al Hussein Bin Abdullah II said that the world is facing a formidable challenge, terrorism and extremism, which may be the greatest challenge to world peace and security, with the youth being its prime victims.

The Crown Prince made the remarks as he chaired a United Nations Security Council's Meeting on "Maintenance of international peace

and security: The role of youth in countering violent extremism and promoting peace" Prince Al Hussein said: "While youth are most susceptible to the present situation and its consequences, they can also have the strongest impact on the present and the future. This has been evident in the recent events in my region. As a young man, who is part of this generation, I take part in debates about the challenges facing my generation and the need to empower youth.

"There is much talk about youth being a marginalized segment of society. Allow me to say that they are not marginalized group, but rather a targeted group. They are targeted for their huge potential, self-confidence and ability to change the world," the Crown Prince said.

He also expressed Jordan's readiness to host the first international conference on "The Role of Youth in Making Sustainable Peace", in partnership with the UN in August this year, noting that this event is aimed at enhancing the capabilities of young peace-makers in confronting extremism and terrorism.

Their Majesties King Abdullah II and Queen Rania Al-Abdullah at Crown Prince Graduation ceremony (Georgetown University, 22/05/2016, majoring in international history)

H.R.H. Crown Prince Al Hussein bin Abdullah II attending the launch of two strategic initiatives, carried out by the Public Security Department (PSD) in partnership with Cisco and the Vocational Training Corporation (VTC).

H.R.H. Crown Prince Al Hussein bin Abdullah II meets with Jordanians with special needs winners in the Beirut Marathon.

H.R.H. Crown Prince Al Hussein bin Abdullah II accompanied by His Majesty the King Abdullah II

THE HASHEMITE KINGDOM OF JORDAN
FROM ABDULLAH I TO ABDULLAH II

H.R.H. Crown Prince Al Hussein bin Abdullah II on a visit to the Civil Defense Directorate.

H.R.H. Crown Prince Al Hussein bin Abdullah II launches schools central heating project.

H.R.H. Crown Prince Al Hussein bin Abdullah II on a visit to Gendarmerie of the public security.

H.R.H. Crown Prince Al Hussein bin Abdullah II attends Friday prayers at Mosque.

H.R.H. Crown Prince Al Hussein bin Abdullah II on a visit to Ministry of Foreign Affairs.

H.R.H. Crown Prince Al Hussein bin Abdullah II chairing the first meeting of the Crown Prince Foundation' board of trustees.

H.R.H. Crown Prince Al Hussein bin Abdullah II opens The Royal Society for the Conservation of Nature.

H.R.H. Crown Prince Al Hussein bin Abdullah II on a visit to one of the charities in Jordan.

H.R.H. Crown Prince Al Hussein bin Abdullah II sworn in as Regent in His Majesty King Abdullah.

- **His Majesty King Hussein bin Talal (The Father of Modern Jordan)**

King Hussein bin Talal bin Abdullah bin Al Hussein Al Hāshimī; King of the Hashemite Kingdom of Jordan (1999 – 1935 AD). He was born in Amman on November 1935, 14, to Prince Talal bin Abdullah and Princess Zein al-Sharaf bint Jamil. King Hussein is survived by two brothers, Prince Muhammad and Prince El Hassan, and two sisters, Princess Basma and Princess Asma (died at birth). After completing his elementary education in Amman, His Majesty attended Victoria College in Alexandria, Egypt, and Harrow School in England. He later received his military education at the Royal Military Academy Sandhurst in England.

His Majesty King Hussein was proclaimed King of the Hashemite Kingdom of Jordan on August 1952, 11. He assumed full constitutional powers on 2 May 1953, amidst a delicate phase in Arab and international politics. Throughout his long and eventful reign, King Hussein was able to achieve the high levels of development — especially in the political and social fields.

He became the builder of a moderate Jordan and succeeded in securing a decent life for his people. Under his leadership, Jordan continued to play its Arab, regional and international role ably and effectively, with keen prescience in terms of development in the level of services, education and scientific advancement.

His Majesty King Hussein was an accomplished aviator, motorcyclist and race-car driver who also enjoyed water sports, skiing and tennis. He was well-known to ham radio operators throughout the world as the friendly voice of "JY1". King Hussein enjoyed surfing the Worldwide Web and used to read about political relations, history, international law, military sciences and Aviation Arts.

By virtue of being king, he was influenced by the revolutionary tide that overwhelmed the Arab arena after the triumph of Free Officers Movement in Egypt, so he asserted Jordanian independence by dismissing Glubb Pasha as the commander of the Jordanian Army in 1956, and replacing all the British officers with Arab Jordanians. King Hussein also abrogated the Anglo-Jordanian Treaty and refused

to take advantage of the English bases in Jordan to attack Egypt.

In 1958, he formed the Arab Federation of Iraq and Jordan which lasted only six months after the overthrow of the monarchy in Iraq by a military coup.

Early on, King Hussein concentrated on building an economic and industrial nation, leading to the development of the main industries -including phosphate, potash and cement, and a network of highways was built throughout the kingdom.

In 1960, only %33 of Jordanians were literate, while by 1996 during the reign of King Hussein, this number had climbed to %85.5. UNICEF statistics show that between 1981 and 1991, Jordan achieved the world's fastest annual rate of decline in infant mortality -from 70 deaths per 1000 births in 1981 to 37 per 1000 in 1991.

King Hussein also struggled throughout his -47year reign to promote peace in the Middle East. After the 1967 Arab-Israeli war, he was instrumental in drafting UNSC Resolution 242, which calls on Israel to withdraw from all the Arab lands it occupied in the 1967 war in exchange for peace. King Hussein played a pivotal role in convening the Madrid Peace Conference, and providing an "umbrella" for Palestinians to negotiate their future as part of a joint Jordanian-Palestinian delegation. In addition to the 1994 Peace Treaty between Jordan and Israel (sometimes referred to as Wadi Araba Treaty).

On 7 February 1999, King Hussein died of complications related to lymphoma cancer; he used to visit Mayo Clinic (Rochester, Minnesota) for treatment.

Shortly before his death, King Hussein named his eldest son Prince Abdullah as the Crown Prince.

King Hussein's funeral was held on 8 February after bidding

farewell in the Royal Court. The massive global presence in the funeral was for several reasons, most notably the good and strong relations of his Majesty with the most of world leaders.

- **Works of King Hussein Bin Talal:**

    - Uneasy Lies the Head. (1962)

    - My "War" with Israel. (1969)

    - Mon Métier de Roi. (1975)

- King Hussein's book "Mon Métier de Roi" is a practical lesson and an example of the faithful rulers, who prefer watching over the interests of their peoples and enrich them with the personal experiences full of lessons.

- **Wives, sons and daughters of King Hussein Bin Talal:**

    - Her Royal Highness Princess Dina Al Hussein

    - Her Royal Highness Princess Alia bint Al Hussein (born 1956).

    - Her Royal Highness Princess Muna Al Hussein

    - His Majesty Abdullah II, King of The Hashemite Kingdom of Jordan (born 1962).

    - His Royal Highness Prince Faisal bin Al Hussein of Jordan (born 1963).

    - Her Royal Highness Princess Aisha bint Hussein (born 1968).

    - Her Royal Highness Princess Zein bint Hussein (born 1968).

    - H.M. Queen Alia Al Hussein

    - Her Royal Highness Princess Haya bint Hussein (born 1974).

    - His Royal Highness Prince Ali bin Al Hussein (born 1975).

    H.M Queen Noor al Hussein

    - His Royal Highness Prince Hamzah bin al Hussein (born 1980).

    - His Royal Highness Prince Hashim bin Al Hussein (born 1981).

    - Her Royal Highness Princess Iman bint Hussein (born 1983).

    - Her Royal Highness Princess Raiyah bint Hussein (born 1986).

- **Brothers of King Hussein Bin Talal:**

    - Prince Mohammed bin Talal

    - Prince Al Hassan bin Talal

- **Sisters of King Hussein Bin Talal:**

    - Princess Asma bint Talal Princess (died at birth)

    - Princess Basma bint Talal (aunt of His Majesty King Abdullah II)

- **Wives of King Hussein Bin Talal**

Her Highness Princess Dina Abdul Hameed

She was the first wife of King Hussein. Born in Egypt, she is a graduate of Cambridge University and a former lecturer in English literature at Cairo University. She is the mother of H.R.H Princess Alia bint Hussein.

Her Royal Highness Princess Muna Al Hussein

She was the second wife of Hussein. Mother of His Majesty King Abdullah II ibn Al Hussein ; and Their Royal Highnesses Prince Faisal bin Al Hussein, Princess Aisha bint Al Hussein and Princess Zein bint Al Hussein.

HRH Princess contributed to the founding of the Princess Muna College of Nursing in 1962. She is the founder of Jordanian Nursing Council in 2002 as part of her early commitments to the provision of quality nursing and the advancement of nursing services, practice and research in the nursing profession. H.R.H has a wide range of activities at all levels at home and abroad.

Her Majesty Queen Alia Al Hussein

She was the third wife of King Hussein. She is the Mother of His Royal Highness Prince Ali bin Al Hussein and Her Royal Highness Princess Haya bint Al Hussein.

She felt free to do anything that she believed in and considered that it is important to know all peoples who share our world. She always expressed her opinion frankly (Do not pay attention to what people think as long as you know that you behave properly, she said).

Her Majesty Queen Noor al Hussein

She was the fourth wife of King Hussein. She is the Mother of their Royal Highness Prince Hamzah bin al Hussein, Prince Hashim bin Al Hussein, Princess Iman bint Hussein and Princess Raiyah bint Hussein.

H.M Queen Noor focuses on the Jordanian culture and the rights of children and women. She also contributes to numerous non-governmental organizations. Queen Noor, in conjunction with students from Yarmouk University, founded the Jerash Festival for Culture and Arts.

Under the title "Leap of Faith: Memoirs of an Unexpected Life"; Queen Noor wrote and published her autobiography in 2003. H.M Queen Noor is also active in many fields around the world.

- **His Majesty King Talal bin Abdullah**

His Majesty King Talal bin Abdullah bin Al Hussein (26 February 7 – 1909 July 1972); the second King of the Hashemite Kingdom of Jordan from 20 July 1951 until 11 August 1952.

He studied at the British Army's Royal Military College, Sandhurst, from which he graduated in 1929. King Talal ascended the Jordanian throne after the assassination of his father, Abdullah I, in Jerusalem. His son, Hussein, who was accompanying his grandfather, was also a near victim. King Talal is also judged as having done much to soften the previously strained relations between Jordan and the neighboring Arab states of Egypt. His grandmother is Saleha Bint Gharm Al Shehary, whose father is Prince Knight Gharm Al Shehary (A prince of Asir region, Namas city in the southern region of Saudi Arabia), descendants of Hagar bin Al Hnoa' bin Al Azd bin Al Ghaws bin Nabt bin Malik bin Zaid bin Kahlan bin Sabaa' bin Yashgoub bin Yaa'roub bin Qahtan, a grandfather of Bin Shahr tribe in Saudi Arabia.

He was unable to continue in power due to his illness. On August 1952 ,14, a Regency Council was appointed, under a constitutional resolution, until King Hussein came of age.

He spent the rest his life in Istanbul; his biography was published in the Rose Al-Youssef magazine in a book issued in 1972.

- **His Royal Highness Prince El Hassan bin Talal**

His Royal Highness Prince El Hassan bin Talal was born on 20th March 1947. His Royal Highness is the youngest son of Their Late Majesties King Talal and Queen Zein El Sharaf. In April 1965, His Royal Highness was officially invested as Crown Prince to the Hashemite Throne of Jordan, until the changes in succession brought about by His Late Majesty King Hussein in January 1999.

He is one of the outstanding intellectuals and economists in the Arab world and has a prominent presence in global intellectual and economic conferences.

Prince Hassan initiated, founded and is actively involved in a number of Jordanian and international institutes and committees, H.R.H established:

- Prince Hassan chaired the committees overseeing the first development plan (1975-1973) and the three subsequent development plans (1985–1981, 1980–1976 and 1990–1986).

- The Royal Scientific Society, in 1970.

- The annual Bilad Al-Sham Conference, in 1978.

- The Al al-Bait Foundation, in 1980.

- The Arab Thought Forum, in 1981.

- The Higher Council for Science and Technology, in 1987. Including: Human Resources Development Center, the National Information Center, Diplomatic Institute.

- The Islamic Scientific Academy, administrated by him.

- The tri-annual conferences on the History and Archaeology of Jordan

- The Hashemite Aid and Relief Agency

- Al al-Bait University in Mafraq

- Having always been interested in young people, and a true believer in the importance of their community, the Forum Humanum, in 1982 (renamed the Arab Youth Forum, in 1988);

- the Crown Prince Award, in 1984 (renamed the El Hassan Youth Award, in 1999)

- Prince Hassan chaired and was a member of a number of international committees and organizations.

- Chairman of the Policy Advisory Commission for the World Intellectual Property Organization (WIPO)

- Member of the Executive Committee of the Club of Rome

- Founding Member and President of the Foundation for Interreligious and Intercultural Research and Dialogue.

- Member of the International Board of the Council on Foreign Relations;

- Honorary Member of UNESCO World Commission on Culture and Development

- Board member of the Committee of UNESCO International Inter-religious Advisory Committee

- Chairman of the Board for the Center for Peace Studies and Conflict Resolution at the University of Oklahoma International Programs Center, since 1999.

- **His books:**

    - A Study on Jerusalem (1979)

    - Palestinian Self-Determination (1981)

    - Search for Peace (1984)

    - Christianity in the Arab World (1994)

    - Essere Musulmano Co-authored with Alain Elkann – (2001)

(Italian, French, Spanish) To Be A Muslim

- In Memory of Faisal I: The Iraqi Question (2003)

- Q and A: Contemporary Issues, 2003.

- **His Family:**

H.R.H prince El Hassan was married to H.R.H Princess Sarvath El Hassan; having three daughters and a son: HRH Princess Rahma, HRH Princess Sumaya, HRH Princess Badiya, HRH Prince Rashid.

- **H.R.H. Prince Muhammad Bin Talal**

H.R.H. Prince Muhammad Bin Talal bin Al Hussein bin Ali (born 2 October 1940) is the second son of King Talal and Queen ZeinSharaf. He is the Personal Representative of His Majesty the King.

Prince Muhammad spent his primary education at the Islamic Scientific College in Amman and then attended the École Beau Soleil in Switzerland. He then went to Bryanston College in the United Kingdom where he finished his secondary education.

Between 1957- 1956, he attended the Military Academy in Baghdad. Upon his return to Jordan, he joined the Jordan Arab Army and served in the first Royal Guard Regiment before becoming Aide de Camp to His Majesty King Hussein.

Prince Muhammad has served his country in many official capacities: from 1962-1952, he was Crown Prince of the Hashemite Kingdom of Jordan. In 1970, he was appointed by His Majesty King

Hussein as the Head of the Council of Tribal Chiefs. In 1973, a Royal Decree invested him as the Personal Representative of His Majesty King Hussein.

He then headed the Supreme Committee for Tourism in Jordan. He has also served as Regent and as Head of the Regency Council on numerous occasions in the absence of His Majesty the King.

He holds the honorary rank of Full General in the Jordanian Armed Forces, as well as many high decorations from Jordan and other countries.

Prince Muhammad speaks fluent Arabic, English and French and understands German and Ottoman Turkish. Prince Muhammad practices and promotes various sports including Karate, chess, shooting and hunting. He is the Honorary President of the Jordanian Chess Federation and the Jordanian Shooting Federation. He is also the Honorary President of the British Federation of Koyokoshinkie Karate holding a first Dan and honorary fifth Dan in that martial art. In 1960, he earned his Private Pilot's License.

- **His Brothers:**

    - King Al Hussein bin Talal.
    - King El Hassan bin Talal.

- **His sons:**

    - H.R.H. Prince Talal, the Director of the National Security Council (b. 26 July 1965)

    - H.R.H. Prince Ghazi, Personal envoy and adviser for religious and cultural affairs of his Majesty King Abdullah II (born on 15 October 1966).

He has played a major role in the scientific, religious and cultural fields, in addition to demonstrating the leading role of the Islamic religion and its truth, tolerance and love for humans and asserting that Islam safeguards the human's dignity, honor, property and soul regardless of his belief. He also showed the extent of moderation of this religion and its openness to others, especially people of other monotheistic religions, which represent a part of the spirit of religion and its teachings, and the extent of co-existence and rapprochement that could arise and last between these monotheistic religions. "How can we get up together towards progress, civilization, values, equality and love, hand in hand in the light of human dignity, especially in the face of extremism experienced by the Nations now?" he always inquired.

H.R.H has had outstanding activity and consistency in the field of coexistence and rapprochement among religions. His Highness has exerted remarkable efforts in the World Interfaith Harmony Week, as His Highness patronized the ceremony held at Al Maghtas (Baptism Site of Christ, peace be upon him), acting as the delegate for His Majesty King Abdullah II and distributed the prizes of World Interfaith Harmony Week 2013 organized by Al al-Bait Foundation in the Convention Center at Al Maghtas (Baptism Site of Christ, peace be upon him) East of the Jordan River in the District of South Shouna.

The most gratifying matter about the World Interfaith Harmony Week was the innovative formula and the content of the initiative (the love of God and love of neighbor), the formula that had not been used before in the world or in the United Nations as declared by HRH Princess Areej Ghazi Chairperson of the Board of Judges during the event.

- **Her Royal Highness Princess Basma bintTalal**

Her Royal Highness Princess Basma bint Talal is the only sister of His Majesty the late King Hussein, His Royal Highness Prince Mohammed and His Royal Highness Prince Al Hassan.

Princess Basma received her primary education at the Ahliyyah School in Amman, and her secondary education at Benenden School in England. She went on to specialize in languages at Oxford University.

Princess Basma was awarded a D.Phil. degree from Oxford University. Her thesis entitled, "Contextualizing development in Jordan: the arena of donors, state and NGOs," examines the evolution of Jordan's development process as shaped by political and economic factors. The thesis traces the growth of civil society entities, particularly those working in social development, as they respond to conditions at the local, national and international levels.

For nearly thirty years, Her Royal Highness has worked nationally, regionally and internationally to promote a range of global issues.

Princess Basma believes in the need to strengthen local communities and social organizations and strengthen its capabilities with full focus on the cultural dimensions of positive values and national heritage.

Her Highness is the chairperson of the Board of Trustees of the Jordanian Hashemite Fund for Human Development.

On the international level, Princess Basma is Honorary Human Development Ambassador for the United Nations Development Program (UNDP), Honorary President of the Jordanian Society for the Family Protection and Planning and a Member of the International Planned Parenthood Federation.

On the international level, The Princess played a prominent role before and during the Fourth International Conference on Women in Beijing, where Her Highness was a member of the International Consultative Group of Secretary-General of the United Nations to prepare for the conference. She also chaired the Arab preparatory meetings for the conference.

HRH Princess Basma has participated in a number of specialized conferences and seminars in the field of sustainable development.

At the national level, In 1991, HRH Princess Basma launched a national campaign in the face of the problems of poverty across Jordan under the name (Goodwill Campaign).

Her Highness focused on work in order to improve educational and living conditions of children, particularly in pre-school stage. In 1994, HRH Princess Basma became the president of Mabarrat Um Al Hussein, established by her late Majesty Queen Zein Al Shara and considered to be one of the first competent bodies to take care of orphaned children and provide full care, education and vocational

training services to them.

Her Highness, in the context of her efforts to support children and the youth, chaired the Jordanian Society for the care of children and Jordanian Association for Boy Scouts and Girl Guides.

HRH Princess Basma is the Honorary President of many local and national institutions and associations, including: the General Federation of Jordanian Women (GFJW), Jordanian women police, Young Women's Christian Association, Arab Women Media Association, Inner Wheel Club, Amman Children Association, Private Schools Education Forum, Friends of Kidney Patients Society and Home and Garden club.

The Rest of Family Members of His Majesty King Abdullah II:

- Princess Iman bint Abdullah II bin Al Hussein (born 27 September 1996)

- Princess Salma bint Abdullah II bin Al Hussein (born 26 September 2000)

- Prince Hashem bin Abdullah II bin Al Hussein (born 30 January 2005)

Their Royal Highnesses ..... The Hashemite Princes

His Royal Highness
Prince Faisal bin Al Hussein

His Royal Highness
Prince Ali bin Al Hussein

His Royal Highness
Prince Hamzah bin Al Hussein

His Royal Highness
Prince Hashem bin Al Hussein

Their Royal Highnesses ..... The Hashemite Princes

His Royal Highness
Prince Ghazi bin Muhammad

His Royal Highness
Prince Talal bin Muhammed

His Royal Highness
Prince Raad bin Zaid

His Royal Highness
Prince Ali Bin Nayef

His Royal Highness
Prince Assem bin Nayef

His Royal Highness
Prince Rashid bin Al Hassan

His Royal Highness
Prince Mired Bin Raad

His Royal Highness
Prince Zeid bin Raad

His Royal Highness
Prince Firas bin Raad

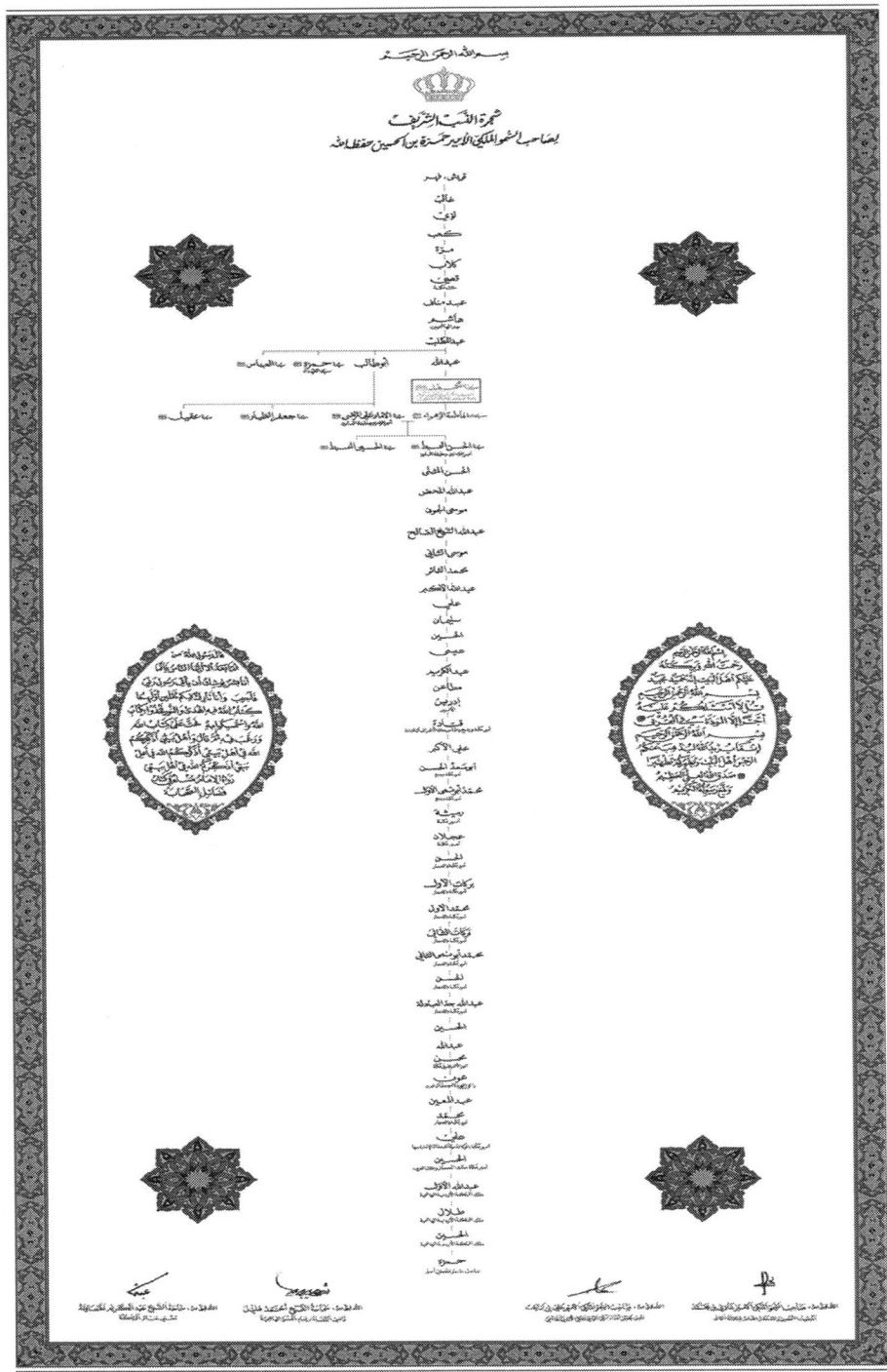

THE HASHEMITE KINGDOM OF JORDAN

CHAPTER THREE

FACTS ABOUT JORDAN

CHAPTER THREE
FACTS ABOUT JORDAN

The Hashemite Kingdom of Jordan, an Arab kingdom in south west Asia, lies in the heart of the Middle East due to its location in the southern part of the Levant, and the northern part of the Arabian Peninsula. Jordan is bordered by Syria to the north, Israel, Palestine and the Dead Sea to the west, Iraq to the north-east, Saudi Arabia to the east and south, and the Red Sea (Gulf of Aqaba) in its extreme south-west where Port of Aqaba is located (the only port in Jordan). Located on the East Bank of the Jordan River, Jordan is named after the Jordan River.

Jordan is a country that, remarkably, combines various Arab cultures and dialects. Jordan has no natural boundaries with its Arab neighbors except of the Jordan River and Yarmouk River, which are parts of its border with Palestine and Syria. The remaining part is an extension of Levant "al-Sham" desert in the north and east, and the

An Nafoud desert in the south, and Wadi Araba to the south-west.

Jordan terrain varies dramatically; the most important mountains are Ajloun Mountains in the north-west and the Sharah in the south. The highest mountain peak can be found in Jabal Umm ad Dami: 1,854 m (6,083 ft). The lowest point is in the Dead Sea at 408- m. (Also, lowest point on Earth.)

In 1921, Prince Abdullah Bin Al Hussein founded the Emirate of Transjordan with the help of Britain and under the British Mandate

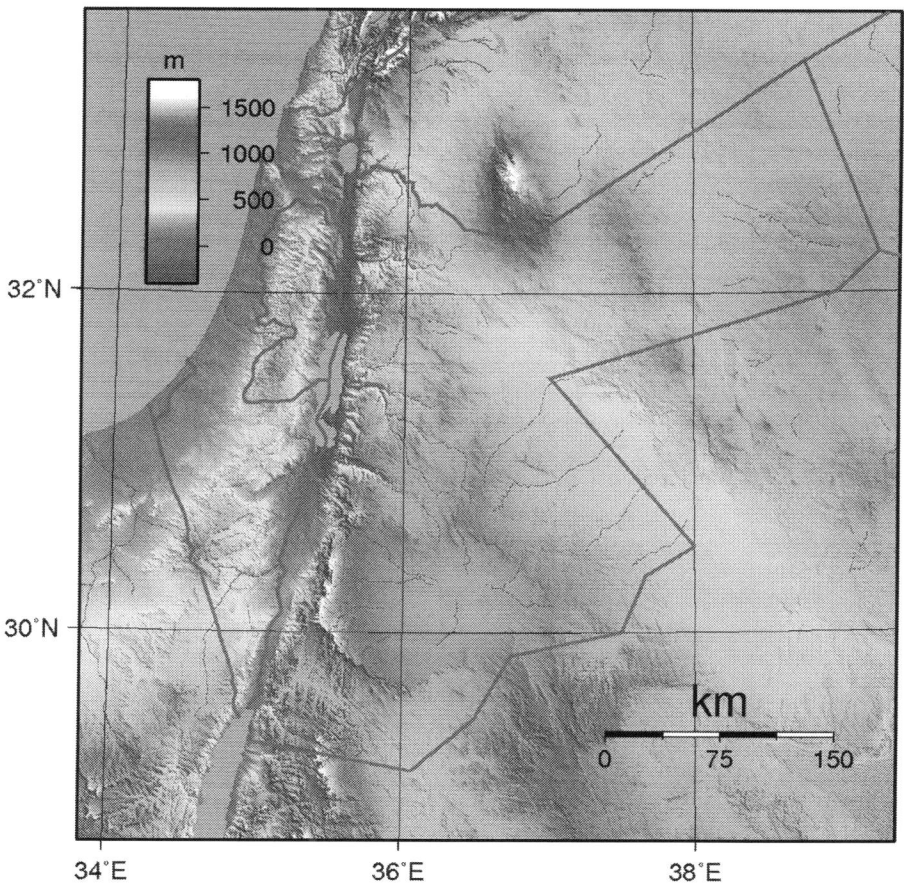

for Palestine. Transjordan gained independence in 1946, and Prince Abdullah was proclaimed King of the Hashemite Kingdom of Jordan the king.

The Hashemite Kingdom of Jordan is a constitutional monarchy with a representative government. The king exercises his executive authority through the prime minister and the Council of Ministers, or cabinet. The cabinet is responsible before the elected House of Deputies which, along with the House of Notables (Senate) (appointed by the king), constitutes the legislative branch of the government. The judicial branch is an independent branch of the government.

- **Ancient Period:**

Since ancient times, Jordan has been continuously inhabited, where it has witnessed various civilizations. The Semitic migrations settled in Jordan and established flourishing cultural communities all over Jordan.

Jordan has witnessed the settlement of great civilizations and kingdoms that have made their mark on the history of such eras. The people of the Amorites, descendants of Canaan, lived in Jordan, and the Canaanites settled in Palestine and named it land of Canaan, while Jordan has carried several names, as we find in the Old Testament itself: the general name of the country was (Trans Jordan). The other names of Jordan refer to the kingdoms that inhabited it, and the special part of the name refers to the geographical areas which are the country's components carried out by such kingdoms. Each kingdom and its people were named after those areas, such as the Edomites (Edom), Moabites (Moab), Heshbonites (Heshbon, Hasbannowadays), and the Ammonites (Rabbath Ammon, Amman nowadays), in addition to Bishanites (Bishan, Bisan nowadays), and the Kingdom of the Nabataeans being related to their name instead of the name of the area. These Arab tribes migrated from the Arabian Peninsula to the land of Jordan, where each tribe settled in an area separated from other tribes through natural landmarks, the tribes had a friendly and good relations. Such tribes emerged in Jordan since about two thousand years BC.

At about the same time, Edomites lived in Jordan and established their capital (BOZRAH), which is currently located in Tafila. Moabites lived in Jordan and established their kingdom, its capital was Dibon north of Wadi Mujib, then moved to the ker Moab (Karak) during King Mesha time. Karak and Dhiban were the main capitals of them, and their chief god was Chemosh. Mesha was their greatest king; his victories were recorded on the Mesha Stele (also known as the "Moabite Stone"). The Assyrians and Babylonians occupied it later, where Kingdom of Moab became a Babylonian state at the time of King Nebuchadnezzar.

Ammon or Rabbath Ammon, now known as Amman, was the capital of the kingdom of Ammon. The Ammonites were concentrated in northern and central Jordan, and Amman retains the ancient capital location.

Being featured by the nomadic life, Ammonites established their kingdom around the year 1250 BC, as a strong and wide kingdom where its borders extended from Mujibin south to Zarqain north and the desert in east to the Jordan River in the west. Taking into account Amman's strategic geographical location, the Kingdom of the Ammonites underwent invasion and destruction several times but it had always recovered. "Tobiah" was the last king of Ammonites and was linked to the Iraq al-Amir and Qasr Al-Abd in Al Wadi Al Seer. Amman area was inhabited in the Iron Age (1200 BC 330- BC), such period was characterized by using the wheel in pottery industry, and that the region witnessed a development in the use of iron in the arms and house ware industry. Amman Citadel (in Amman) represents a landmark of Ammonites, in addition to the remains of Ammonites' palaces which lie in Amman Citadel like walls and wells drilled in limestone.

Four statues of the kings of the Ammonites, dating back to the eighth century BC, were found in Amman Citadel in addition to other statues found in the suburbs of Amman, in Khirbet Hijaz and Abu Alanda and Arjan.

After the defeat of the Assyrian capital of Nineveh, all peoples under the Assyrians rule revolted. The last king of Assyria (Opali) fled to Harran and Babylonians took control after the Assyrians. Babylonians tried to take possession on the eastern Mediterranean, including the east of the Jordan. Kings of Moab, Ammon, Tyre and Sidon formed a union to fend off the Babylon attacks. However, the Babylonian King Nebuchadnezzar managed to beat them and reached Jerusalem in the year 586 BC, then he managed to defeat Sidon, Moab and Ammon; Tyre's siege lasted for thirteen years till he was be able to conquer it. Nebuchadnezzar captured a large number of Jews from Jerusalem and Palestine to Babylon. Shortly thereafter, Babylon was defeated by the Persians in 540 BC. Jordan remained under Persian rule till Alexander the Great wars in 333 BC, in which Alexander defeated the Persian king Darius and extended the Greek rule to include Jordan and neighboring countries.

After the death of Alexander the Great, Greek empire was divided into three parts: Egypt was for the Ptolemaic, the Levant was for the Seleucids. However, Ptolemy managed in 312 BC to the take over the southern Levant (Jordan and Palestine) to become part of the Ptolemaic Kingdom who were based in Egypt. The Greeks accorded great importance to it, being the property of the Egyptian Ptolemy, where they rebuilt it and granted it a new name: Philadelphia instead of Rabbeth Ammon.

Greeks remained in Amman for nearly one hundred years after this occupation, until being expelled by the Nabataeans who originated their kingdom after seizing the state of the Edomites.

Nabataean empire borders extended from the Gulf of Aqaba to the Yarmouk River and from Sirhan Valley in the east desert to the Jordan River and the Jordan Valley in the west.

- **Boundaries:**

Except for small sections of the borders with Palestine and Syria, Jordan's international boundaries do not follow well-defined natural features of the terrain. The country's boundaries were established by various international agreements and with the exception of the border with Israel none was in dispute in early 1989.

Jordan's boundaries with Syria, Iraq, and Saudi Arabia do not have the special significance that the border with Israel does; these borders have not always hampered tribal nomads in their movements, yet for a few groups borders did separate them from traditional grazing areas and delimited by a series of agreements between the United Kingdom and the government of what eventually became Saudi Arabia). The borders were first formally defined in the Hadda Agreement of 1925.

In 1965, Jordan and Saudi Arabia concluded an agreement that realigned and delimited the boundary. The realignment resulted in some exchange of territory, and Jordan's coastline on the Gulf of Aqaba was lengthened by about 18 kilometers (11 mi). The new boundary enabled Jordan to expand its port facilities. The agreement also protected the pasturage and watering rights of nomadic tribes inside the exchanged territories.

Jordan is bordered by Syria to the north, Iraq to the north-east, Saudi Arabia to the east and south, and Palestine to the west.

- **Emirate of Transjordan:**

Emirate of Transjordan is an autonomous political entity existed within the area of Mandatory Palestine since 1923 and up to the date of declaration of independence of the Hashemite Kingdom of Jordan in 1946. Emirate of Transjordan included most of the land located in east of the Jordan River, and so it gained its name.

Prince Abdullah left Ma'an and headed to Amman to discuss matters with the people of the region and the British. In 1921, the establishment of the young emirate was declared, soon thereafter, Transjordan became under the British Mandate, and was not covered by the Balfour Declaration.

- **Arab - Islamic rule in Jordan:**

Jordan remained under Roman rule until the Islamic conquest of the Levant ending the Byzantine rule by Arab Muslims coming from the Arabian Peninsula. During Islamic rule, the region which was composed of the Levant countries yielded to military district (called Ajnad) during the reign of Caliph Omar ibn al-Khattab, leading to the division of the Levant to many sectors named after its district, including Jund al-Urdunn.

After the death of the Caliph Omar, Uthman ibn Affan took over Caliphate till the end of his rule in 33 AH, 656 AD. Muawiya remained the ruler of the Levant "al-Sham" where he was appointed by the Caliph Omar ibn al-Khattab in 640 after the death of his brother Yazid ibn Abi Sufyan. After the death of Uthman, Ali ibn Abi Talib was chosen to be the Caliph, but Muawiya refused to pledge allegiance to him, leading to a series of wars between the two teams. Abdul Rahman bin Muljim al-Moradikilled the Caliph Ali ibn Abi Talib, then people swore allegiance to his son, Hassan, but he waived the Caliphate to Muawiya.

Muawiyah founded the Umayyad Caliphate, choosing Damascus as its capital. Due to the proximity of Jordan to the capital of Islamic rule and its prominent geographical location, Jordan became at a crossroads of pilgrims heading to the Holy Land of Mecca and Medina. Jordan witnessed a flourished life, cities and palaces were built such as Qasr al-Hallabat, Qasr al-Kharana, Mushatta Palace, Qasr Amra and others.

Umayyad remained so until the state had been eliminated in 749 at the hands of Abul `Abbas as-Saffaḥ. Abbasid Caliphate was named after the uncle of the Prophet Muhammad "Abbas".

Abul Abbas selected Baghdad instead of Damascus to be the capital of the Abbasid Caliphate as one of his first actions.

Knowing that Baghdad was capital of the caliphate, Jordan's locations was no longer important compared with its role in the previous Caliphate. Thus, the desert castles, built by the Umayyads to practice hunting and to be a place to rest for commercial and pilgrims' convoys of heading to the Holy Land, were abandoned.

The 10th and 11th century witnessed the growing influence of the Fatimids, who ruled Egypt and took over Jordan in 969. At the beginning of the twelfth century, the Levant was attacked by Crusades, which led Jordan to a raging war.

King Baldwin I built a series of castles in Jordan main areas in order to protect the roads leading to Jerusalem. Then Baldwin I unified Syria and Egypt under his rule. Saladin was able to expel the Crusaders from Jerusalem in 1187 AD after the battle of Hittin, freeing the country from the foreign presence and accordingly Jordan became free of the foreign domination.

Jordan flourished in the Ayyubid and Mamluk times. It formed a union with Egypt and Syria leading it to have a prominent position among its neighbors. Jordan's forts and hostelries were reconstructed to host pilgrims on their way to Mecca and Medina, and in order to strengthen the protection of trade and communications ways.

In that period, Jordan Valley flourished where sugar refining plants were established.

The region came under a new attack by the Tartars in 1401 AD, leading to the weakness of governments and the spread of diseases in some areas in addition to the weakness of the whole region. The Ottoman "Turks" defeated the Mamluks in 1516 AD; then, Jordan became a part of the Ottoman Empire and remained so throughout 400 years.

Eastern desert of Jordan and central mountainous areas are rich in historical monuments dating back to different Islamic eras. Monuments and historical palaces, castles and fortified towers are deemed to be landmarks of Jordan. There are many castles that were built over the centuries to be the home of safety and security to defend the country. Azraq Castle is an example which dates back to the era of the Romans and the Arabs. Also, al-Rabd Castle is another monument which represents the architectural styles of Arab Muslims; it was built to monitor the movements of the Crusaders and the exploitation of iron mines in the mountains of Ajloun, called Warda Grotto, in addition to protecting the trade routes with Damascus and northern Syria. Karak and Showbak Castles dating back to the period of the Crusades, located in mountainous areas, filled with arcades and towers and fortifications that indicate the martial arts style of the Middle Ages. In addition to these castles, there are other castles in Aqaba, Al-Hassa and Qatraneh that represent different eras in the history of Islam.

- **Ottoman era:**

Jordan came under Ottoman rule in the wake of the defeat of the Mamluks by the Ottomans in 1516 in the Battle of Marj Dabiq. Jordan remained part of the Empire from 1516 until 1918.

Arab countries were under direct Ottoman rule and Syria enjoyed autonomy. Sultan appointed Janbirdi al-Ghazali as a governor of it. After the death of Sultan Selim, Janbirdi al-Ghazali declared himself as a ruler of the Levant, and its independency from the Ottoman Empire. The Ottoman army defeated him, so he surrendered and was executed in 1521. Thus, the Levant returned under the Ottoman governors' administration and yielded to the Ottoman Sublime Porte.

Ottoman Empire divided Levant into three states namely: Damascus, Aleppo, and Tripoli. Jordan was part of Damascus state.

In 1831, Muhammad Ali Pasha "Governor of Egypt" sent his son Ibrahim Pasha to the Levant as the leader of a big army that was able to triumph over the Ottoman army and take over the Levant.

Muhammad Ali was characterized by his reformist rule, being interested in education and tried to impose taxes and its regulations. Soon thereafter, he was forced to leave it, where Britain, Russia, Austria and the Ottoman Empire gathered in 1840, and threatened to expel him out of Egypt in case that he hadn't called the army back from the Levant. His army withdrew in 1841 and was forced to stay in Egypt and Sudan only.

In general, Jordan suffered from negligence that affected the development of its infrastructure in the Ottoman era due to several aspects including that the construction works of the Ottoman Empire were executed only if it was of religious significance (like Al-Qatraneh Castle that was built to protect convoys of pilgrims), most schools and hospitals, baths, wells, orphanages were very neglected.

The most important works and construction projects at the time were "Hejaz Railway" project, starting from Damascus to reach Medina. The railway became a useful tool for the transfer of the Ottoman armies and Supply during the First World War to reach the heart of the land of Hijaz; such purpose exposed the railway for many attacks during the Great Arab Revolt, which revealed a new phase in the history of Jordan, and the entire region.

- **Greater Syria:**

On June 1919 ,10, King-Crane Commission arrived in Jaffa and visited a lot of cities in Palestine, Jordan and Syria. The commission received 1800 petitions carrying 300.000 signatures. On July 2, the commission met with Prince Faisal in Damascus as well as members of the General Syrian Congress. The Commission completed its work on August 1919 ,28 and submitted its report to the Allies who did not adopt any of its clauses. Report of the commission remained confidential until it was published in a US newspaper in 1922; where included: The Levant should be deemed one state, because it is consistent with the people's wishes, language, economy, culture and traditions; Lebanon shall enjoy autonomy within this state. The regime shall be a constitutional monarchy headed by Prince Faisal bin Al Hussein. Jewish immigration to Palestine must be stopped.

On March 1920 ,7 AD, The General Syrian Congress was held and issued the Declaration of Independence. The declaration stated the rejection of any division of the country and stressed its cooperation with Iraq. The congress acknowledged "Faisal Bin Al Hussein" as constitutional monarch king of Syria, Faisal I. The congress acknowledged the autonomy of Mount Lebanon and administrative decentralization of all other areas.

The declaration was unilateral action without the prior consent of the allies. British consul in Damascus advised Faisal I as well as the General Syrian Congress to postpone the declaration of independence beyond the San Remo Conference.

- **Independent Government in Transjordan:**

The British government prepared the Mandate of Transjordan. The Land east of the Jordan River was excluded from all the provisions dealing with jurisdiction over Jewish settlements, and the provisions of the Mandate of Palestine.

The Prince, during a visit to London in October 1922 AD, called for the full independence of Transjordan. Negotiations continued for a long time, during which the cabinet headed by Ali Reda Al-Rikabi resigned. A new cabinet was formed, headed by Mazhar Ruslan, in February 1923 AD. The new cabinet tried to resume negotiations with the British for independence, but to no avail.

On 25 May 1923 AD, Herbert Samuel, the British High Commissioner for Palestine, according to his government's orders, declared in Amman that:

"Subject to the approval of the League of Nations, His Britannic Majesty will recognize the existence of an independent Government in Trans-Jordan under the rule of His Highness the Amir Abdullah, provided that such Government is constitutional and places His Britannic Majesty in a position to fulfill his international obligations in respect of the territory by means of an Agreement to be concluded with His Highness".

Jordan deemed this declaration as the recognition of its independence from Britain. April 1921, 11 AD, the first Jordanian cabinet headed by Rashid Tali'a was formed. It is worth mentioning that the first five governments carried the name "House of Councilors". The fifth cabinet was formed under the name "Council of Ministers", the sixth and seventh cabinet "the board of trustees" and the eighth cabinet "Executive board". The cabinet carried the name "The Council of Ministers" as of the ninth cabinet, in the forties of the twentieth century.

- **Modern history:**

First World War was declared between the Allies and the Axis Powers in July 1914 AD. In October 1914, the Ottoman Empire entered the war alongside Germany, where its fleet bombarded Russian ports on the Black Sea. On the October 1914 ,2 AD, Russia declared war on the Ottoman Empire and three days after England and France declared war on the Ottoman Empire.

Committee of Union and Progress (CUP) started the application of Turkishness and Turanism policy, on the grounds of racism, and this was an abuse of the rule under the Ottoman Empire. CUP adopted the Turkish nationalism with the abandonment of Islam, which combines the Turks and Arabs. Sultan Abdul Hamid II, a friend of the Arabs where they depended on him to resist the ambitions of the fanatic Turkish leaders, was removed in 1909 AD. Such action made the Arabs angry toward them, especially after adopting the Turkification of peoples other than Turkish people in the state.

The Arab States asked the Ottoman empire to grant them autonomy and to make Arabic an official language in the Arab States in order to limit the recruitment of Arab youths as stated in the decisions of the Arab congress in Paris in 1913 AD.

The Ottomans refused to meet the demands of the Arabs. In the meantime, the Arabs nationalists, who founded the national associations, especially the Al-Fatat (the Young Arab Society) in touch with Sharif Hussein bin Ali through his son Faisal bin Al Hussein, who met with Arab nationalists in Damascus, and agreed to the ARAB REVOLT led by his father. Damascus Protocol aimed at the establishment of a single unified Arab state, where Sharif Hussein acting as president, from the Taurus Mountains to the Arabian Sea, and from the Red Sea to the Gulf. In the meantime, Jamal Pasha was executing nationalists including Arab officers. Sharif Hussein started the negotiations and correspondence through the McMahon-Hussein Correspondence (1916 AD) which resulted in the agreement on the establishment of a revolt against Turkey to be backed, recognized and protected by Britain. Britain also provided it with money and weapons, in exchange for the participation of Arabs in the war alongside the Allies against the Turks. Also, the British promised the Arabs to recognize their independence.

The Arab revolt began in Mecca on June 1916, 10 AD. Sharif Hussein bin Ali declared the holy war against the Turks in the reign of Sultan Mehmed V Reşâd. Sharif Hussien marched with his army from the Hijaz to Syria and was able to conquer Mecca and Taif, Jeddah and Medina. The Jordanian tribe Huwaitat, in southern Jordan, was the first to join the Arab Revolt. Sheikh A'wdah Abu Tayeh communicated with Prince Faisal, the northern Arabian army chief, and announced that his tribe would join the revolt. Sharif Hussien headed to Damascus, shortly thereafter, Prince Faisal Bin Al Hussein was able to capture it in early October of 1918 AD.

As such, the fate of Jordan at that stage, during Faisal I reign, was associated with what was going on in the Levant and the Al-Mashreq in general. Gen. Edmund Allenby appointed Ali Reda Al-Rikabi as the prime minister of an interim cabinet of the Levant on October 1918, 1 AD. Rikabi was confirmed in office as prime minister upon Prince Faisal's arrival to Damascus. Prince Faisal left to visit Homs, Hama and Aleppo, then commissioned by his father to be the representative at the Paris Peace Conference after the Allied victory in World War I, he left Syria in November 1918 AD, leaving his brother Prince Zeid bin Al Hussein to act as his deputy for protocol affairs, and Ali Al-Rikabi for actual management.

Faisal I was disappointed during his visit to Paris, as it became clear that the Allies would not agree to establish the Great Arab state, in spite of the promises of autonomy granted to Sharif Hussein. The Sykes-Picot agreement, which was agreed by the British and the French, flouted such promises and everything that came in his correspondence with McMahon. Sykes-Picot proved to be fact and not rumors as claimed by the British during the war. The Balfour Declaration was a great disaster, and Prince Faisal was forced to admit under an agreement signed with Chaim Weizmann.

- **Geography of Jordan:**

Jordan's latitude and longitude is °34.52 to °39.15 N and °59 to °31 E. The territory of Jordan covers about 89.213 Km34.445) ^{2} mi^2), land areas cover 88.884 km34.318) ^{2} mi^2) and water areas 329 km (127 mi^2). Jordan lies strategically between the Levant and the Arabian Peninsula, south of Syria (borders of 375 km), west of Iraq (border line of 181 km), northwest of Saudi Arabia (border line of 744 km) and east of Israel (border line of 238 km) and the West Bank and the territories of the Palestinian National Authority (border line of 97 km).

Jordan has its longest border line with Saudi Arabia, and it is the Arab state which has the longest border with Israel. Jordan has a coastline of 26 km; its territorial water covers 3 nautical miles. Despite its small size, Jordan's terrain, topography and climate reflect its diversity.

- **Topography:**

Jordan consists mainly of a plateau in east and mountainous areas in west. The Great Rift Valley lies between the eastern and western banks of Jordan River. Jordan land consists of three regions, namely: The Great Rift Valley, the mountainous areas and desert plateau.

- **Climate:**

Jordan has a combination of Mediterranean and arid desert climates, with Mediterranean climates prevailing in the north and west of the country, while the majority of the country is desert. Generally, the country has warm, dry summers and mild, wet winters.

Jordan has a diverse climate; where the tropical dry climate prevails in the Jordan Valley, warm steppes climate prevails in the mountainous area, and Mediterranean climate prevails in the mountainous area, as well. The Mediterranean cold climate prevails in the high mountain peaks like Ajloun, steppes climate prevails in the eastern slopes, and dry desert climate prevails in East plateau.

The annual temperature ranges from 15-12 degrees Celsius (-54 77 Fahrenheit) in the winter and up to 46-40 degrees (115-105 F) in the summer in the desert. Rainfall averages vary from 50mm 1.97 inches) annually in the desert to 580mm (22.8 inches) in the northern highlands on which snow might even fall, especially the highlands in the north, center and south of the kingdom and be very heavy and accumulated in some cases.

- **Nature:**

Dana Biosphere Reserve is the home to more than 800 plant species, three of these species may not be found anywhere in the world but in the Dana Biosphere Reserve.

Scientists in Jordan recorded about 78 species of mammals, belonging to seven orders and 26 families. This list includes: carnivores, meat-eaters, such as Striped Hyena, Wolf, Golden Jackal, and the different species of foxes and wildcats. Others are herbivores, plant eaters, such as the Nubian Ibex, Arabian Oryx, and the different gazelle species. Interestingly, the largest groups of mammals are the rodents and the bats which make up almost two-thirds of the mammals in Jordan. In Jordan, there are five types of amphibians and 97 species of reptiles. More than half of these reptiles are lizards, nearly 55 species; whereas there are 37 species of snakes, of which only 7 are poisonous. The majority of Jordanian herpetofauna is not critically endangered; however, about 14 species are relatively rare and 4 -2 species might be already extinct

Jordan's location by the Great Rift Valley makes the country one of the most important flyways for migratory birds, where hundreds of thousands of birds cross the area yearly. The -425bird species recorded in Jordan belong to 58 families (Ian Andrews, 1995). Of which more than 300 are migrant, 95 are resident with definite breeding records, 111 are winter visitors, 202 are passage migrants, 83 are vagrants, and 63 are different summer visitors. Jordan hosts breeding populations for some globally threatened species including Lesser Kestrel (Falco naumanni) and Syrian Serin (Serinus syriacus). In addition to these, there are several globally threatened species that are recorded in Jordan at different times of the year. This includes Imperial Eagle, Palled Harried, Lesser Spotted Eagle and Sociable Lapwing. Fifteen bird species are threatened, while 21 are on the CITES appendices.

Jordan's flora is rich and highly diverse. Around 2,500 species of vascular plants have been recorded, belonging to 152 families, representing about %1 of the total flora of the world. One hundred species are endemic, representing about %2.5 of the total flora of the world (a high rate being compared to the global standards). 349 plant species recorded in Jordan are considered to be rare, 76 threatened species, in addition to 18 species listed on the IUCN lists.

Gulf of Aqaba is home to some of the finest marine life in the Middle East, where its reef is unmatched in the world. Gulf of Aqaba contains a wide range of marine life, such as jellyfish, sea horses, sea cucumbers, crabs, shrimp, sea urchins, and many types of fish, worms that burrow their homes in the sandy bottom of the sea. A variety of seaweed may be found in shallow water.

Perhaps one of the most important attractions for divers in the Gulf of Aqaba is the colorful coral reefs, especially those in the southern part of the Jordanian coast. The Gulf contains about 100 species of Scleractinia, also called stony corals. Algae that require light to the process of photosynthesis are mainly found in shallow water. Also, there are several hundred species of fish which have made their homes among the coral, and live by feeding on some of the algae that grow on coral reefs.

THE HASHEMITE KINGDOM OF JORDAN

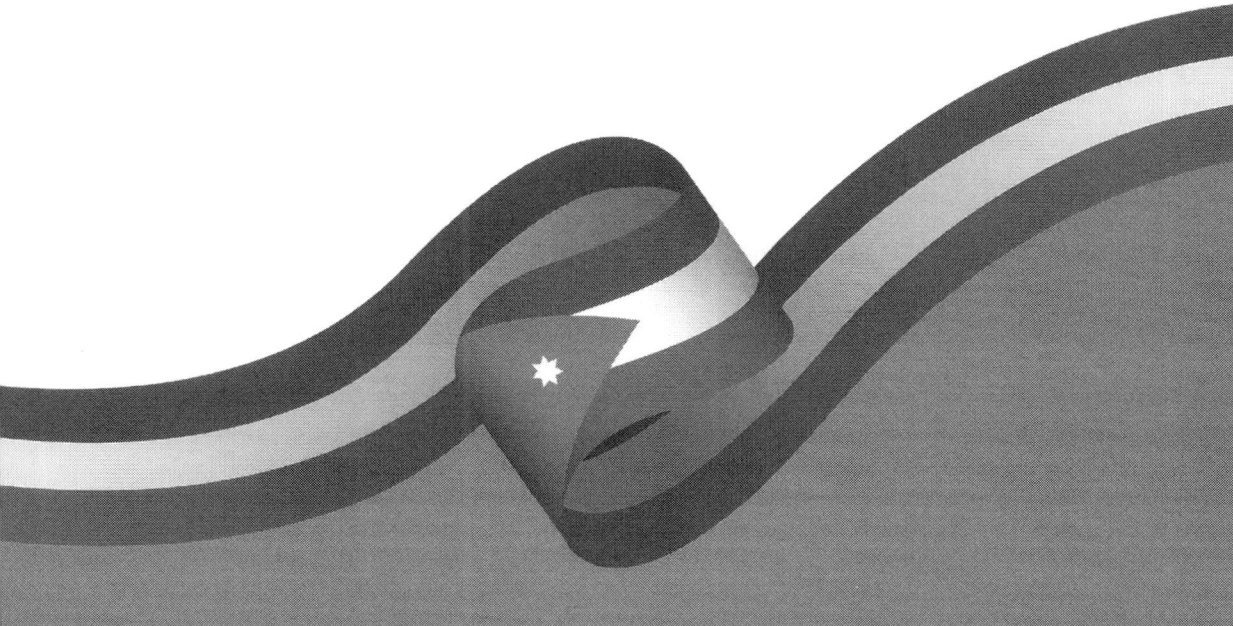

CHAPTER FOUR

AN OVERVIEW OF JORDANIAN POLITICS

CHAPTER FOUR
AN OVERVIEW OF JORDANIAN POLITICS

Constitution of the Hashemite Kingdom of Jordan states that its system of government is parliamentary with a hereditary monarchy, the Nation is the source of all powers. The Nation shall exercise its powers through three authorities, namely: Executive, Legislative, and Judicial Authority.

(THE CABINET)

The Legislative Power is to be vested in the National Assembly and the King. The government is the Supreme executive and administrative authority in Jordan. Governmental and administrative work shall be implemented by the Cabinet which is responsible for the management of all internal and external affairs of the state.

The Cabinet consists of the prime minister as the chairman, and a number of ministers. The Prime Minister oversees the work of the government, and presides over the Cabinet. The prime minister shall be associated with a wide range of institutions and bodies, councils, departments and government offices in order to conduct and follow-up the affairs of state, including the following:

- The General Intelligence Department

- Audit Bureau

- The Civil Service Bureau

- Legislation and Opinion Bureau

- Ombudsman Bureau

- Jordan Investment Commission

- Jordan Atomic Energy Commission

- Higher Education Accreditation Commission

- Audiovisual commission

- Anti-Corruption Commission

- Hashemite Commission for Disabled Soldiers

- Greater Amman Municipality

- Central Bank of Jordan

- Petra Development and Tourism Region Authority

- Jordan Radio and Television Corporation

- Jordan News Agency, Petra.

- The National Resources Investment & Development Corporation 'Mawared'

- The Economic and Social Council (ESC)

- Economic Social Association of Retired Servicemen and Veterans

- Supreme Judge department / Orphans Funds development corporation

- Aqaba Special Economic Zone Authority / The Ports Corporation

- The Supreme Council for Youth / National Fund for Support of Youth and Sport Movement

- Jordan Securities Commission

- the General Fatwa Department

- Higher Council for Affairs of Persons with Disabilities

- Jordanian Nursing Council

- Higher Council for Science and Technology

Jordan succeeded through decades of regional political turmoil in maintaining its stability and building a solid foundation for economic growth. Jordan has become in recent years a regional hub for investors and business owners. Investors have shown their confidence in Jordan by opening a lot of investment companies and commercial projects of multinational companies. Investors' efforts have contributed to the creation of high momentum of economic growth and development of the country, where its effects are reflected in the prosperous urban, industrial and tourism movement.

Jordan has a sophisticated, well-trained and effective army and a police force. Its effectiveness has been proven by maintaining security, stability and speed in dealing with any emergency.

According to the Global Competitiveness Report 2008 – 2007, Jordan ranks among the top group of safe countries in Middle East and the world. Jordan was ranked 14th in the world and first in the region, in terms of the effectiveness of the police service, while Egypt was ranked 57th, Israel 53rd, USA 20th, Britain 29th.

Jordan, in terms of the fight against organized crime, was ranked ninth in the world (ranked first among the Middle East countries), while Egypt was ranked 32nd, Israel 36th, Britain 43rd, India 68th, China 92nd. These statistics prove that Jordan is one of the most secure countries in the world.

His Majesty King Abdullah II Bin Al Hussein has shown a sustained commitment towards the social sector reform.

In addition to offering support to the large-scale initiatives of democratic reform, this is reflected in the responsibilities borne by the cabinets during his reign. Each cabinet exerted its best to achieve its impact, responsibilities and results within the comprehensive reform initiatives led by His Majesty.

A quick review can clarify the vision that His Majesty seeks to achieve and enforce its effect on the realpolitik life, where the citizen can see its landmarks in all areas of the aspired reform.

- **Jordanian Cabinets during the reign of His Majesty King Abdullah II:**

- **The cabinet of H.E Dr. Abdelraouf al-Rawabdeh**

    1999/03/04 AD.

    1999/09/01 AD: Cabinet reshuffle

    2000/05/01 AD: Cabinet reshuffle

- **The cabinet of H.E Eng. Ali Abu al-Ragheb**

    2000/06/19 AD

    2001/06/16 AD: Cabinet reshuffle

    2001/10/27 AD: Cabinet reshuffle

    2002/01/14 AD: New Cabinet

    2002/09/26 AD: Cabinet reshuffle

    2003/01/12 AD: Cabinet reshuffle

- **The cabinet of H.E Mr. Faisal al-Fayez**

    2004/10/25 AD

    2004/10/25 AD: Cabinet reshuffle

    2005/02/20 AD: Cabinet reshuffle

- **The cabinet of H.E Dr. Adnan Badran**

    2005/04/07

    2005/07/03 AD: Cabinet reshuffle

- **The cabinet of H.E Dr. Marouf al-Bakhit (1st time)**

    2005/11/27 AD

    2006/11/22 AD: Cabinet reshuffle

    2007/09/02 AD: Cabinet reshuffle

- **The cabinet of H.E Eng. Nader al-Dahabi**

    2007/11/25 AD

    2009/02/23 AD: Cabinet reshuffle

- **The cabinet of H.E Mr. Samir Rifai**

    2009/12/14 AD

    2010/07/29 AD: Cabinet reshuffle

    2010/11/24 AD: New Cabinet

- **The cabinet of H.E Dr. Marouf al-Bakhit (2nd time)**

    2011/02/10 AD

- **The cabinet of H.E Mr. Awn Shawkat Al-Khasawneh**

    2011/10/24 AD

- **The cabinet of H.E Dr. Fayez al-Tarawneh (2nd time)**

    2012/05/03 AD

- **The cabinet of H.E Dr. Abdullah Ensour**

    2012/10/11 AD

    2013/03/30 AD: New Cabinet

    2013/08/21 AD: Cabinet reshuffle

    2015/03/02 AD: Cabinet reshuffle

    2015/11/09 AD: Cabinet reshuffle

- **The cabinet of H.E Dr. Hani Al-Mulki**

    2016/05/29 AD

Some ministries have undergone limited amendments that we have not. We just wanted to show that these ministries, its statistics and amendments were a part of the ongoing quest for comprehensive reform (social, political, judicial and economic), which took place during the reign of His Majesty King Abdullah II to achieve the overall vision that His Majesty is trying to achieve in order to raise the profile of the homeland and the citizen.

In the past few years, the Jordanian government worked to

improve the legal and regulatory frameworks for Jordan, supporting reforms in the legal field, in order to achieve full independence of the judiciary.

Many of democratic institutions and civil society organizations are not organized enough, and have no political skills to perform their role in an effective and influential way. In addition, nongovernmental organizations (NGOs) face a legal and administrative framework that does not help too much on growth and expansion in this area. Media reports on Jordan's political arena are less sophisticated than what is found in Western democracies. There is also a relatively low participation level of civil society in the decision-making process. The Jordanian government has initiated a dialogue with a wide range of relevant groups, including political parties and professional syndicates, in addition to working on increasing the freedom of the press, and activating the role of the media.

Regarding human rights, Jordan entered into six of the seven United Nations conventions on human rights, including; International Covenants on Civil and Political Rights and on Economic, Social and Cultural Rights "(1975), in addition to the" The Convention against Torture and Other Cruel, Inhuman or Degrading Treatment or Punishment" (1991). Jordan also entered into seven of the eight International Labour Organization conventions on human rights.

Prime Minister's speech, on the day of the Universal Declaration of Human Rights in 2015 AD, confirmed that the government has worked to develop a comprehensive system of human rights in the Kingdom, based on the recommendations contained in the report of the human rights

situation in the kingdom, issued by the National Centre for Human Rights in 2014 AD, received by His Majesty King Abdullah II who instructed to study it and enforce its recommendations.

The Prime Minister stated, in a speech marking the Day of Universal

Declaration of Human Rights, annually observed on December 10, that the report confirmed that the government has taken many of the necessary immediate actions to enforce such recommendations without delay, and to prepare a comprehensive national plan for human rights befitting the homeland and the citizen within the time frame, priorities and indicators measuring the performance of good execution.

The Prime Minister pointed out that the government's effort to develop such a system is based on the principles necessitated by the Constitution of the Hashemite Kingdom of Jordan and the royal directives on various occasions, especially discussion papers concerning the interest in human rights, preservation of his dignity and the promotion of his freedoms as a prelude to make Jordan one of the leading countries of the region to care about the development of a comprehensive integrated system dealing with human rights within the reformist approach adopted by Jordan for years.

The Prime Minister pointed out that the public framework of the mechanism, adopted for the work of the Intergovernmental Coordination Group for the human rights, shall highlight the positive aspects of Jordan that have been made in all areas in terms of the implemented legislation, policies, practices and procedures. Also, this is implemented with the aim of maintaining the harmony of Jordanian society's values with observance of human rights and ensuring the consistency of legislation and decisions with the covenants and conventions relating to the human rights in the ministries and institutions. This goes side by side with the mandatory application of the principles of human rights to all, without discrimination on the basis of race, color or creed and activating the means of communication between the service recipient and the service provider.

The Prime Minister stressed that the tireless and sincere measures and follow-ups carried out by the government represent a part of the great work about the human rights system.

It is becoming clear the extent of the seriousness and concern for human rights, caring about his interests, the promotion of freedoms and preservation of his dignity, pointing out that these measures and follow-ups contribute to the promotion and development of the human rights system.

The Prime Minister emphasized that the Universal Declaration of Human Rights is one of the most important achievements of countries that respect human rights during the last century; where one of its most important pillars states that the recognition of the inherent dignity and of the equal and inalienable rights of all members of the human family is the foundation of freedom, justice and peace in the world, pointing out that the disregard and contempt for human rights have resulted in barbarous acts which have outraged the conscience of mankind, and the advent of a world in which human beings shall enjoy freedom of speech and belief and freedom from fear and want. Whereas it is essential, if man is not to be compelled to have recourse, as a last resort, to rebellion against tyranny and oppression, that human rights should be protected by the rule of law.

The premier stressed that the government seeks to promote the different living, economic, social and political aspects of the citizen, within the framework of the analysis of the human rights situation in Jordan, through a participatory approach with the National Center for Human Rights, international and regional organizations concerned with human rights, civil society organizations and all parties at different levels.

Jordan contains most types of human rights institutions ranging from national institutions to parliamentary committees and non-governmental organizations concerned with human rights.

THE HASHEMITE KINGDOM OF JORDAN
FROM ABDULLAH I TO ABDULLAH II

THE HASHEMITE KINGDOM OF JORDAN

CHAPTER FIVE

PARLIAMENTARY LIFE AND POLITICAL PARTIES IN JORDAN

CHAPTER FIVE
PARLIAMENTARY LIFE AND POLITICAL PARTIES IN JORDAN

- **Senate Speakers:**

  - His Excellency Mr. Tawfiq Abu Al Huda

  - His Excellency Mr. Ibrahim Hashem

  - His Excellency Mr. Sameer Al-Rifai

  - His Excellency Mr. Saeed Al-Mufti

  - His Excellency Bahjat Al-Talhouni

  - His Excellency Mr. Ahmad Al-Tarawneh

  - His Excellency Mr. Ahmad Al-Lawzi

  - His Excellency Mr. Zaid Al-Rifai

  - His Excellency Mr. Tahir Al-Masri

- His Excellency Mr. Abdelraouf Al-Rawabdeh

- His Excellency Mr. Faisal Al-Fayez

- **Speakers of the House of Representatives:**

  - Mr. Khalid Abu Al Huda

  - Sheikh Abdallah Al- Sarraj

  - Mr Ibrahim Hashem

  - His Excellency Mr. Tawfiq Abu Al Huda

  - His Excellency Mr. Sameer Al-Rifai

  - Mr. Hashem Khair

  - Mr. Abdulqader Al-Tal

  - Mr. Omar Matar

  - Mr. Saeed Al-Mufti

  - His Excellency Mr. Abdallah Al Kulaib Al Sheridan

  - His Excellency Mr. Hikmat Al-Masri

  - His Excellency Mr. Abdulhalim Al-Nimer

  - His Excellency Mr. Ahmad Al-Tarawneh

  - His Excellency Mr. Mustafa Khalifa

  - His Excellency Mr. Salah Touqan

- His excellency Mr. Akef Al-Fayez

- His Excellency Mr. Qasim Al- Rimawi

- His Excellency Mr. Kamel Erikat

- His Excellency Mr. Suleiman Arar

- His Excellency Dr. Abdullatif Arabeyyat

- His Excellency Mr. Taher Al-Masri

- His Excellency Eng. Saad Hayel Al-Srour

- His Excellency Eng. AbdelHadi Al-Majali

- His Excellency Mr. Faisal Al-Fayez

- His Excellency Mr. Abdelkarim Al-Doghmi

- His Excellency Eng. Atef Al-Tarawneh

- **Parliamentary Life:**

The Basic Law of the Emirate of Transjordan - which was issued in 1928 - gave constitutional legitimacy to rule over the country, and this Basic Law included the first law mandating parliamentary elections to elect Jordan's first legislative council. Five councils were elected during the Emirate era. The first one was elected in 1929, while the last one was elected in 1947.

It is noteworthy mentioning that these councils had powers that were limited to passing laws drafted by the executive council without having the power of proposing them. Also, these councils

were stripped of the powers of checks and balances on governmental policy. For instance, the council had no right in directing any question or inquiry at the government or making it undergo a vote of confidence. As for its term, it was three years, with the Emir possessing the right to prolong it for a period of two years s. After the formation of the Hashemite Kingdom of Jordan and the issuance of the new Constitution, the bicameral system was adopted and was called National Assembly, and it consisted of an elected House of Representatives and a Senate appointed by the King.

The House of Representatives had a term of four solar years, and the Constitution did not give the National Assembly the power to propose laws, but instead, it only gave this power to the executive authority. However, the Constitution gave the National Assembly the powers of checks and balances on the executive authority in the form of questions and inquiries although the power of having votes of confidence was still an exception and was still not granted by the Constitution to the National Assembly.

The first House of Representatives was elected on the 20th of October, 1947 and parliamentary life continued until it was disrupted due to the circumstances of the occupation in the West Bank. During that period, nine Houses of Representatives were elected before being replaced with the National Consultative Council of which three were formed during that period, starting from April 1978, 20 and ending in 1984, where each of these councils had a term of two years.

Afterwards, the National Assembly was asked to convene forming the tenth House of Representatives.

Then, the elections of the eleventh House of Representatives followed in 1989, followed by the twelfth in 1993, the thirteenth in 1997, the fourteenth in 2003, then the fifteenth in 2007, the sixteenth in 2010 and then the seventeenth in 2013.
There were numerous amendments to the elections law between 2010 and 2016, the last one being the Parliamentary Election Law of 2016.

The Jordanian Parliament has adopted the bicameral system:

1- Senate: Its members are appointed by the King.

2- House of Representatives: Its members are elected by universal suffrage.

So, the Parliament of Jordan consists of two chambers which are the Senate and the House of Representatives.

- **Political Parties in Jordan:**

Partisan life has been a crucial part in the Jordanian political history, probably because it was present during the early beginnings of laying the foundations of the modern Jordanian state. The Jordanian political parties have always been a part of the social fabric in the country and an expression of the rich diversity and the will of participation and positive interaction with events, whether from the position of opposition to governments and their policies or from the position of support. Jordan has known partisan life early on. Since the formation of the Emirate of Transjordan in April 1921, political life of partisan nature has been going on in parallel with existing efforts in the country to build and develop the young and emerging nation amongst complicated regional and political circumstances.

It is noteworthy to note the early cooperation between the Arab Independence Party and the Founder King of Jordan -Prince Abdullah bin Al Hussein at that time- in laying the first foundations of the new state. Although the Arab Independence Party was working back then within the framework of Greater Syria, its early participation in the founding of the Jordanian state had compelled researchers to consider it Jordan's first political party on the basis of its manifesto and organization. It should be noted, however, that the party ceased its activities in Jordan due to British pressures exerted in August 1924.

Nevertheless, political life in Jordan quickly rebounded on the hands of the Jordanian People's Party which was founded in March 1927 and filled the political vacuum that was left by the Arab Independence Party.

The partisan experience was launched in 1989 and was deepened with the issuance of the Political Parties Law No. 32 of 1992, according to which a large number of political parties from the different political currents in the country were legalized. Nevertheless, the issuance of Law No. 19 for 2007, which made it mandatory for parties to have 500 founding members at least, had rendered them obsolete.

However, there are many different opinions regarding this issue. For instance, some people see that the large number of political parties and the similarities between their manifestos is an obstacle to political life and prevents its natural evolution. While in this phase, mature manifestos that provide a clear vision and benefit the nation and governments alike to deal with internal and external challenges are needed. On the other hand, there is a different opinion that Dr. Mohammed Al-Hammouri expressed by saying: "The right to form political parties should be mandated by Clause 2 Article 16 of the Jordanian Constitution which states that" Jordanians are entitled to establish societies and political parties provided that the objects of such societies and parties are lawful, their methods peaceful, and their by-laws not contrary to the provisions of the Constitution".

The contemporary partisan experience witnessed growth and expansion, but it also faced many obstacles. For instance, recently, there were many voices of MP's and political activists saying that amending the political parties law and executing it democratically to strengthen partisan life is not enough, as long as other laws that regulate the political life stay as they are, especially the election law. Such voices also stress the importance of connecting both the political parties' law and the election law since reform and progress must come within an integrated system.

- **Political Parties and the Judiciary:**

The Constitution states that the judiciary is the responsibility of courts with their numerous types and classifications, and all the rulings are issued according to the law in the name of the King.

The Constitution also states that the judges are independent and answer to no authority other than the law.

The judicial system in Jordan consists of civil and special religious courts. The civil courts consist of: Magistrate Courts, Elementary Courts, Courts of Appeals and the Supreme Court of Justice (the Judicial Council after the Judicial Independence Law). As for religious courts, they consist of specialized courts that deal with personal status cases for Muslims and religious courts for non-Muslims. Also, there are special courts that may be formed for very specific purposes. These include military tribunals and the police court. These specialize in ruling over cases involving members of the Armed Forces and the Public Security.

- **A synopsis about the Judicial Council:**

The Jordanian Judicial Council represents, according to the Judicial Independence Law, the top of the Judiciary in the Kingdom. Along with the National Assembly and the Cabinet, it represents the principle of separation of powers. The Judicial Council is the one with legal powers to supervise all regular judges in the Kingdom and all related issues including nomination, mandation, secondment, promotion, transfer, accountability, discipline and retirement.

The council also deals with the development of the judiciary and submission of legislative drafts pertaining to the judiciary, the Public Prosecution and the judicial procedures, so that the government can be guided when drafting different bills and acts.

The Jordan Judicial Council consists of eleven members, of which all are regular judges:

1- President: President of the Cassation Court

2- Vice President: President of the Supreme Court of Justice

3- President of the Public Prosecution of the Cassation Court

4- The two most senior judges in the Cassation Court

5- The Presidents of the Appeal Courts of Amman, Irbid, and Ma'an

6- Senior inspectors in the regular Courts

7- Secretary General of the Ministry of Justice

8- The President of the First Instance Court

The Judicial Council meets upon invitation from its President in the headquarters of the Cassation Court in the New Palace of Justice in Amman or any other venue that the President determines, and the meeting becomes legal whenever seven members of the council attend at least. Its decisions are made either by consensus or supermajority of the members. When the votes are equal, the most senior judge in the Cassation Court joins the council.

The Judicial Council sessions are of secret nature, and disclosure of their proceedings is equivalent to the disclosure of court deliberation.

The legal system in Jordan is based on Islamic Sharia and French laws, and new judicial revisions of new legislations are carried out by the Supreme Judicial Council.

Jordan has not ratified the compulsory jurisdiction of the

International Court of Justice. There are more than 30 political parties, but the only active party in the Legislative Council is the Islamic Action Front.

Examples of Such Parties:

- The United Jordanian Front party

- The Jordanian Arab Socialist Ba'th Party

- The Jordanian Communist Party

- The Islamic Action Front (IAF)

- Al Wasat (Middle) Islamic Party

- The Jordanian Democratic Popular Unity Party

- The Arab Progressive Ba'ath Party

- Al Fursan (Knights) Jordanian Party

- The National Constitutional Party

- The National Movement for Direct Democracy Party

- The Jordanian Movement for Citizens' Rights

- The Workers Communist Jordanian Party

- The Social Left Jordanian Party

The political parties can be classified into four categories:

1- **Islamists:** Represented by the Islamic Action Front in addition to other Islamist forces like the Duaa Islamic Movement and others.

2- **Leftists:** Represented by numerous parties such as the Popular Unity Party, the Jordanian Communist Party and the Jordanian Democratic People's Party (HASHD)

3. **Nationalists:** Represented by the two Ba'athist parties: the Jordanian Arab Socialist and the Arab Progressive Party.

4. **Liberals:** Represented by Al Wasat (Middle) Current, Al Ahd (Oath) Party, the Future Party and others.

It is to be noted that these parties do not have a large impact on the political process due to their lack of a clear vision or strategy and also due to internal disputes within these parties.

THE HASHEMITE KINGDOM OF JORDAN

CHAPTER SIX

JORDANIAN AUTHORITIES

CHAPTER SIX
JORDANIAN AUTHORITIES

The King is head of state and sits on the Kingdom's throne as well as holds the position of the Supreme Commander of the Armed Forces. The King practices his executive powers via the Prime Minister and the Cabinet. The Cabinet is considered responsible in front of the elected House of Representatives which along with the Senate represent the legislative arm of the government, and this arm works with complete independence.

King Abdullah I reigned over Jordan after its independence from the United Kingdom. After he was assassinated in 1951, his son - King Talal - reigned briefly. King Talal's most prominent achievement was the issuance of the Jordanian Constitution on January 1952 ,8. He abdicated on August 1952 ,11 due to health reasons. At that time, his eldest son, Hussein was still young to reign (17 years old), so a regency council took over until Hussein reached the age of majority to reign according to the 1952 Constitution which is 18 lunar years.

After Hussein reached the age of 18, he ascended the throne of the Kingdom and reigned from 1953 until his death in 1999, suppressing many challenges to his reign, relying on his army's loyalty and

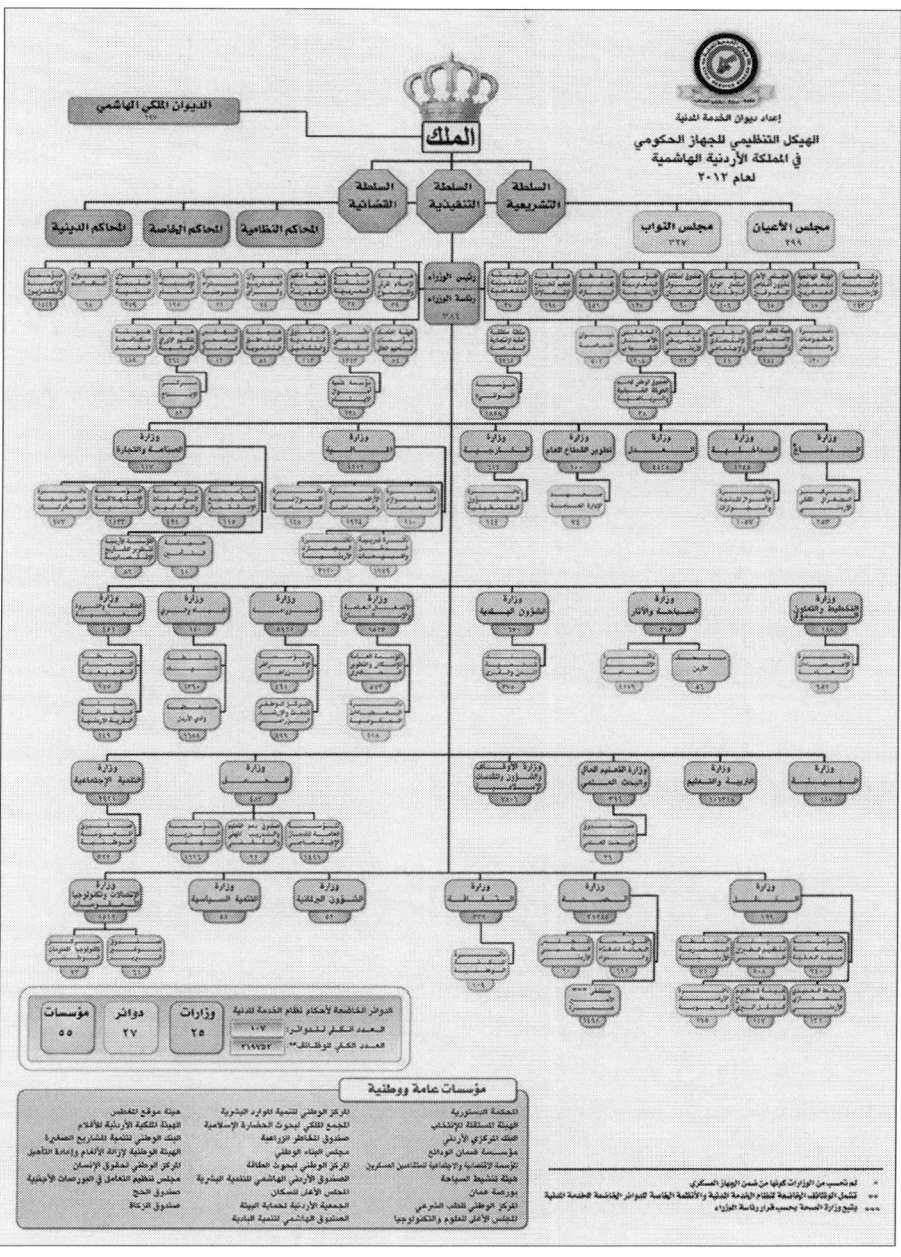

by being a symbol of unity among both Bedouin and Palestinian communities in Jordan.

King Hussein ended Martial laws in 1991 after imposing them in 1970. In 1992, the King allowed the formation of political parties, and in 1989 and 1993, Jordan had free and fair parliamentary elections. However, some amendments to the elections law had made the Islamist parties boycott the 1997 elections.

King Abdullah II succeeded his father Hussein after his death in February 1999. King Abdullah was quick in reassuring the peace treaty with Israel and Jordan's relations with the United States. During his first year in power, he worked on redirecting the governmental policy on economic reform.

Jordan's continuous struggle with economic restructuring, its population growth and the more liberal political environment have all led to the appearance of a number of political parties.

In its quest for more independence, the Jordanian Parliament had accused some high ranking officials of corruption, and the Parliament became the biggest forum where different political viewpoints are expressed, including those of Islamist politicians. The Parliament plays a vital role in governance. King Abdullah remains, however, the supreme authority.

On the June 2004 ,28, King Abdullah appointed his eldest son, Hussein, who was born in 1994, as heir apparent to the throne.

- **The Royal Hashemite Court:**

The Royal Court is considered the main and primary link between King Abdullah II bin Al Hussein and the central government, the Armed Forces and the Security Services. It is also considered the point of contact between the King and the Jordanian people.

The Royal Court has grown to include numerous departments and to handle all other royal family members' affairs. These departments take care of several aspects of social development as well as educational and military cases. The Royal Hashemite Court is connected with the National Security Council, and the Court fully supports the relationship between the King and the Cabinet and considers this support and role as essential to ensure the proceeding of the constitutional process and the Jordanian Government's role.

The Royal Hashemite Court also supports humanitarian issues for all sects and classes of the Jordanian society. It also supports desperate people with health conditions who have no resort other than the Royal Hashemite Court. The Court also supports educational cases to enable different classes of society achieve the academic

The Royal Hashemite Court

status that this nation and its citizens deserve to attain in their pursuit towards development and progress.

The position of the President of the Royal Hashemite Court is considered to be one of the most important positions in the Royal Court and is constantly filled with well-known figures.

- **Legislature:**

The legislature in political systems functions as an active authority performing a legislative and checking role within the state's hierarchy and structure, and it can absorb new currents in society and contain them. It also sorts out national priorities and the needs that the society has due to its development and change. **In any political system, the legislature performs two primary tasks:**

1- Performing checks and balances on the executive power.

2- Legislating laws

In theory, the main goal behind the existence of the legislature is passing laws that the government and society need. Therefore, we find the legislature carrying out the following:

- Drafting and passing laws.

- Political supervision of the tasks carried out by the executive.

- Guidance of the government towards keeping up with the public interest.

- Raising awareness among members of the society about issues of governance and public policy.

- Representation; representing individuals and groups in the process of political decision making.

- General discussions in public affairs.

- Imposing financial supervision on issues of the annual state budget and its passing.

According to Article 25 of the Jordanian Constitution, legislature is the responsibility of the National Assembly and His Majesty the King. The National Assembly consists of the Senate and the House of Representatives. Article 36 of the Constitution states:

"The King appoints members of the Senate, and appoints the Speaker from amongst them and accepts their resignation". The number of members of the Senate is limited, according to the Constitution, to half the number of members of the House of Representatives. As for the House of Representatives, and according to Article 67 of the Constitution, it consists of members elected by secret and universal suffrage according to the election law which guarantees the integrity of the election process and the candidates' right to observe the voting process and keep it from being sabotaged. The Speaker of the House of Representatives shall be elected at the beginning of each ordinary session for a period of one calendar year according to Article 69 of the Constitution. But he may be re-elected. If the House of Representative meets in an extraordinary session and has no speaker, the House shall elect a Speaker for a term of office which shall terminate at the beginning of the ordinary session.

- **Parliamentary Life in Brief:**

The Basic Law of the Emirate of Transjordan, issued in 1928, gave governance of the country a constitutional legitimacy. And so, the first election law was issued to elect the first legislative council, and five legislative councils were elected in the era of the Emirate with the first being elected in 1929 and the last in 1947.

It is noteworthy to mention that these councils' powers were limited to passing law drafts proposed by the Executive Council without having the power of proposing them. As for supervisory powers of the governmental policies, these councils were stripped of such powers and could not direct any questions, inquiries, ask for a discussion of policy or have a vote of confidence in the Cabinet.

These councils had a term of three years with the Emir having the right of prolonging it for a period of two years.

Parliamentary life is considered a pillar of the democratic establishment in Jordan, and it passed through numerous phases:

- **First Phase:**

    On March 1946, 22, the Second Jordanian British Treaty was issued, and according to which, the United Kingdom recognized Jordan's independence. This was followed by transforming the Emirate to a Kingdom and the issuance of the Constitution of the Hashemite Kingdom of Jordan. In April 1947, the election law of the House of Representatives was issued, and it stated that every Jordanian citizen who had reached 18 years of age had the right to vote. The National Assembly then consisted of 20 deputies elected directly by universal suffrage and 10 senators appointed by the King. The term of the National Assembly was fixed at four years, and it was the first National Assembly to be established in the history of the Kingdom of Jordan. It was dissolved on January 1950, 1 to have new elections including both the East and West banks on basis of their presumable unity.

    After the unity between the East Bank and the West Bank, the second Jordanian National Assembly was formed.

It included deputies and senators from both banks of the Kingdom. And following the unity, several amendments were made to the Constitution and the election law. These had doubled the number of members of the National Assembly making the number of senators 20 and the number of deputies 40. This new National Assembly held its first sessions on May 1950 ,20. It remained in session until May 1951 ,3. The third National Assembly was elected on September 1951 ,1 and ended its term on June 1954 ,22. During the term of this National Assembly, His Majesty the late King Hussein assumed his constitutional powers. The 1952 Constitution was also issued during the same period. The fourth National Assembly was then elected on October 1954 ,17 and ended its term on June 1956 ,26. On October, 1956 21, the fifth National Assembly was elected and completed its constitutional term on October 1961 ,21. The King, however, prolonged its term for a period of one year according to the power granted to him by Article 68 of the Constitution.

During the term of the fifth National Assembly, a new election law was issued in 1960. It included an increase in the number of deputies to sixty; thirty of which were from the East Bank and thirty from the West Bank. The number of senators also increased and became thirty. On November 1961 ,22, the sixth National Assembly was elected and ended its term on October 1962 ,17. On November 1962 ,27, the seventh National Assembly was elected and ended its term on April 1963 ,21. On July 1963 ,8, the eighth National Assembly was elected and ended its term on January 1966 ,23. On April 1967 ,18, parliamentary elections of the ninth National Assembly were held.

On June 5 of the same year, Israel launched its offensive on Arab countries and occupied the West Bank. The National Assembly remained in session, and it completed its constitutional term in addition to a term extension of two years until April 1973, 18.

This was followed by the decision of the Arab summit in Rabat in 1974 which recognized the Palestinian Liberation Organization (PLO) as the sole and legitimate representative of the Palestinian people. Therefore, a royal decree was issued to dissolve the House of Representatives on November 1974, 23.

- **Second Phase:**

To avoid constitutional confusion in the performance of the state's responsibilities, a national consultative council was formed with the task of voicing its opinion, giving consultancy and discussion of the public policy of the state in the framework of cooperation with the government to preserve public interests. It was reassured that the formation of this council is not an alternative to any of the constitutional institutions, as well as not being an alternative to elections. The National Consultative Council remained active until a royal decree was issued to dissolve it as of January 1984, 7.

Then, the House of Representatives gained back its powers following a royal decree that asked the previous National Assembly (Ninth) to convene in an exceptional session starting from January 1984, 9. On March 1984, 13, by-elections were held to fill the vacant East Bank seats in the House of Representatives. The House also elected members for the West Bank vacant seats, thus, bringing Parliamentary life back to Jordan. This was called the tenth National Assembly, and it remained until July 1988, 30 after it had completed its constitutional term with an extension before it was dissolved prior to the disengagement from the West Bank.

- **Third Phase:**

After the legal and administrative disengagement from the West Bank on July 1988, 31, new amendments were made to the election law to suit the new situation. The electoral constituencies in the Kingdom were only present in the East bank. The general elections of the eleventh National Assembly were then held on November 1989, 8, and for the first time since 1967, according to the Jordanian Election Law No. 22 for 1986 and its amendments in 1989. This National Assembly consisted of eighty deputies representing the various governorates in the Kingdom and hailing from multiple political, partisan and religious sects. The royal decree also appointed the senators who numbered forty.

The eleventh House of Representatives was dissolved on August 1993, 4 and the elections were held on November, 8 1993 according to the Temporary Election law No. 15 for 1993 and its amendment which was issued on August 1993, 17, which stated that each citizen had one vote to cast instead of the previous law No. 22 for 1986 which allowed the voter to vote for a number of candidates equal to that allotted to his/her constituency. The elections process was held on time and in fairness and neutrality and without any intervention of the government in favor of any side. These elections were held in light of the partisan participation that was established by the Constitution and the Political Parties Law No. 32 for 1992.

A royal decree that dissolved the twelfth National Assembly was issued on September 1997, 1 in accordance with the Temporary Election Law No. 24 which was issued on May 1997, 15 and, in accordance with which, the constituencies' division table appendix was amended.

It also included an amendment to Article 39 and mandated

the power of voting extension to the head of the President of the Central Commission. In addition, Article 46 related to the illiterate votes was also amended.

A royal decree that dissolved the thirteenth National Assembly was issued on June 2001, 16. The elections of the fourteenth National Assembly were held on June 2003, 17.

The Jordanian Parliamentary system has adopted the bicameral system:

1- Senate: Its members are appointed by the King.

2- House of Representatives: Its members are elected by universal suffrage.

- **Legislative Role:**

The National Assembly had a vital and active role in deciding the legality of the election law draft after it was amended and proposed by the Cabinet, as was the case with the Temporary Law No.5 of 2010 where the National Assembly's decision to refer the law to the ad-hoc committee (the legal committee). The National Assembly and the committee had several remarks including:

The Seventeenth National Assembly had agreed in its non-regular session on October 2013, 3 on the Legal Committee Decision No. 5 of February 2013, 24 regarding the temporary law and ruling it as repealed by law.

The National Assembly also had a role in later amendments:

Article (1): This law shall be called (Law on the Election of the House of Representatives 2016) and it shall be effective from the date of its publication in the Official Gazette.

Article (65): The Election Law of the House of Representatives No.25 of 2012 and its amendment shall be repealed with the executive orders issued in accordance with it remain valid until they are changed in accordance this law.

This gives a true example of the legislative life in the National Assembly and its role in passing and repealing laws in line with current and future national interests. This indicates the vitality of the National Assembly (the Senate and the House) and its performance of its legislative role in light of the democratic and partisan system that the political life in Jordan is based on under the patronage of His Majesty King Abdullah II bin Al Hussein and in his blessed tenure.

- **Executive:**

The executive includes the Prime Minister, his Ministers, his Counselors and the Heads of various different executive departments. This system is followed in most countries that follow the Parliamentary system.

In accordance with the Jordanian political system, the executive power is vested in His Majesty the King who exercises it via his Cabinet in accordance with Article 26 of the Jordanian Constitution which states "The Executive Power shall be vested in the King, who shall exercise his powers through his Ministers in accordance with the provisions of the present Constitution". His Majesty the King is the one responsible for appointing, sacking and accepting the resignation of the Prime Minister and the Ministers in accordance with Article 35 of the Constitution which states that "The King appoints the Prime Minister and may dismiss him or accept his resignation. He appoints the Ministers; he also dismisses them or accepts their resignation, upon the recommendation of the Prime Minister". Therefore, His Majesty then King is the head of state and the symbol of the country, and executive power is vested in him.

Cabinet

The Cabinet consists of the Prime Minister who is chosen by the King in accordance with his constitutional right in accordance with Article 35 of the Constitution.

The Prime Minister recommends the names of the Ministers he wishes to appoint in his Cabinet to the King. This recommendation, however, is not binding to His Majesty the King who can reject any of these names for a reason or another. Afterwards, the Cabinet takes the oath of office in presence of His Majesty the King in accordance with Article 43 of the Constitution which states that "The Prime Minister and Ministers shall, before assuming their duties, take the following oath before the King 'I swear by Almighty God to be loyal to the King, uphold the Constitution, serve the Nation and conscientiously perform the duties entrusted to me'.". The oath of office is considered as the announcement of the Cabinet.

Although His Majesty the King is the head of the executive, he possesses constitutional immunity manifested in him not being responsible before the National Assembly concerning issues of governance, and this is what Article 30 of the Constitution states

"The King is the Head of the State and is immune from any liability and responsibility".

• Judiciary:

The state draws its essence from the presence of law that organizes the behavior of individuals and their relationship with it (the state). The goal behind the judiciary is law enforcement. The legal rules that organize individuals and groups are the work of specialized legal bodies of the state, and judges generally do not propose laws but enforce them instead.

In the Jordanian political system, the judiciary is considered independent from the other branches of government. It is carried out by the different courts which rule in accordance with applicable laws in Jordan. This is what Article 27 of the Constitution states "The Judicial Power is independent and shall be exercised by the courts of law in their varying types and degrees. All judgments shall be given in accordance with the law and pronounced in the name of the King".

Courts in Jordan are open to all and are immune against involvement in their affairs, meaning that all individuals, agencies and various establishments have the right of litigation, and no intervention in the proceedings of courts from neither an official or non-official party is permitted.

In addition to the principle of judicial independence and the principle of equality before the judiciary, the judicial system in the Kingdom has adopted the principle of free judiciary. This system includes that whoever goes to the courts does not pay litigation fees, and that all members of the judiciary are paid by the state.

To ensure the principle of proper administration of justice, the

Jordanian judiciary adopts the system of litigation in two classes in order to give a chance to the individual or the agency that is ruled against to take the dispute up to a court of a higher class to get a second ruling on the dispute in order to strengthen the instinct of justice among individuals and establishments.

Judges have, in accordance with the Jordanian Constitution, full independence, and they answer to no other authority other than the law. The process of appointment, promotion and dismissal of judges is performed in light of decisions made by the Judicial Council and associated with royal decrees in accordance with Article 98 of the Constitution.

In accordance with The Judiciary Independence Law No.49 of 1972 and its amendments in The Temporary Law No.13 of 1989, the Judicial Council is made up of President of the Cassation Court, President of the Supreme Court of Justice, President of the Public Prosecution of the Cassation Court, the two most senior judges in the Cassation Court, the Presidents of the Appeal Courts of Amman, Irbid, and Ma'an, senior inspectors in the regular Courts., the secretary General of the Ministry of Justice and the President of the First Instance Court.

The Ministry of Justice carries tasks of managerial supervision on all courts and judges.

The Minister can, voluntarily, and in light of recommendation from the president of the court, give notes to the judges of various courts. In accordance with Article 99 of the Constitution, there are three types of courts in the Kingdom: Regular courts, religious courts and special courts.

- **Constitutional Court:**

Constitutional courts generally specialize in control and regulation of the constitutionality of laws. This is done by either prior regulation like France and partially in Algeria, Lebanon and Bahrain, **or by subsequent regulation which falls under two types:**

1- Regulation by repeal of the entire non-constitutional legislative text.

2- Regulation by abstain from enforcement of the non-constitutional legislative text.

There are countries with a separate constitutional court and others with supreme courts that have the responsibility of checking the constitutionality of legislations. An example of these is The Supreme Court of the United States which is the oldest constitutional court in the world as it was the first court in the world to address the repeal of a law passed by the Congress (The Legislature) in the case of "Marbury vs. Madison". This is in spite of the fact that it is not a separate constitutional court.

The Constitutional Court in Jordan, and in accordance with Article

4 of its Law of 2012, specializes in the following:

- Regulation of the constitutionality of laws and applicable regulations.

- Interpretation of the constitutional texts.

As for the specialization in the examination of constitutionality of laws, it refers to law in its broad sense.

This includes every general and abstract legal basis like systems and regulations of the following parties exclusively (Article -9A) and has the right to appeal the constitutionality of applicable laws and regulations directly in court: The Senate, the House of Representatives and the Cabinet.

Also, any party of a lawsuit before courts regardless of their types and classes can appeal for the unconstitutionality of any law or applicable regulation regarding the subject of the lawsuit (Article -11A).

The appeal of unconstitutionality before the court considering the lawsuit is done in accordance with a memorandum where the appealer states the name of law or regulation that is appealed for non-constitutionality, its number and the range of the appeal in a clear and specific way. According to (Article -11B), evidence to support the unconstitutionality should be given along with evidence that this specific law is applicable to the subject of the lawsuit. A description of its alleged clash with the Constitution should be given as well. Any other party in the lawsuit can submit their response within the period specified by the court, on the condition that it does not exceed fifteen days from the date of application of the memorandum of unconstitutionality if the concerned court finds that the law or regulation that is appealed for unconstitutionality is applicable on the issue of the lawsuit, and that the unconstitutionality is serious, it stops looking into the lawsuit and refers the lawsuit to the Court of Cassation for purposes of determination of the issue of the lawsuits' referral to the court.

The decision of the court considering the lawsuit is subject to appeal along with the lawsuit subject. For the purposes of determination of the lawsuit's referral to the court, the Court of Cassation convenes with a committee of three members at least, and it issues its decision within thirty days from the date of the lawsuit's referral to it. If the Court of Cassation accepts the lawsuit's referral, it informs the involved parties. If an appeal of unconstitutionality is referred to the Court of Cassation or the Supreme Court of Justice, then they start the process of determination of the referral immediately in accordance with the provisions of the article.

- **Introducing the first Constitutional Court in Jordan:**

The constitutional amendments issued on October 2011, 1 included a special chapter on the formation of the formation of the Constitutional Court in Articles 60, 59, 58 and 61. The Law

No. 15 of 2012 was issued on October 6, 2012. Article 58 of the constitutional amendments stated that "A constitutional court shall be established by a law and based in Amman and shall be deemed an independent and separate judicial body. It shall consist of at least nine members, including the president, all of whom shall be appointed by the King". His Majesty the King has been keen in his directives for the Royal Committee of Constitutional Amendments to stress that the committee performs its vital role in the reform process, and that it is an essential step to reinforce the principle of separation of powers, and to stop the encroachment of different branches of the government on each other and defend liberties and rights of people in accordance with the Constitution especially after its amendment that meets international standards in rights and liberties.

A royal decree was issued appointing the following gentlemen as president and members of the first Constitutional Court in the country. The members took the oath of office on October 6, 2012 before His Majesty the King:

- His Excellency Mr. Taher Hikmat	President
- His Excellency Mr. Marwan Dudin	Member
- His Excellency Mr. Fahd Abu Al-Athm Al-Nsour	Member
- His Excellency Mr. Ahmad Tubeishat	Member
- His Excellency Dr. Kamel Al-Saeed	Member
- His Excellency Mr. Fouad Sweidan	Member
- His Excellency Mr. Yousef Al-Hmoud	Member
- His Excellency Dr. AbdelKader Al-Toura	Member
- His Excellency Dr. Mohammed Salim Mohammed Al Ghazwi	Member

The court has assumed its duties since October 6, 2012 and is still active. In addition to being a prominent constitutional requirement, the Constitutional Court is considered a prominent symbol of civilization and an important step in the comprehensive and gradual reform process led by His Majesty the King prior to the Arab Spring. The Constitutional Court is an independent authority with effective decisions. Its judges are independent, and it draws its power from the Constitution that it preserves and is preserved by it.

If we take a look at the members of the Constitutional Court, we find that they are people of specialty, long experience and bright minds who are able to take suitable decisions regarding what is referred to the court from cases whether for interpretation of the Constitution or issuance of required rulings for entities that possess the right to appeal directly to the court on the constitutionality of laws and regulations and the interpretation of the Constitution. These entities are:

1- The Senate

2- The Chamber of Deputies

3- The Cabinet

Any party involved in a lawsuit in a court regardless of its type and class has the right to claim the unconstitutionality of any applicable law or system concerning the issue of the lawsuit according to the specific rules in the Law of the Constitutional Court.

The Court determines its decision regarding the appeal referred to it within a period that does not exceed one hundred and twenty days starting from the date of the referral. The court has the right to request any data or information it deems necessary for that purpose.

All the decisions of the court are issued in the name of the King, and the decisions are considered final and binding to all authorities.

- **Anti-Corruption Commission:**

The establishment of the Jordanian Anti-Corruption Commission was a manifestation of the royal message that His Majesty King of the Hashemite Kingdom of Jordan, Abdullah II bin Al Hussein, sent to the Cabinet of His Excellency Dr. Adnan Badran on June 2005 ,26 conveying the supreme leadership's faith in the importance of the formation of an independent reference that deals with anti-corruption, as it promotes prevention of corruption and raises awareness of its dangers in accordance with the requirements of the United Nations Treaty of Anti-Corruption that Jordan ratified on October 2003 ,31. The ratification was in accordance with Law of Ratification No.28 of 2004 which was published in the Official Gazette No.4669, and the instrument of ratification was deposited with the General Secretary of the United Nations on February 2005 ,24.

As a result, the Anti-Corruption Commission Law No.62 of 2006 was issued, and it determined accordingly the goals and tasks of the commission and outlined the actions that are to be considered as corruptive. The law was amended in accordance with the Amended Law No.10 of 2012 and was published in the Official Gazette No.5151 on April 2012 ,3. The new amendments included numerous legal articles intended to provide protection for witnesses and whistleblowers in corruption cases, in addition to granting the commission the power of stopping any contract or franchise that was obtained as a result of a corruptive action.

The commission was granted the power of international cooperation to provide and request mutual legal help. The amendment also excluded statutes of limitations for corruption crimes and their penalties. The law was amended in accordance with the Amended Law No. 16 of 2014 and was published in the Official Gazette No.5278 on March 2014, 2. In accordance with the Amended Law, several acts were added to the list of criminalized corruption acts in Article 5 of the Anti-Corruption Commission Law No.62 of 2006 and its amendments. These acts include crimes of money laundering and illegal earning and the non- declaration of assets or investments that may lead to a conflict of interest if the laws and regulations required so and the non- deceleration would bring personal direct or indirect benefit to the party not declaring.

The Anti-Corruption Commission is considered the responsible authority of the prosecution of any party that commits any of the criminalized acts of corruption in accordance with the Commission Law No.62 of 2006. It is also responsible of exerting efforts to dry up the sources of corruption and raise awareness among the people about its dangerous and negative effects on economic, social and political development as well as its fatal impact Jordan's reputation among investors and international institutions.

- **Security Services:**

The Jordanian security services include Public Security, Civil Defense, General Intelligence and the Gendarmerie. Here is an outline of the evolution of these services.

- **Public Security:**

Public security had remained part of the military force founded by His Highness Prince Abdullah, King Abdullah I bin Al Hussein later on, from 1921 until 1956.

In 1956, a law was issued that separated the security forces from the army. Therefore, the Public Security forces were made under the authority of the Ministry of Interior. The Public Security force has remained in constant development until it has become now comparable to the best security forces in the world.

- **Duties of Public Security:**

The Public Security Law of 1956 determined the following duties for the security forces:

1- **Preventive Duty:** Police is considered one of the arms of the executive being granted the task of maintaining order, security and public safety.

2- **Social Duty:** Police is considered one of the social defense forces concerned with the behavior of individuals and their values as well as society's morals and traditions. Due to its position and links with the public, it is considered the most capable force in prevention in the first place and care and reform in the second place.

A big role in social reform was, in fact, granted to the police, and the force became required to transcend general prevention to a deeper and more comprehensive role. This is in order to rehabilitate inmates (either prisoners or those under house arrest), rehabilitate them psychologically, educationally, socially and vocationally and place them back in society as healthy individuals.

- **Civil Defense:**

Duties of the Civil Defense:

- Organization of firefighting, ambulance and rescue operations.
- Prepare qualified personnel to perform the tasks and duties of the force.
- Securing vehicles, equipment and essential communication - devices on the basis of self-sufficiency in each governorate.

- Supervision of digging and setting up shelters in cooperation with responsible authorities.

- Formation of volunteer civil defense teams in the numerous areas and population centers, so that they can be an aid to the official authorities in cases of emergency. These volunteer teams are also trained to carry out Civil Defense tasks like firefighting, rescue and first aid.

- Cooperation with the official authorities to bring life back to normal after the occurrence of natural and human disasters.

- Raising awareness among citizens and officials in ministries and in private and public institutions about the prevention and safety procedures to ensure protection of lives as well as public and private property.

- **General Intelligence:**

The General Intelligence Directorate was founded in accordance with the General Intelligence Law No. 24 of 1964, and it answers

directly to the Prime Minister.

Duties of the General Intelligence:

- Gathering and submission of information to the government, so that it can utilize it to plan suitable policies.

- Combat of subversive activities of secret and non-authorized organizations on Jordanian territory.

- Combat of terrorism and terrorist organizations that target the state's security and the people's safety.

- Combat espionage.

- **Gendarmerie:**

The Gendarmerie is an independent field pavilion with high readiness and different duties than those of the Public Security force. It answers directly to the Minister of Interior and was established in 2008.

Duties of the Gendarmerie:

- Maintenance of public order.

- Containment of any disruption in internal security, unauthorized demonstrations that may disrupt public order or hooliganism.

- Dealing with dangerous criminals.

- Reinforcement of feelings of comfort of society members, maintenance of security and order and dealing with exceptional and emergent cases.

- Combat of riot and disobedience and resolving quarrels and

clashes relying on rapid intervention to prevent the occurrence of clashes.

- Protection of foreign embassies, governmental institutions and critical and vital institutions in the country.

- Participation in foreign missions as part of peacekeeping forces.

• **Jordanian Army:**

The Arab Jordanian Army, aka the Arab Army, is considered one of the top armies in the region in terms of efficiency and professionalism and is looked upon as highly trained.

The Jordanian Armed Forces (JAF) consists of the Royal

Jordanian Land Forces (RJLF), Royal Jordanian Marine Forces, the Royal Jordanian Air Force, the Joint Special Operations Command (SOCOM) as well as the Directorate of Public Security (which follows the Ministry of Interior, but becomes part of the Armed Forces in times of war and crisis).

Males perform the military service when they reach 18 years of age for two continuous years without interruption. However, conscription was suspended in 1999 before being resumed again in 2007 to provide training for youth to join the job market. All males under 37 years old are asked to register. Females are not conscripted but they might volunteer in the army in non-combat roles.

The lack of resources has greatly strained Jordan's military expenses. But, during the years of equipment modernization, the Special Jordanian Armed Forces were given utmost importance by working on the reinforcement of its abilities of rapid response to any threats to state security. As for the Air Force, it possesses a high

degree of professionalism, but its capabilities are damaged, however, due to the lack of funding and the unavailability of advanced combat systems like the ones possessed by the Israeli Air Force.

Jordan has restructured its Armed Forces in order to deal better with a group with potential threats. Most focus was given to rapid response and Special Forces. The Joint Special Operations Command (SOCOM), which was founded in the mid-nineties, has focused on internal security and security of the borders to support the peace process in the Middle East.

Finally, the Joint Special Operations Command pays a special attention to smuggling across the Iraqi border, infiltration across the Syrian border as well as its focus in a more special way on critical zones along the West Bank border.

The Jordanian forces have become flexible and more mobile with reliance on the system of battalions which improved the ability of rapid response in emergencies.

Jordan has also set up a defensive strategy to preserve forces that can deter any offense no matter how superior the offender is, which has made it known that the Jordanian forces would fight back any potential offense, and that any offense against Jordan would be of severe consequences. Jordan has become keen on protection of its land, maintaining its internal security and securing its interests.

Jordan has been a strong supporter of UN peacekeeping missions and has units deployed among these missions in various areas around the globe.

- **Defense Industry and Peacekeeping Process:**

Jordan entered the market of defense industry with its establishment of "King Abdullah II Design and Development Bureau or KADDB" in 1999. It operates as an independent military establishment under the umbrella of the Jordanian Armed Forces, and it specializes in research and development to provide optimum solutions in defensive and commercial fields in Jordan especially and the Middle East in general. The bureau also designs, develops and modifies defense and security systems using modern technology to meet the needs of the user and find optimum solutions for them. The bureau has expanded

its network of business relations on local and international levels and has concluded foreign trade agreements with Yemen, Brunei, Azerbaijan and other countries

There are now about 50,000 Jordanian soldiers working with the UN in peacekeeping forces deployed all over the globe. They carry out duties that include everything from military defense, training the local police, medical aid and charities. Jordan ranks third globally in the level of participation in UN peacekeeping forces. Jordan sent many field hospitals to conflict areas and areas affected by natural disasters around the world.

These include Iraq where aid was given to more than a million people, around a million in the West Bank, 55000 in Lebanon, 750000 in Afghanistan in addition to Haiti, Indonesia, Congo, Liberia, Ethiopia, Eritrea, Sierra Leon, Pakistan and others. Jordan also provides training for security forces in Iraq, the Palestinian Territories and Gulf countries.

THE HASHEMITE KINGDOM OF JORDAN

CHAPTER SEVEN

FOREIGN AND ARAB RELATIONS

CHAPTER SEVEN
FOREIGN AND ARAB RELATIONS

Jordan's foreign policy is considered moderate somehow but is closer to the West. Jordan has had historic close ties with the United States and the United Kingdom. These ties were damaged in the beginning of the nineties when Jordan announced neutrality during the Gulf War and kept its relations with Iraq especially after the Iraqi invasion of Kuwait. After the end of the war, relationships started to recover slowly between Jordan and the West through Jordan's participation in the peace process in the Middle East and its help in the implementation of international sanctions imposed on the Iraqi regime.

Jordan shares exceptional relations with the Palestinian Authority as it is considered to be the closest to Palestinians historically, especially since the West Bank was a part of the Hashemite Kingdom of Jordan for more than 38 years until the disengagement in 1988.

At the same time, Jordan is currently the sole gate of the Palestinian economy to the world.

Numerous headquarters of the Palestinian Liberation Organization (PLO) are found in Amman due to the historic intermingling between the two peoples and the official Palestinian presence in the Kingdom for decades. The PLO took part in the Madrid Conference in 1991 in a joint delegation with Jordan.

As for the Arab-Israeli conflict, Jordan was considered for decades as one of the frontline countries against Israel, and the relations were hostile from both sides as most Palestinian resistance attacks used to launch from Jordan. In addition, Jordan fought three wars against Israel, two of which were fought directly.

This hostility from both sides persisted until the Jordanian Israeli peace treaty was signed in Wadi Arabah in 1994. Jordan is one of three

Ministry of Foreign Affairs and Expatriates

Jordanian Embassy in London

out of twenty two members of the Arab League to have diplomatic relations with Israel, the other two being Egypt and Palestine.

As for the rest of countries in the region, Jordan shares close relations with Syria, Egypt and Saudi Arabia especially since the establishment of the Arab League in 1946.

Jordan generally tries to be moderate in its policy in the region which coincides with the policies of several countries active in the region.

The World Bank allocates an annual budget for supporting the Jordanian government. The United States also allocates annually about 360 million dollars of its budget as aid to Jordan. This aid has increased by 100 million dollars after the events of the Arab Spring in 2011. The Gulf countries, the European Union, Japan and China

Jordanian Embassy in Washington D.C

all support the Jordanian economy whether via major investments, commercial exchange or by granting aid from time to time to support development projects in the country.

With regard to Jordan's diplomatic relations with the European Union, the year 1977 witnessed the ratification of the cooperation treaty which went into effect in 1978. The framework that organizes the mutual and multilateral relations between Jordan and the European Union consists of several aspects. These aspects begin with the Euro-Mediterranean partnership that was launched during the Euro-Mediterranean Conference in Barcelona 1995 to set ambitious policies and long term goals for the sake of reinforcement of cooperation between the European Union and the Mediterranean countries in light of three aspects included in the declaration of Lisbon which are: political and security partnership, economic and financial partnership and partnership in social and cultural affairs.

There are also the Jordanian- European Partnership Treaty and the European Neighborhood Policy (NEP).

The first provides a comprehensive framework for the economic, political and social dimensions for bilateral cooperation which was signed on November 1997, 24 and went into effect on May 2002, 1 to replace the General Cooperation Treaty of 1977. The goal of this treaty is the establishment of a free zone between both sides, the preparation of a comprehensive framework for political, social and financial cooperation and the increase in economic growth. The goal of the second treaty (the NEP) has the goal of creating an ambitious partnership policy with neighboring countries where it provides neighboring countries of the European Union the chance to get large shares in the internal market of the Union and paves the way for more economic integration. This is all in return for achieving actual progress in these countries and the effective implementation of political, economic and institutional reform. The basis of this policy was laid by the European Commission in March 2003.

Jordan and Israel have had official relations since 1994 after the leaders of both countries signed a peace treaty between them. It started with the Non-Aggression Treaty with Israel (Washington Declaration) in Washington D.C on July 1994, 25. This was followed by the ratification of the historic peace treaty on October 1994, 36 between Jordan and Israel in the presence of President Clinton accompanied by his Secretary of State, Warren Christopher. The United States had discussions with both Jordan and Israel on issues regarding the division of water resources, infrastructure projects, commercial and financial cases, in addition to security issues and working on the development of the Jordan Rift Valley.

In comparison to other Arab countries, Jordan's relations with Israel are considered quite better. There were several diplomatic clashes, however, that strained the relation due to provocative acts performed by Israel in The Temple Mount.

- **Jordan's Role in Maintaining World Peace via Peacekeeping Forces:**

Jordan participates effectively in peacekeeping forces deployed all over the world, as it ranks first on the list of countries participating in the peacekeeping forces. Jordan also participates in multilateral peace talks within the framework of the European Union.

In 1996, Jordan and the United States reached an agreement to make Jordan a major non-NATO ally, and recently, a free trade treaty was signed with the United States.

Jordan is an active member of the United Nations and its numerous agencies. These include the Food and Agriculture Organization (FAO), the International Atomic Energy Agency (IAEA) and the World Health Organization (WHO) in addition to being a member in the World Bank, the International Monetary Fund (IMF), the Organization of Islamic Conference (OIC), the Non-Aligned

Movement and the Arab League.

As for Jordan's relations with the Eastern bloc, it had been generally frosty but it improved significantly nowadays through military cooperation and in the fields of nuclear energy research, tourism and other fields.

With all that mentioned, Jordan's foreign policy succeeded in setting an example of balance of relations with Arab and International spheres. This is evidence that the Jordanian openness has started moving into a balance of relations and does not remain confined within the axis of "moderation" with reliance on American support. Jordan has also taken few steps towards strengthening relations with several Arab countries which was preceded with openness to Hamas. This also signifies that the foreign policy is determined carefully and accurately in accordance with Jordan's national interests, and that Jordan has no interest in maintaining hostility towards any Arab country or in aligning with an Arab country against another.

It is noteworthy to point out that Jordan is a founding member of the Arab league and the Organization of Islamic Conference and a member in the World Trade Organization, the Arab Fund for Economic and Social Development, the Arab Monetary Fund, the International Monetary Fund, the International Criminal Court, the Greater Arab Free Trade Area, the Economic and Social Commission for Western Asia and the European Neighborhood Policy. Jordan is also now part of the system of the Gulf Cooperation Council and used to be a member in the Arab Cooperation Council.

Jordan ratified the Free Trade Treaty between Arab countries on February 2004, 25 in accordance with the "Agadir declaration" that was ratified by Jordan, Tunisia, Morocco and Egypt on May 2001, 8 which targets establishing a free zone in the first phase gradually between the ratifying countries with the possibility of other Arab countries joining later. Jordan also welcomed the initiative of Union

for the Mediterranean which was launched by the French President "Nicola Sarkozy" in its keenness to ensure the success of efforts to reinforce the Euro-Mediterranean relations, and following that, Jordan participated in the Paris Summit on July 2008 ,13.

- **Jordanian Palestinian Relations:**

Jordan and Palestine form the southern part of the area known historically and geographically under the Islamic era as "Bilad al-Sham" (the Levant), and it continued to be known by that name until the last days of the Ottoman Empire. In the post-World War I period, it was known as sometimes Greater Syria and others as General Syria.

This region had remained a single entity with its land and population until the end of the Arab government that King Faisal formed in Syria after the end of the Great Arab Revolt. After the end of Faisal's reign in July 1920, the colonial governments started dividing the region into areas of influence in a way unprecedented in the region. This division was preceded by the decree issued by the British Secretary of State for Foreign Affairs in 1917 which he promised to establish a national homeland for Jews in Palestine. The Palestinian people fought against this decision with stubborn persistence resulting in many Palestinian revolutions, the most important of which were AlBuraq Uprising in 1929 and then the Great Palestinian Revolt in 1936. In light of common national responsibility and the unity of the common legacy, the Jordanian people gave a hand of help and support to the Arab Palestinian people to aid them in the armed revolutions aiming to liberate Palestine and maintain Palestinian sovereignty on it.

In spite of Jordan being under the British mandate at that time, the Jordanians used their available abilities and took part in the Palestinian national uprisings and provided martyrs for the sake of the freedom of Palestine and its people. To be more specific, the beginning of the Jordanian support to the Palestinians was the help given by the Jordanian tribes in attacking the Jewish settlements in 1920, and this was their first armed clash with the Jews. Kayed Mefleh Al Obediat from the village of "Kufrsum" was the first Jordanian martyr to fall in Palestine.

This support had persisted throughout the mandate period, and when the United Nations General Assembly issued the decision of division of Palestine between Arabs and Jews on November ,29 1947, the Palestinians rejected the decision and the Jordanians were among the first of the Arab volunteers to answer the call of duty to support their Palestinian brothers.

After the Arab Israeli War broke in 1948, the Arab Jordanian Army took part in repelling Zionist attacks on Palestine and was able to preserve the lands it was ordered to defend by the Unified Arab

Command, thus, preserving the Jordan Rift Valley and the cities of Jerusalem, Ramallah, Lod and Ramla.

- **Jordanian Palestinian Unity in 1950:**

After the end of the war in Palestine, in light of the Arabs' acceptance to sign a lasting truce with Israel, a large number of Palestinian and Jordanian community leaders found that the best way to guarantee the preservation of the Palestinian Territories was the unification of what remained of the Palestinian Territories with Transjordan. So, in order for the unity to be legitimate, several popular conferences were held including: the Arab Palestinian Conference in Amman (Amman Conference), another conference in Jericho and another in Nablus. All those conferences called upon unity with Transjordan and swore allegiance to King Abdullah bin Al Hussein as the constitutional monarch of Jordan and Palestine. When the outcomes of the Jericho Conference were presented to King Abdullah by a Palestinian delegation presided by Sheikh Mohammed Ali Al-Jaabary, King Abdullah bin Al Hussein conveyed the desires of the Palestinian people to the Cabinet to look into the Arab Palestinians' desire and voice their opinions in this regard. .

After the Jordanian Cabinet studied the decisions of the conference, it issued a statement that appreciated the Palestinian people's desire of unity and considered that to be in accordance with the aims of the Jordanian people and government, and it promised that the government would seek this aim in constitutional and international ways.

This step was taken out of respect and appreciation for the Arab countries that gave a lot of their efforts to liberate Palestine through peace and war alike. To complete the unification, the Cabinet referred

the conference's desire to the Jordanian National Assembly to voice its opinion as the request was about the future of the country.

When the Jordanian National Assembly agreed with the unification, the Cabinet issued a number of laws to facilitate the process of unification. One of the most important laws was a new for Public governance which became to be known as Law No. 17 of 1949, and this was the law under which the Jordanian government canceled the positions of Jordanian military governors, who were appointed to govern what was left of Palestine, and substituted them with civil officials. Then, this step was followed by even a more important one, which was the Palestinian participation in the government. And so, on May 1949, 7, the first joint Jordanian Palestinian Cabinet was formed, and it included three Palestinian ministers to represent the West Bank.

- **Jordan, the country of immigrants and helpers:**

Jordanians take pride in the fact that their country is a safe haven of stability and is a country of helpers and immigrants; a country which takes refugees who find no other place to go and will remain so with its people's awareness and its sons' wisdom.

Historically, no relationship is similar to the Jordanian Palestinian relationship with the exception of the Muhajirun (Immigrants) and Al-Ansar (helpers) in the advent of Islam.

History repeats itself as Palestinians who were expelled out of their country due to Western Zionist conspiracies were forced to settle in diaspora in the Arab world and outside it. Those who ended up in Syria, Lebanon, Egypt, and Saudi Arabia do not call them citizens of Palestinian origin but rather as Palestinian resident in those countries.

With the exception of the Palestinians living in Jordan who take pride in calling themselves Jordanians of Palestinian origin. This is because only Jordanians welcomed Palestinians like Al-Ansar welcomed Al-Muhajirun, and this relationship was reinforced by the Hashemite leadership who manifested national unity between the two peoples and considered its breach as a line that must not be crossed.

- **Taking Care of Holy Places with Official Authorization:**

Jordan, with its Hashemite leadership, is committed to accepting its historical responsibility in taking care of the holy places,

preserving the Islamic identity of Al Aqsa Mosque and the Dome of the Rock and supporting the steadfastness of the people of Jerusalem in face of Israeli policies that aim to judaize the city and ethnically cleanse its population.

The royal Hashemite support for Jerusalem is continuous and never ending. This is manifested in the numerous Jordanian foundations working for the city of Jerusalem, especially the Ministry of Awqaf and Islamic Affairs and its departments present in Jerusalem. This is in order to stand up to these policies that ignore international decisions and efforts aiming to bring just peace to the region.

Hatem Abdulqader, Jerusalem's caseworker in the Palestinian movement of Fatah and the ex-Minister of Jerusalem, revealed that the Jordanian Palestinian agreement which was signed by King Abdullah II and President Mahmoud Abbas came after Israeli leaks spoke about Israel's intention to attempt and remove the Jordanian custody and impose a new fait accompli next September.

Abdulqader considered, while speaking to "Maan" Palestinian agency, that this agreement was a strategic step to defend the Arab identity of Jerusalem and protect Al Aqsa Mosque.

Abdulqader, who warned previously of Israeli attempts to remove Jordanian custody of Al- Aqsa, added that this agreement allows Jordan and the King to have a lot of options on the political and legal levels to thwart Israeli attempts to divide Al -Aqsa Mosque.

He pointed out that although the agreement is an upholding of the status quo since 1924, there is fear that Israel might use recognition of the State of Palestine as an excuse to remove Jordanian custody of Al-Aqsa Mosque, since the agreement stated that Jerusalem is part of the 1967 Palestinian territories.

Abdulqader also clarified that this agreement does not contradict with the political mandate of the Palestinian Authority in Occupied Jerusalem including Al Aqsa Mosque, but that Jordanian custody of Al Aqsa shall remain until liberation of the holy city.

He also added: "The agreement comes in a time when Israeli attempts to violate Al Aqsa Mosque are getting more frequent. These attempts are not exclusive to extremists anymore and Israeli officials and military and judicial authorities are taking part in them now".

THE HASHEMITE KINGDOM OF JORDAN

CHAPTER EIGHT

COMPONENTS OF THE SOCIETY DEMOGRAPHICS OF JORDAN

CHAPTER EIGHT
COMPONENTS OF THE SOCIETY DEMOGRAPHICS OF JORDAN

Jordan's total population is estimated at about 9,531,712, while the number of the Jordanian population estimated at about 6,613,587 makes up %69.4 of the total population of Kingdom.

Jordan's population has doubled more than 10 times during 55 years. The largest increase was in the past decade, especially since 2011 AD (According to the General Census of the Department of Statistics "Census" during the period from November 30 to December 2015, 10 AD). The population of the capital, Amman, exceeded the four million in 2015 AD.

The country's population is growing rapidly, and the demographics in Jordan will change dramatically over the next fifty years.

Most Jordanians are Arabs descended from different origins, who migrated to the region over the years from various areas. In addition, there are Kurds who inhabited the area with armies of Saladin and settled in several cities such as Salt and Karak and Irbid, as mentioned in the Yaqut Al-Hamawi's book, as well as some Kurdish immigrants in the time of the Ottoman Empire. In addition, there are the Circassians who are descendants of Muslims displaced by the Russia invasion in the Caucasus in the nineteenth century and a small group of Chechnya. Also, there are small numbers of Armenian population. It is difficult to count the number of Bedouins, where most of Jordan's Bedouins live in the vast wasteland that extends east from the Desert Highway throughout the south and east of the country.

It can be said that many of the characteristics of the Jordanian and Arab society are found in their strongest form in Bedouin culture. For instance, Bedouins are most famous for their hospitality and generosity.

Some Jordanians are of Palestinian origin, having been forced from their homeland during the 1948 and 1967 wars with Israel. Jordan was the only Arab state to grant all Palestinians the right to Jordanian citizenship, on the basis of administrative and legal ties with the West Bank, which lasted until 1988 AD, and many have exercised that option, playing an important part in the political and economic life of Jordan.

Some Palestinians continue to live in a number of refugee camps in Jordan, where the United Nations Relief Works Agency (UNRWA) is responsible for the welfare of the refugees, including their health and education.

About %70 of Jordan's population lives in cities (Urban); and less than %6 are residents of rural areas.

Circassians first arrived in masse in Jordan in 1878 AD, where they settled in Amman, Wadi Seer and Na'ur. Today, Circassian populations can be found also in Jerash, Sweileh, Zarqa, Azraq and other parts of northern Jordan. Estimates of the Circassian population vary from 20,000 to 80,000. Until the 1940s, they continued to overwhelmingly prefer service in the army or government, but now they are represented in a diverse assortment of sectors and professions. Circassian culture places strong emphasis on respect for the elderly and closely-knit extended families. Circassians are also well known for their honesty. In fact, Jordanian Circassians constitute King Hussein's ceremonial guard.

A small community of Druze lives in Jordan, mainly near the Syrian border. There is also a community of Druze in Azraq, in the east of the country. The north Jordan Valley hosts a small community of Turkomans and Baha'is, who moved from Iran to Jordan to escape persecution in 1910 AD.

In the late nineteenth century, Chechens, another Caucasian people, migrated to Jordan from Grozny in waves. Over the years, they have assimilated into Jordanian society, while maintaining their special culture and charm. For example, it is a marriage tradition among the Chechens, for the groom to capture his future bride with her consent and against the will of her family. This was seen as a measure of manhood, horsemanship and bravery. Today, this practice continues, but has taken on more of a ceremonial nature.

A large number of Iraqis live in Jordan. They fled the US invasion and escaped from the turbulent political situation in their country. There are a number of Syrians living in Jordan but their number has increased significantly for up to 1,300,000 after the Syrian crisis in 2011 AD (According to the General Census of the Department of Statistics "Census" during the period from November 30 to December 2015, 10 AD). %34 of that population is concentrated in the capital, Amman, according to the census.

There is a large foreign labor segment in the country, compared with the population. There are hundreds of thousands of workers who are hosted by Jordan. Most of them come from Egypt, Syria, Indonesia and Southeast Asian countries, as that Qualified Industrial Zones Conventions with the United States have helped to increase their numbers. Most of the workers are from China and Bangladesh, in addition to some residents of Lebanese descent who came to Jordan upon the civil war in their home countries, others by the year 2006 war between Israel and Hezbollah, and most of these workers reside in Amman.

In the late 1980s, Jordan experienced more than one form of migration. Large segments of the labor force worked abroad, and rural-urban migration continued unabated.

In rural areas, substantial numbers of men were employed outside the villages or were engaged in military service. Jordan often has been referred to by economists as a labor-exporting country.

With the oil boom of the 1970s in the Persian Gulf countries and Saudi Arabia, substantial numbers of the well-educated and skilled labor force, from both rural and urban areas, temporarily emigrated for employment. Government figures for 1987 stated that nearly 350,000 Jordanians were working abroad, a remarkably high number for such a small domestic population. Approximately 160,900 Jordanians resided in Saudi Arabia alone. Jordan was affected by the repercussions of the Gulf war because of the return of thousands of workers.

- **Community and Culture:**

Jordan's traditions are the same as the Arab traditions in the region, including generosity, hospitality and good treatment between persons and others. Jordan does not differ from the rest of the Arab countries; however, Jordan is characterized by homogeneity and intermingling between its culture and the culture of the surrounding countries, such as Saudi Arabia, Iraq, Palestine and Syria.

In the late 1980s, social life and identity in Jordan was a family-centered one. The household was composed of people related to one another by kinship, either through descent or marriage, and family ties extended into the structure of clans and tribes. Gender and age were important determinants of social status.

Age greatly influenced an individual man or woman's standing in society; generally, attaining an advanced age resulted in enhanced respect and social stature.

The formation of an educated middle class that included increasing numbers of educated and working women led to some changes in the traditional pattern. Men and women now interact in public--in the universities, in the workplace, on public transportation, in voluntary associations, and at social events.

- **Art and Architecture:**

Art and Architecture in Jordan is closely linked to art history and

(AL-SALT: ARCHITECTURAL ICON IN JORDAN)

patterns in neighboring Arab region. Jordan has had a significant impact in the Levant region as it has paved the way for the emergence of civilizations that have left many important effects in fine arts and architecture.

For example, the pottery industry in Jordan, in the Nabataean era, is marked by skill and fine texture. Pottery was decorated with geometric shapes and colors of red, brown and black. Nabataean sculpture was developed, as example; god Helios statue, Eros statue and the head of the god Hermes. Floor mosaics art, in the east of the Jordan, dates back to the Byzantine period (the fifth and sixth centuries); one of the most famous available pieces was "Madaba Mosaic Map" showing the Holy Land "visits sites", stating their names in Byzantine characters, other mosaic representing three queens to symbolize the cities of Madaba, Gregoria and Rome.

Jordan, in recent twentieth century decades, has made government efforts to encourage private art, and made some galleries available for photography, sculpture, painting, engraving and decoration. The traditional applied arts and handicraft professions pursued its march, for example calligraphy, rugs, carpets, leather, pottery and porcelain, seashell inlay and small statues of olive wood. "Jordan Art Symposium" was founded in 1953 AD. The College of Fine Arts at Yarmouk University was founded in 1980 AD.

The Royal Society of Fine Arts was established in Amman in 1979 AD, followed by the establishment of The Jordan National Gallery in 1980 AD featuring artworks of Jordanian and Arab artists.

Urbanization and construction movement in Jordan has been active since the early twentieth century.

Major cities included government buildings and private residences were built using Jordanian stone. Jordanian architecture features the styles of contemporary architecture in an attempt to relate it to the local style, and inlay it with elements inspired by Arab heritage.

Stone is the main building material in Amman, being used in strengthening buildings' facades throughout the cities. A lot of major cities, such as Amman, are characterized by the beauty of architecture, the presence of services and five-star hotels. Most ministries have been established on the basis of distinct standards in architecture and construction. The stones, used in the construction of Amman City, added a distinctive art to this city, in addition to the aesthetic touch to its architectural character that enabled engineers to show their creativity in a wide variety of styles of architecture using stone.

A group of architects, who took over the production of models of architecture in Jordan, confirmed that the architecture in the country is affected by the Islamic, Roman and Greek architecture and cultural heritage of the city of Amman, but most of them stressed that Islamic art is their wish and aim. Engineers censure some of the buildings which they call «assembly» buildings, in-which the design has the features of the West Building designs paired with the style in the region without taking into account the architectural character of the region, its history and other cultural and civilizational considerations. Some engineers design buildings with facades that have more than one culture and heritage; the engineers named it «glamour style» buildings. This kind has no content or heritage and unsuccessful in terms of engineering. They have mentioned a number of those models in various places in Jordan. Engineers did not deny the need to introduce some modern materials to building process such as glass and metal sheets within a thoughtful design taking into account the development of Arab architecture and argued that this interference is required and in good standing.

Jordan contains numerous and unlimited number of architecture styles, where it varies according to the architectural culture of

Jordanian engineers graduated from East and West. Such engineers returned after graduation to apply their culture about different schools of architecture in the corners of the nation. In spite of such multiple models, the common use of the Jordanian stone in buildings prevented the architectural chaos; leading to a wide use of stone available in sufficient quantities due to the geographic and topographic nature of the country.

- **Literature:**

In fact, anyone keeping abreast of literary movement in Jordan can monitor its path through three phases:

1- Literature in Emirate of Transjordan time (1946-1921)

2- Literature between Nakba (Palestinian exodus) and Naksa (setback) (1967-1947) Unification of the Two Banks time.

3- Literature after Naksa (setback) (-1967 till today)

Poetry and prose flourished in the Emirate time; Mustafa Wahbi Al-Tal, better known as 'Arar', is considered to be the pioneer of Jordanian patriotism, distinguished by his eloquent versified poetry closer to the spirit of the people. Al-Tal was a daring spokesman for the nation's poor and oppressed people in that period. In the field of prose; Muhammad Subhi Abu Ghunaymah wrote his book "night songs", a group of social, ethical and moral stories.

After the unification of the two banks, a new literature emerged from the blending of the Jordanian and Palestinian identity, leading to Palestinian and Jordanian novel writers such as Jum'a Hamad and

Mofied Nahla, Jordanian and Palestinian poets like Khalil Zktan and Fadwa Toukan.

1950s and 1960s were the establishment stage of Jordanian real literature, wherein specialized literary magazines, supporting literature and encouraging writers, emerged. There were many literary schools beside the increasing authorship in this stage. The Jordanian Writers Association was established in 1976 AD, including hundreds of poets and writers in its activities.

There are writers and poets who made a clear mark in the Jordanian cultural scene, the story and the novel field, literary article and thoughts field, traditional literature studies field and short story field.

- **Music, Theater and Cinema:**

Jordanian Bedouin Singing looks like the Bedouin Arabs singing in the various deserts, characterized by short simple tone and narrow vocal scope. This singing consists of Al-Samer and Al-Hageeny type of music. Al-Samer type includes "Al-Qassoud" dance performed by men with one girl in the middle "al-hashi" and accompanied by Rababa music.

The rural singing is similar to the Arab folk dance "Dabke" found in Levant countries in addition to Al-Mawwal and Zajal. There are hybrid types that combine Bedouin and rural singing like «Haddadi». Rural melodies are short and repeated with narrow vocal scope but contain some melodic additions. Modern music in Jordan includes several musical trends according to what influence it like the folkloric heritage, the foreign style or the traditional Arab heritage.

Theater in Jordan was known in its infancy in the early twentieth century through some of the historical, religious, social and translated plays as well as some attempts regarding local authoring by some amateurs in Jordan. In its second phase, Professor Hani Snobar, graduated from "Codman Theatre" in the United States in 1957 AD, has emerged in the art scene. He settled in Amman and worked on attracting theatrical art amateurs from Radio Jordan (Drama Department), the University of Jordan and some amateurs. This group founded the Jordan theater family at that time.

In the third phase, 1970s witnessed the graduation of academic directors from Arab and world universities, institutes and academies, where plays of the masterpieces of the Arab theater and some of local performances were introduced.

The fourth phase (1980s); it witnessed an increase in the number of graduates from Arab and world academies, universities and technical institutes, as well as the establishment of the Faculty of Arts at Yarmouk University and the Theater Training Centre under the Ministry of Culture. A number of old and new directors introduced their new experiences away from the authoring and traditional art pattern. The fifth phase (1990s) witnessed the growth and widespread of Jordanian theater after the Gulf War as a result of the lack of demand on the Jordanian Arab TV works; leading the artists towards the theater where the theater groups performed a lot of plays with help of the Ministry of Culture, which organized culture festivals (especially theater festivals) Jordanian theater festival and Jerash Festival for Culture & Arts, which is held annually since 1980 until now.

Cinema in Jordan has not experienced prosperity unlike the theater. Many attempts were successful, in spite of resource constraints, lack of cinematic devices and experiences and the scarcity of specialized institutions. News and documentary movies have appeared since 1948 AD.

- **Language and religion:**

All Jordanians, regardless of ethnicity or religion, speak Arabic, the official language of Jordan. Throughout Jordan, the language exists in three forms: the classical Arabic of the Quran, the literary language developed from the classical and known as Modern Standard Arabic, and the local form of the spoken language (Colloquialism). Each area in Jordan owns its dialect that distinguishes it from other area. There are dialects of the people of the north, south and center in addition to Rural Jordanian - Bedouin Jordanian - Urban Jordanian. All these dialects are close to each other and differ only in pronunciation or being affected by border areas or being independent in the form of a combination of several dialects; in spite of the existence of the common terms and expressions. English is used widely in the field of trade and government and French language is taught in some private schools. Circassians, Armenians, Chechens and Kurds use their own languages in their areas in spite of mastery of the Arabic language.

In addition to being the official religion of the kingdom, Islam is the dominant religion in Jordan, and also the religion of the majority of Arabs and non-Arabs. The overwhelming majority of them are Sunnis. About %6 of the population is Christians, who mostly live in Amman, Irbid, Madaba, Karak and Salt. The majority of Christians belong to the Greek Orthodox Church. Also, there are small communities of Roman Catholics, Syrian Orthodox, Coptic Orthodox, Assyrian, Chaldeans Catholic, Armenian Orthodox, and a few numbers of Protestant Christians in Amman. In addition, a small number of the population follows the Shiite and Druze sects.

The Jordanian constitution guarantees freedom of religious belief. This means that Jordan contains ethnic and religious diversity, and it offers complete freedom for its citizens in the formation of and participation in their own clubs, schools, associations or places of worship in addition to the right of ethnic groups to learn their own languages for free.

- **Healthcare:**

Jordan is one of the most developed countries in the region in the field of medicine and pharmaceuticals as it competes with developed countries in this field. Jordan ranks first among the Arab countries in terms of healthcare according to Arab Competitiveness Report in the Arab World.

In Amman, there are a lot of hospitals specialized in the treatment of cancer, heart diseases, eye diseases, infertility, family medicine and other medical specialties. King Hussein Medical City is one of the most important medical centers in the region. The Jordanian hospitals deservedly got the International Accreditation which is an important advantage regarding the hospital's reputation at home and abroad.

The revenues of health care sector in Jordan have grown steadily in recent years, where a share of GDP of total public expenditure is allocated to it each year; as well as private hospitals and clinics revenues have doubled over the years.

The country's health care system is divided between public and private sectors. There is a large number of hospitals which are affiliated to the Ministry of Health; the military's Royal Medical Services runs its own hospitals; in addition to quasi-governmental hospitals like the Jordan University Hospital and King Abdullah University Hospital.

It is worth noting that the cost of treatment in a Jordanian hospital is less than other countries. The Ministry of Health operates healthcare centers divided according to classification as follows: comprehensive health care centers, primary health care centers, health care sub-centers, maternity centers and dental Clinics.

The pharmaceuticals sector in Jordan has existed since the 1960s.

At present, local companies operate in this sector. Pharmaceuticals sector account for a large proportion of contribution to GDP. The pace of industrialization has grown to a great extent, as revenues of

(King Hussein Medical City)

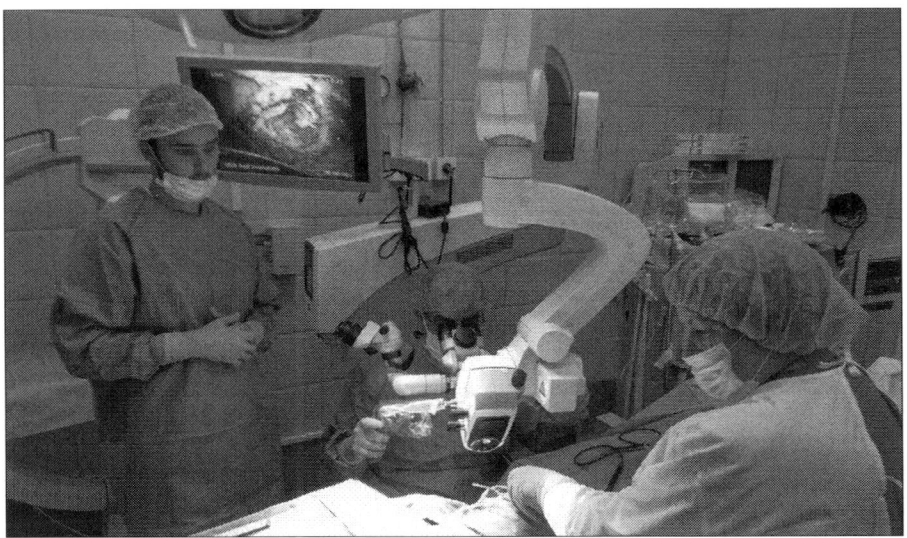

(The Royal Medical Services conducted cochlear implants operations in Russia)

the sector amounted to hundreds of millions of dollars per year. The volume of exports has witnessed a relatively large increase, where Jordan exports many pharmaceuticals to many countries around the world. Investment in the pharmaceutical sector has exceeded hundreds of millions of dollars; the most important export markets are Saudi Arabia, Iraq, Algeria and other countries.

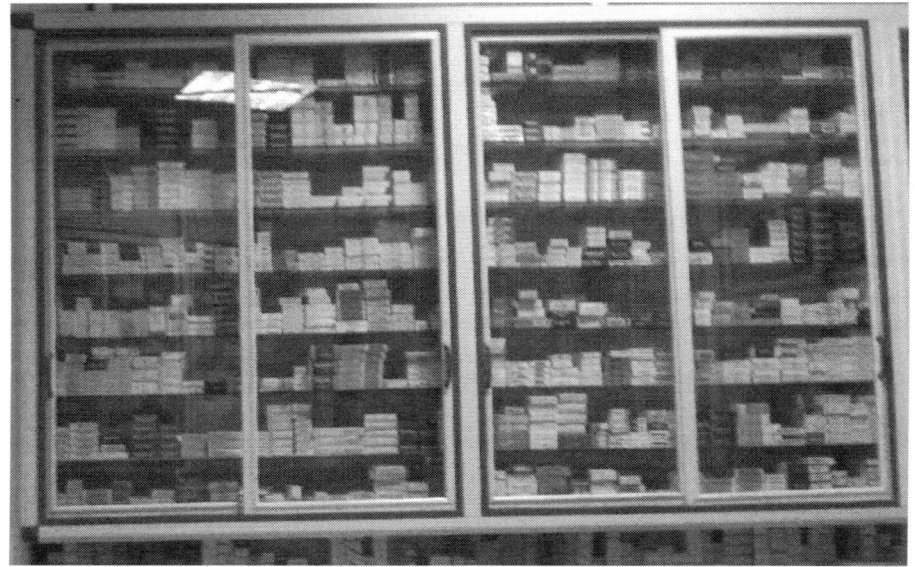

THE HASHEMITE KINGDOM OF JORDAN

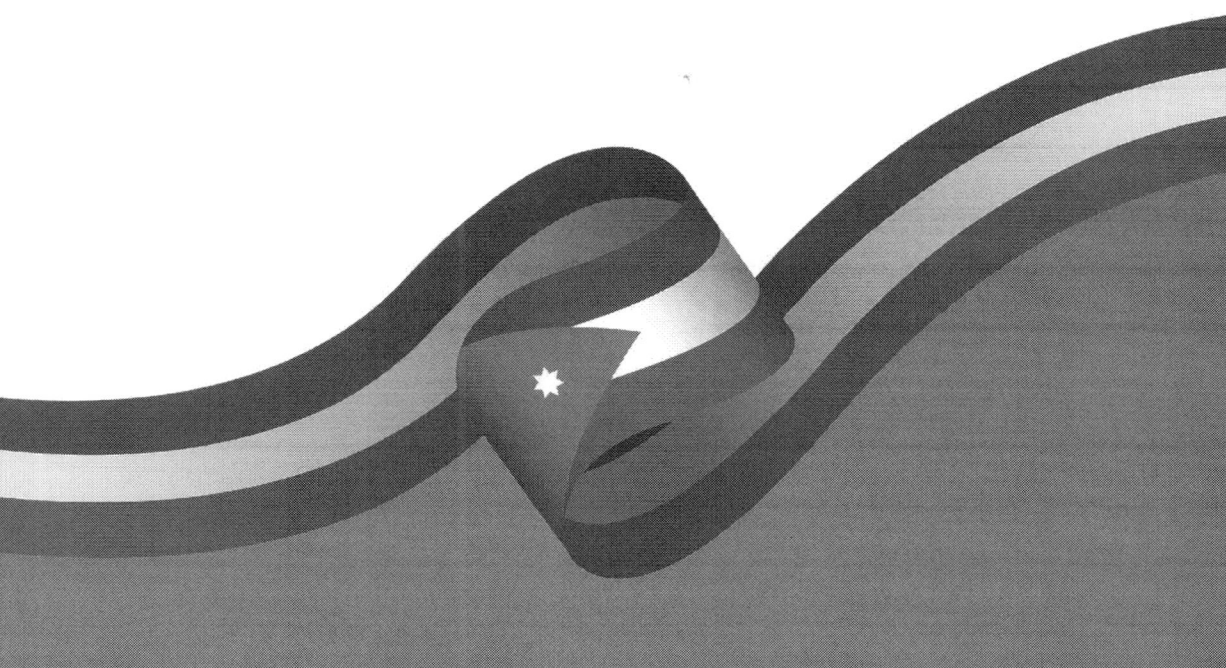

CHAPTER NINE

**JORDAN'S ECONOMY
AND
ITS BRANCHES**

CHAPTER NINE
JORDAN'S ECONOMY AND ITS BRANCHES

According to a study published by The Arab Investment & Export Credit Guarantee, the average income per capita in Jordan amounted to $ 4852 for the year of 2012 AD, compared to $ 4542 for the year of 2011 AD.

The economic report and the study, which their data relied on figures from the International Monetary Fund (IMF), highlighted the evolution of the average annual income level for the Jordanian citizen and in the Arab world in general.

Statistical data, issued by the World Economic Forum (WEF), estimated the family income in Jordan to be 57 Dinars per day, income per capita to be $ 5174 per year, equivalent to 3,663 Dinars in 2015 AD.

The economy of the Kingdom depends mainly on the services sector, trade, tourism, and some extractive industries such as fertilizers and medicines.

The phosphate mines, south of the Kingdom, make Jordan the third-largest source of this material in the world. Among the most important resources are extracted potash and other minerals, natural gas and limestone. Agricultural land space is limited and water resources are quite rare. Around %78 of Jordan's population lives in urban areas. The proportion of young people is considered to be one of the highest among the countries of the lower middle-income countries; the age of at least %35 of the population is lower than 14 years. It is also one of the countries with the best education indicators in the region. Allah has granted Jordan special advantages that strengthen the kingdom's ambition to shift to a knowledge-based economy.

Since His Majesty King Abdullah has assumed his constitutional powers as a King of the country in 1999 AD, the government introduced liberal economic policies that have led to the prosperity of the Jordanian economy in general. Jordan is now one of the most liberal and competitive economies in the Middle East. The banking sector in Jordan is sophisticated and modern so that it has become a favorite investment destination as a result of the conservative policies adopted which helped Central Bank of Jordan (CBJ) avoid the global financial crisis, such as the global financial crisis in 2009 AD.

Jordan's economy grew by almost %10 during the previous years. Jordan has concluded free trade agreements exceeding any other Arab country. Jordan enjoys a supreme status with the EU; along with tight integration with the GCC. The access to such markets will hopefully bring significant economic benefits to the kingdom in the coming years.

Jordan's economy is a knowledge-based economy on the path of education development, privatization, and economic liberalization; with economic restructuring to ensure a knowledge-based economy. The main obstacles for Jordan's economy are scarce water sources and complete reliance on oil imports in order to obtain energy in addition to regional instability.

Jordan, at an accelerated pace, has privatized state-owned sectors, liberalized the economy; thus stimulating unprecedented growth in urban centers in Jordan such as Amman and Aqaba in particular. It also has plenty of new industrial zones that produce goods in textile, pharmaceutical and cosmetics sectors; in addition to defense and aerospace industries and telecommunications and information technology.

Jordan pins its future hopes on tourism and exports of uranium, in addition to oil shale, trade and information and communication technology leading to economic growth in the future.

Jordan's Natural Resources Authority (JNRA) estimates that phosphate formations cover about %60 of the total area of Jordan. Also, Jordan is one of the richest countries in terms of oil shale reserves in the world. The Jordanian energy sector's strategy aims to introduce the oil-shale as one of the alternatives to primary energy sources to reach %11 of the total energy mix by 2015 AD and %14 by 2020 AD. There are also very large quantities to be commercially exploited in the central and northwestern regions of the country.

Jordan has discovered massive amounts of uranium that make it the eleventh largest country in the world. Such reserves of uranium grab the attention of many countries. Furthermore, Jordan seeks to establish the first nuclear reactor for this purpose, where the kingdom imports %95 of its energy needs.

- **Oil-shale in Jordan:**

There are very huge quantities of oil shale to be commercially exploited in the central and northern regions west of the country. According to the World Energy Council Jordan reserves approximately 40 billion tons, which established it as the second richest state in rock oil reserves after Canada (estimated), and first at the world's level of proven discoveries at a rate of extraction of oil up to between %8 and %12 of content, and could be the production of 4 billion tons of oil from the current reserve, which puts the quality of Jordanian oil on the one hand extraction, on an equal footing with their counterparts in western Colorado in the United States, which its estimated amount may rise to 20 billion tons. The moisture content and ash within is relatively low. The total thermal value is 7.5 mega joules/kg, and the content of ointments reach %9 of the weight of the

organic content. Reserves, available to be exploited, are accessible, since most of them lie in open and shallow mines.

- **Shale Oil Production Plant:**

The Government of the Hashemite Kingdom of Jordan and Enfit signed a 10+40 year Oil Shale Surface Retort Concession Agreement (SRCA), for the distillation of oil shale, giving exploration and production rights for about 2.3 billion tons of oil shale.

Enfit has prepared and provided a comprehensive economic feasibility study for the exploitation of oil shale to produce synthetic crude oil. A plant will be established for such a purpose at a capacity of about 40 million barrels per day. Such quantity is enough to cover %40 of the current daily energy needs of Jordan, saving about 700,000,000 Jordanian dinars per year of energy expenditure.

- **Benefits for Jordan:**

Enfit projects in Jordan will have a significant impact on the economic and social levels in the Kingdom, to be reflected positively on the local economy as a whole. The most prominent advantage of these projects can be reflected in enabling Jordan to achieve the independence and safety in the field of energy and reduce Jordan's dependence on import of oil derivatives. **The following are examples of these advantages:**

- Jobs (more than three thousand jobs during the construction phase and permanent thousand jobs).

- Independence and safety in the field of energy.

- Inward investment.

- Strengthening of national wealth.

- **Jordan Atomic Energy Commission (JAEC):**

The Jordan Atomic Energy Commission was established at the beginning of 2008 as successor to the Jordanian Nuclear Energy Commission. The development and promotion of peaceful uses of nuclear energy were transferred to the Commission. The work of the Atomic Energy Commission focused on two main areas, namely, the construction of nuclear power plants for the production of electricity and desalination of water using those nuclear reactors, and also the project to use the natural nuclear resources found in Jordan, namely, the uranium.

Jordan, through the establishment of a nuclear power plants for the production of electricity, aims to reduce the cost of producing electricity, which is proportional to the price of oil and is affected by the frequent interruptions of Egyptian natural gas.

- **Jordan's nuclear program (for peaceful purposes):**

  Jordan's nuclear program consists of two major projects:

To construct a nuclear power plant for the production of electricity and the desalination of water using nuclear reactors.

Exploitation of the natural nuclear resources present in Jordan, primarily uranium.

The program includes construction of the Jordanian nuclear research reactor with a capacity of 5 to 10 MW as an important part of the infrastructure of nuclear technology and the focal point of the Centre for Nuclear Science and Technology. The research reactor will be used to train a new generation of nuclear scientists and engineers, and to provide support for a variety of services in the medical and health, as well as agricultural and industrial fields.

The Authority (JAEC) plans to build a second reactor within two to three years after the first reactor begins to operate with the purpose of providing power to transfer water from the Red Sea and the energy needed to desalinate and pump it.

The long-term plans for the nuclear program includes four nuclear reactors for peaceful energy during the next two decades that will not only generate enough electricity for Jordan's needs, but will also make it possible to export electricity to neighboring countries.

- **Shams Ma'an Power Generation Solar Photovoltaic Power Plant:**

Shams Ma'an Power Generation PSC is a 52.5MW photovoltaic power plant (PVPP) that went into production of clean energy from the sun by the end of 2016 led by an agreement with the National Electric Power Company (NEPCO).

It is one of the largest PV plants in the region and the largest in Jordan that is privately developed and owned at a total investment of approximately $ 170 million.

Shams Ma'an occupies 2 million square meters, installed by world class thin film technology by First Solar, producing around 160 GWh per year, almost %1 of Jordan's electricity current generation, and preventing around 90,000 tons of CO_2 emission. In addition to the positive impact, the citizen will be able to see its significance on social and economic levels in the Southern area.

(Solar cells)

- **Agriculture and Livestock:**

The agricultural sector is one of the important sectors in Jordan. Agriculture plays an important role regarding economic and social system of rural communities. It is closely linked to efforts to preserve the environment and its sustainability.

The Jordanian agricultural sector is facing problems and challenges represented in the successive years of drought, the fluctuation of rainfall, lack of agricultural land, the scarcity of water resources and different risks.

The agricultural sector contributes at a rate of %2.8 of GDP and employs %3.5 of the total workforce. Agricultural exports make up %11 of the total exports of the Kingdom, %92 of which goes to the Arab markets.

Jordan has achieved self-sufficiency regarding a number of agricultural products such as olive oil and milk, except that a lot of basic food products as types of wheat, dairy products, sugar, red meat and vegetables are imported from abroad.

The most important countries from which we import the products (in general, not just agricultural products) are Saudi Arabia, China, the United States, Germany and Egypt. Exports of agricultural products have grown and its value increased. The most important agricultural exports: tomato, hydrogenated oils, cigarettes. The most important countries that import our exports are: Iraq, United Arab Emirates and Syria.

Jordan has entered into international cooperation agreements, leading to establish a special relationship with the ministries of agriculture and research centers in the majority of countries with which Jordan has diplomatic relations. Jordan seeks to strengthen its role internationally in the field of agriculture through participation in regional groupings and relevant international organizations in this sector.

Renewable groundwater can be found in Jordan in 12 defined basins. Jordan faces an imbalance in water resources / population equation. Per capita share of renewable water resources is considered to be one of the lowest quotas in the world; per capita percentage of water is defined to be 180 cubic meters approx. Conventional water resources in Jordan consist mainly of groundwater and surface water. In addition, the treatment of sewage is increasingly exploited for irrigation in the Jordan Valley. Fresh water resources are estimated to be 850 million cubic meters per year.

Regarding the plant wealth, the area planted with fruit trees grows every year. The most fruit trees are, namely, olive, almond trees, citrus and apples and grapes. Also, the production of olive is growing from year to year because of its local and international importance in order to obtain olive oil.

Livestock is considered to be a key component of the agricultural sector as it contributes about %55 of the value of agricultural production. The contribution percentage of the various livestock sectors in agricultural production varies, where the poultry sector ranks first, followed by cattle sector and sheep sector (sheep and goats).

Sheep sector has importance related to the social perspective of this sector. About %48 of the pastoral communities living in the desert depend on it.

- **Industry:**

Jordan enjoys a strategic location and distinct security and stability in the region, making it a center for attracting foreign and domestic investments in various sectors, especially the industrial sector.

Despite the fact that Jordan is relatively poor country regarding natural resources, it is rich in human resources.

Industry in Jordan is divided into the following:

Manufacturing industry, including: Garments and Leather Industries, Therapeutic Industries and Medical Supplies, Chemical and Cosmetics Industries, Plastic and Rubber Industries, Engineering, Electrical and Information Technology Industries, Wood and Furniture Industries, Construction Industry, Ration, Food, Agriculture and Livestock Industries, Packaging, Paper, cardboard, printing and supplies Industry. Manufacturing contributes with an average %17 of the GDP of Jordan annually.

Extractive industry, including: mining industries, which contributes with a percentage of about %3 of GDP annually.

Regarding the electricity and water sector, the contribution percentage of this industry to GDP is almost %2. Small and medium-sized industrial facilities constitute a ratio of about %98.7 of the number of industrial facilities in general, by adopting the standard number of workers and the invested capital for the classification of industrial facilities.

- **Science and technology:**

Given the limited resources, Jordan depends on the human factor to achieve economic and social progress.

Due to the quality of services available in this country and its wealth of educated and talented people, Jordan achieves internally success, and is also capable of exporting human expertise and skilled manpower to other countries in the region.

Jordan has also strengthened its ability to conduct scientific research, in order to take advantage of human talents in Jordan. Encouraging science and technology ranked first in the list of priorities for both the public and private sectors.

The Higher Council for Science and Technology, the Royal Scientific Society and the research and development programs supported by various private companies represent the main components of the science and technology sector in Jordan. Traditionally, Jordan is interested in education and pays much attention to it. The proportion of college graduates to the total population matches those in many developed countries.

- **Transportation:**

Transportation sector contributes more than %10 of GDP, with strong growth by up to %6 per annum. Jordan has also been able to develop its infrastructure to allow companies and individuals to conduct their businesses efficiently with no obstacles. Jordan provides all service to ship the goods and the delivery of services to regional and global markets without any obstacles or complications. Jordan has a well-developed infrastructure of road networks with more than 7891 km representing the main road network.

There are two border-crossings between Jordan and Israel- Bisan "Beit She'an" (Sheikh Hussein Bridge) in the north and Wadi Araba in the south. In addition, there is the King Hussein Bridge crossing (or Allenby bridge) which is located between Jordan and the West Bank.

The total length of the railway reaches 507 kilometers. A journey from Amman station to the Giza Station takes place on Friday and Saturday of each week. The railway is also used to transport goods to Syria. The Aqaba Railway is used to transport phosphate to Aqaba for export.

Jordan contains many airports. Three airports receive commercial flights, two are in Amman and the third is in Aqaba. The Royal Jordanian is the main air carrier in Jordan. Queen Alia International Airport in Amman is the major international airport in Jordan, established on an area of about 22 thousand dunams. Amman Civil Airport was the main airport in Jordan, but it was replaced by the Queen Alia International Airport. Amman Civil Airport serves several regional routes. King Hussein International Airport serves Aqaba with its links with Amman and several regional and international cities.

- **Royal Jordanian / Royal Jordanian Airlines Company:**

On Dec. 15, 1963, RJ was established by a Royal Decree issued by His Majesty King Hussein, as the national air carrier of the Hashemite Kingdom of Jordan.

Upon issuing the decree, King Hussein said: "I want our national carrier to be our ambassador of good will around the world and a bridge across which we exchange culture, civilization, trade, technology, friendship and better understanding with the rest of the world."

Royal Jordanian shares started to be listed on the Amman Stock Exchange in December 2007, after being privatized.

Jordanians own most of the shares of RJ which is the national carrier of Jordan.

Ever since its establishment, RJ has been an essential contributor to the national economy, bringing in hard currency and playing a key role in attracting tourists from all over the world. It contributes %3 of the country's GDP.

Royal Jordanian's -52year journey has been one of constant progress; during this time, it modernized its fleet, expanded its route network, trained human resources for more efficient work and updated its IT systems.

RJ continues its forward stride under the invaluable guidance of and directives from His Majesty King Abdullah II, who generously lends support to the airline to be more competitive both regionally and internationally.

Royal Jordanian has a vision "To be the Airline of choice connecting Jordan and the Levant with the world". It reaches 56 direct destinations on four continents on its 27 young aircraft.

Its flights are operated from Queen Alia International Airport, with its vastly improved infrastructure and cutting-edge facilities.

The airline's policy has always been to renew its fleet of aircraft; in 2014, it introduced the first five Boeing's 787 Dreamliners dedicated to long- and medium-haul routes. Two more 787s will join the fleet by the end of 2016 and the other one in 2018.

Due to its reputation and in view of the international level of competitiveness, Royal Jordanian joined the oneworld airline alliance in 2007 under which 15 international RJ partners operate. This alliance offers RJ passengers the possibility to fly to more than 1,000 cities in 150 countries from/to Amman with one stop only.

RJ is keen to introduce advanced, state-of-the-art operating systems that are used across the air transport industry, staying on par with global airlines. Other facilities are constantly introduced by RJ to make travel easier for its passengers, who in 2015 reached three

million and were carried on 36,000 flights.

- **Competitiveness of Royal Jordanian:**

Royal Jordanian enjoys a leading position, both internationally and locally, due to the great services it offers its passengers.

As the national carrier of Jordan, RJ plays a strategic role in serving the kingdom, reinforcing its image as a secure and politically stable country. This makes Royal Jordanian an airline of choice for the majority of Jordanians flying to different destinations, either on its direct route network or on the network served by the oneworld alliance.

RJ distinguishes itself through its young fleet of aircraft, which averages five years, and through the top-notch services it offers its passengers. Its clean safety record, which has become its strong trademark, puts RJ in a reputable position globally.

The human resources are the airline's biggest asset; they have the highest level of qualification and expertise in their different areas in addition to the ability to introduce and implement all modern technology means to keep pace with the rapid developments in the global aviation industry.

- **Business plan 2019-2015:**

Royal Jordanian is now implementing its six-pillar business plan for 2019-2015. Top on its agenda is the route network and the fleet.

The company took the decision to close eight destinations due to their poor feasibility: Delhi, Mumbai, Colombo, Accra, Lagos, Milan, Al Ain and Alexandria. It has suspended operations to eight other cities for security reasons. They are: Damascus, Aleppo, Mosul, Tripoli, Benghazi, Misurata, Sanaa and Aden. At the same time, RJ phased out a number of aircraft and introduced five new Boeing 787s.

The second pillar of the plan involves boosting the local market share by directly increasing the number of passengers from and to Jordan and through increasing the transit traffic via the kingdom.

Revenue management is the third pillar of the plan. The company has taken a number of measures to boost revenue, with a focus on ancillary revenues, which is the fourth pillar.

The fifth pillar is the efficient use of fuel in order to lower the cost. The company is implementing a number of initiatives that reduce fuel consumption, including continuously renewing its fleet and negotiating with fuel suppliers to obtain best prices.

The sixth pillar involves an analysis of the aircraft ownership structure as the company is currently studying the best ways to meet its needs and achieve its interests with regard to the operational and capital lease leading to ownership, with application of analysis of the advantages of both options.

- **The Port of Aqaba:**

The Port of Aqaba is the only sea port of Jordan. It has the capacity to handle up to 23 ships of different sizes and types, in addition to 8 ships in anchorage. The port can accommodate oil tankers to 406

thousand DWT and 70 thousand tons of other ships at a production capacity of 28 million tons per year. The port contains all logistic requirements of yards, warehouses and hangars for storage of goods received in the port.

Jordan also has an extensive and modern road network across the kingdom from north to south and from east to west along with its connection with its surrounding neighboring countries through the roads of high specifications. There is also a major road linking the north and south Jordan, and it consists of four lanes along the distance.

Major companies of phosphate and potash

- **Jordan Phosphate Mines Co.**

Jordan Phosphate Mines Co. is a public shareholding limited company, founded in 1949. Its current capital is JOD 75 million. The Company aims at mining and processing phosphate ore in Jordan.

During the last six decades, the Company has assumed its pioneering position among the international companies in the fields of mining and producing fertilizers. It has become a major component of the

Jordanian economic structure and exports.

The activities of the Jordan Phosphate Mines Company can be classified under two complementary sectors: mining sector and phosphate fertilizer manufacturing sector. Through the integration of both sectors, the company has firmly proven its capabilities in the international markets.

The company operates its production activities in the Hashemite Kingdom of Jordan, which has the fifth largest reserve of phosphate in the world, equaling 3.7 billion tons, 1.25 billion tons of which are the reserves of the company's mines. That made Jordan Phosphate

Mines Company to be the second largest exporter, and sixth largest producer of phosphate in the world, with a production capacity exceeding 7 million tons of phosphate annually.

The Company's Headquarter is located in Amman, the capital. Furthermore, the Company owns four mines located in the center and south of the Kingdom, namely: Russaifa, Al-Hassa, Wadi Al-Abiad, and Eshidiya mines, in addition to the Department of Research and Quality in the city of Russaifa, and the Industrial Complex in the city of Aqaba, which aims at transforming the phosphate raw material into other products with added values. The Industrial Complex is considered one of the largest phosphate fertilizers complexes in the Middle East. Furthermore, the Company has constructed the Phosphate Port, located in Aqaba, which is especially used for exporting phosphate. The phosphate port facility is enhancing the operations of phosphate exporting to the various international markets. The Company is currently working on expanding and developing the Industrial Port, and adding certain modifications to adhering to environmental issues.

Today, we feel proud with our capability in continuously offering more job opportunities to the nationals of Jordan. Additionally, we are proud of establishing a solid chain of successful projects with our strategic partners in the international and local markets to produce the phosphate ore, expanding exploration sites, and manufacturing various types of phosphate fertilizers. To maintain that forefront, we are working hard on improving the performance, developing the products, and upgrading the products competitive quality.

- **Arab Potash Company:**

Arab Potash Company, a leading company in Jordan, attracts best talents in various fields and disciplines through best practices in the selection for recruitment and training.

The company is interested in the welfare of its employees and their families, and provides various means of social support and appreciation for their contributions.

The company gives priority to provide a healthy, safe, secure and stress-free work environment within the highest safety standards through a series of procedures, policies and training and awareness programs.

Arab Potash Company works to maximize competitiveness and profitability by constantly searching to procure best resources at optimal prices, and to enhance the efficiency of its processes.

Arab Potash Company runs an active CSR program to address shared concerns and contribute to the communities' sustainable development.

- **Contributions of Companies to Economy and Renaissance:**

Industrial growth has continued and GDP has increased in Jordan. The industry sector has provided the place for the workforce in the country. An industrial base was formed in Jordan, composed of industrial, research and exploration companies that have helped to increase exports and benefit to the overall GDP and income.

In recent years, Canadian, Japanese, American, Austrian and South Korean companies have performed its operations to explore the presence of oil in Jordan. According to the Natural Resources Authority in Jordan, the country's resources are still relatively untapped.

Natural gas was discovered in Jordan in 1987. The estimated size of the reserve discovered was about 400-150 billion cubic feet.

Oil shale reserves in Jordan are estimated at 40 billion tons, mostly located in the southern region about 100 kilometers south of Amman.

The Hashemite Kingdom of Jordan is one of the emerging economies among Arab states. In spite of suffering from a lack of natural resources, it reaches, since its establishment, positive and accelerated indicators, introducing itself as one of the most important Arab economic countries in the region.

Jordan's GDP per capita reached $ 4,940 by the end of 2015 AD.

The following is a list of the most prominent and largest Jordanian companies, according to a report by Forbes magazine for the 500 most powerful Arab companies in 2013 AD:

1- Arab Bank

2- Arab Potash

3- The Housing Bank for Trade and Finance

4- Jordan Phosphate Mines Co.

5- Jordan Telecom

6- Jordan Kuwait Bank

7- Bank of Jordan

8- Jordan Islamic Bank

9- Cairo Amman Bank

10- Ahli United Bank

11- Bank al Etihad

12- Afaq For Energy

13- Arab Jordan Investment Bank

14- Eqbal Investment

15- Arab Banking Corporation (Jordan)

16- Alia - Royal Jordanian Airline

17- Irbid District Electricity

18- Arab International for Education and Investment

19- Jordan Commercial Bank

20- Zara Investment Holding

21- Northern Cement

22- Societe General De Banque – Jordanie

23- Jordan Dubai Islamic Bank

24- Afaq Holding for Investment and Real Estate Development

25- Jordan Duty Free

26- Union Tobacco

27- National Poultry

28- Jordan Insurance

29- Petra Education Company

30- Al-Isra for Education and Investment

31- ZiadManasir Group – Jordan

32- Arab Orient Insurance

33- Jordanian Pharmaceutical Manufacturing

34- Jordan Worsted Mills

35- United Iron and Steel Manufacturing

36- United Iron and Steel Manufacturing

37- Arab International Hotels

38- Siniora Food Industries

39- Jordan Hotels and Tourism

40- Al Zarqa Education & Investment

41- Mediterranean Tourism Investment

42- Al Dawliyah for Hotels and Malls

43- Middle East Insurance

44- Al-Nisr Al Arabi Insurance

45- Deera Investment and Real Estate Development

46- First Finance

47- Al Bilad Medical Services

48- Jordan National Shipping Lines

49- General Investments

50- Arabian Steel Pipes

51- Jordan Mortgage Refinance

52- Masafat for Specialised Transport

53- Al Sharq Investment Projects

54- First Insurance

55- The Consulting and Investment

56- Jerusalem Insurance

57- Jordan Trade Facilities

58- The Arab Pesticides & Veterinary Drugs Mfg.

59- Hayat Pharmaceutical Industries

60- Nakilat – JETT

61- International Cards

62- Comprehensive Leasing Plc

63- Bindar Trading and Investment

64- Islamic Insurance

65- Al Ittihad Private School

66- United Group for Land Transport

67- Arab International Food Factories

68- Jordan Dairy

69- Arab Financial Investment

70- Delta Insurance

71- National Aluminium Industrial

72- Amad Investment & Real Estate Development

73- Yarmouk Insurance

74- International Company for Medical Investment

Praise be to Allah and thanks to the determination of the nation's sons, through the enlightened vision of the Hashemite leadership under His Majesty King Abdullah II; Jordanian and Arab companies have left their mark in the Jordanian economy. The sustainable development example cannot be counted, all that mentioned here are some of them.

THE HASHEMITE KINGDOM OF JORDAN
FROM ABDULLAH I TO ABDULLAH II

- **Banks in Jordan:**

The Jordanian dinar is the official currency of Jordan. The dinar is divided into 1000 fils or 100 qirsh. Banknotes are issued by the government in denominations of 10 ,20 ,50 and 1.5 dinars. Coins are available in denominations of 0.5 and 0.25 dinars, and ,25 ,50 ,100 10 and 5fils.

The Rate of the dinar is pegged to the dollar in general; valued at about $ 1.41 for one dinar.

Amman Stock Exchange (ASE) was established in March 1999 as a private institution with administrative and financial autonomy managed by private sector. It is authorized to function as an exchange for the trading of securities in Jordan. The exchange is governed by a seven-member board of directors. A chief executive officer oversees day-to-day responsibilities and reports to the board. The

ASE membership is comprised of Jordan's 58 brokerage firms.

Amman Stock Exchange maintains strong relationships with other exchanges and is keen to concluding agreements in this domain. The exchange is an active member of the Arab Federation of Exchanges and a full member of the World Federation of Exchanges (WFE) and other exchanges.

The number of Islamic banks in Jordan has risen concurrently with economic boom. The number of the Islamic banks and foreign bank's branches has increased, too Throughout the Kingdom, these banks operate freely under the financial policy of the Central Bank. The bank's policy has contributed to increasing the number of its branches in the Kingdom to cover most of the Kingdom's regions. .The number of branches of Jordanian banks operating abroad has increased significantly, in light of the financial and economic policies of the Kingdom.

These banks have contributed, despite the difference in their own policies under the central bank's financial and economic policies, to supporting the sustainable renaissance and investment based on a comprehensive vision of the general policy of the Kingdom.

Central Bank of Jordan sits at the top of these banks and commercial banks:

1- Arab Bank

2- Arab Banking Corporation (Jordan)

3- Bank of Jordan

4- Cairo Amman Bank

5- Capital Bank of Jordan

6- Jordan Commercial Bank

7- Jordan Kuwait Bank

8- Jordan Ahli Bank

9- The Housing Bank for Trade and Finance

10- Arab Jordan Investment Bank

11- Invest Bank

12- Societe General De Banque – Jordanie

13- Bank al Etihad

- **Examples of foreign banks operating in the Kingdom:**

    1- Standard Chartered

    2- Egyptian Arab Land Bank

    3- HSBC Middle East Limited

    4- Citibank

    5- Rafidain Bank

    6- National bank of Kuwait

    7- BLOM Bank

    8- Bank Audi - Audi Saradar Group

    9- National Bank of Abu Dhabi

- **Examples of the Jordanian Islamic banks:**

    1- Islamic International Arab Bank

    2- Jordan Islamic Bank

    3- Jordan Dubai Islamic Bank

    4- Al Rajhi Bank is also an example of international Islamic banks.

The role of the Central Bank of Jordan focuses on maintaining monetary and financial stability, contributing to increasing the proportion of non-Jordanian ownership in Jordanian banks.

Banking business, in terms of quantity and quality, underwent a

great development by the real growth rates recorded by the Jordanian economy since the beginning of 2004 AD to 2016 AD, accounting for an unprecedented income from GDP.

- **Jordan Chamber of Industry and Commerce:**

The Jordan Chamber of Commerce sought over the past few years to derive inspiration from the royal directives of the leader of the country His Majesty King Abdullah II, may God keep and safeguard him, who has always been keen on boosting the economic growth movement, activating the economic institutions and sectors along with the community, and improving the citizens' standard of living. Indeed, His Majesty is exerting personal efforts in order to realize prosperity in all the fields, make of Jordan a praiseworthy model, and secure a place for the Kingdom on the international investment map, thereby enabling the national economy to integrate into the international economy.

Global circumstances have formed a major economic challenge for many countries in the world. Unprecedented rises in oil, commodity and basic material prices have cast a shadow on the living conditions of the citizens in these countries, especially the poor and developing countries.

Reform policies and programs in addition to hedging measures, taken by the government under the guidance of His Majesty, may Allah protect him, contributed to the alleviation of the repercussions of the global financial crisis on the national economy, the protection of the Jordanian citizen from the repercussions of the global financial crisis on the national economy and the protection of the Jordanian citizen from the repercussions of the cost of living and high prices; through elimination of taxes and customs duties on many food and basic materials, production inputs and requirements, in addition to the postponement of raising gas prices and not to raise bread and feed prices, the exemption of small farmers of their loans' interest from the Agricultural Credit Corporation. beside salary increase and expand segments benefiting from the national aid and providing incentives to encourage young people to work and production, besides implementing the national initiatives of His Majesty the King to provide decent housing for decent living which will provide proper housing for thousands of Jordanian families. In addition, there are a lot of efforts being exerted to improve the level of basic services rendered to Jordanian citizens through quality education and comprehensive health insurance.

So, the Jordan Chamber of Commerce has understood the requirements of this phase and His Majesty's wish to create a very advanced business environment in the Kingdom attractive to both local and foreign investments. The Chamber has, therefore, sought to improve the business environment for the private sector either through the activities organized or through participating in the national, regional, and international meetings and conferences.

The Jordanian private sector represents the strong-arm of the process of construction and development, achieving many accomplishments in various sectors. The Jordanian private sector's organizations have witnessed significant development, casting its shadow on different economy activities in a country that does not have a plenty of natural or financial resources; however, it possesses the inimitable spirit of leadership of His Majesty, may Allah preserve him, who works very hard to make Jordan in a privileged position among the nations of the world. Jordan also has the educated, trained, efficient and creative human resources that form the basis for the launch of the Jordanian economy. We must emphasize that the Jordanian private sector has witnessed unprecedented rapid development, causing a breakthrough in growth rates which are the highest in the region. Foreign trade, imports and exports have grown, as well. Jordan has witnessed a significant increase in investments benefiting from the Investment Promotion Law, in addition to the increase of the central bank reserves of foreign currency.

The private sector is the main driving force for investment and production; assisted by Jordan's openness to the world through the World Trade Organization membership, free trade agreements signed with the Arab states, the United States, the European Union and The European Free Trade Association (EFTA) and others.

Jordan's Chamber of Industry considers the industrial sector as one of the main pillars of the Jordanian economy.

It contributes directly to about a quarter of the national economy (%25 of GDP), in addition to its forward and backward links with many sectors. It also accommodates a part of the Jordanian labor, offering them the chance of qualification and training, which works on raising the technical efficiency and productivity, with an estimated labor percentage of about %15 of the total workforce. It also contributes to cover part of the trade deficit through exports, which constitute an important part of the total exports with estimated industrial exports about %90 of the total merchandise exports.

Industries in Jordan may be divided into three main sectors, namely:

1- Manufacturing industry: It contributes to about (%20) of the GDP. This sector includes the following:

Therapeutic Industries and Medical Supplies, Plastic and Rubber Industries, Chemical and Cosmetics Industries, Garments and Leather Industries, Wood and Furniture Industries, Engineering, Electrical and Information Technology Industries, Construction Industry, Ration, Food, Agriculture and Livestock Industries, Packaging, Paper, cardboard, printing and supplies Industry.

2- Extractive industry, including: mining industries, which contributes with a percentage of about %3 of GDP.

3- The electricity and water sector. The contribution percentage of this industry to GDP is almost %2.5. Jordan Chamber of Industry acts as a national body which consists of all other chambers of industry in Jordan. It seeks to represent the interests of these chambers and to enhance cooperation and full coordination among them.

Jordan Chamber of Industry includes Amman Chamber founded in 1962, Al-Zarqa Chamber founded in 1998 and Irbid Chamber founded in 1999 AD.

The board of Directors comprises elected representatives of all industry sectors, in addition to representatives of the three chambers.

The chamber's mission is to represent industrialists and industrial chambers inside or outside the Kingdom, by enabling them and developing their potential through the provision of excellent services in terms of building and development of human resources, allowing the industrialists to participate in seminars and international conferences related to their sectors and help them to promote their business.

The chamber's effort with the Ministry of Industry and Trade is an undeniable, in addition to the participatory approach of the preparation of plans and strategies that elevate the industrial sector as a whole.

- **Types of tourism in Jordan:**

  Archaeological tourism - Religious tourism –

  Medical tourism

Amman was originally built on seven hills, but now it spreads over at least nineteen hills. It is a city of contrasts, a mixture of ancient and modern, where many civilizations left their mark. Amman continues to grow steadily; its suburbs expand and its population continues to increase. Its homes are characterized being luxurious and spaced.

In 1921 AD, being a small city at such time, Prince Abdullah declared it the capital. Now, it is an inhabited big city.

Nowadays, you can still see many remains from ancient times. The Amman Citadel (Jabal Al Qal'a), the remains of the temple of Hercules, the Ummayyad palace, the Byzantine church and the archaeological museum are just some. Down the hill, you may visit the Roman theatre which seats 6,000 and the nearby Grand Husseini Mosque.

Modern Amman also has a lot of entertainment to offer, like modern shopping centers and popular markets in the commercial heart of the city (downtown area).

Jordan's only port Aqaba lies on the northern tip of the Red Sea. The waters of the Red Sea are crystal clear and have an abundant marine life. The Red Sea is home to more than 140 species of coral and countless species of brightly colored fish. The weather near the Gulf of Aqaba is splendid all year around. Even in the midst of winter the temperature hovers steadily around °20C. The water temperature averages from °22.5C in winter to °26C in summer. These circumstances make Aqaba one of the most rewarding spots for scuba diving and snorkeling in the world. Aqaba is also known for its beautiful sandy beaches.

(PETRA)

Tourism is one of the most important sectors in Jordan's economy. Tourism revenues could reach billions of dollars. Millions of tourists from various countries visit Jordan. Its major tourist attractions include visiting historical sites, like the worldwide famous Petra (UNESCO World Heritage Site since 1985 AD, and one of New Seven Wonders of the World since 2007 AD), the Jordan River, Mount Nebo Madaba, numerous medieval mosques and churches, and unspoiled natural locations (as Wadi Rum and Jordan's northern mountainous region in general), as well as observing cultural and religious sites and traditions.

Jordan also offers health tourism, which is focused in the Dead Sea area and in several other areas where all elements of the natural therapy are available, like warm water rich in salt and the volcanic mud. In addition, hiking and scuba-diving in Aqaba's coral reefs can be practiced. In addition, Jordan is famous in eco-tourism. The Royal Society for The Conservation of Nature has established seven nature reserves in Jordan aiming at the promotion of eco-tourism and the preservation of rare livestock; (such as oryx, ostriches, gazelle and deer).

Jordan is a land steeped in history. It has been home to some of mankind's earliest settlements since the Stone Age. Jordan, throughout the ages, has witnessed numerous civilizations, most notably: the Nabateans, Persians, Greeks, Romans, Mamelukes, Ottomans and Arabs.

Petra and Jerash are the most prominent historical and cultural monuments in Jordan.

Petra is located in a mountainous area; it combines captivating nature and architecture of Nabatieh where you can find theaters, temples, facades of tombs, monasteries and houses carved entirely in pink rocks. UNESCO has placed Petra on the World Heritage List as one of the New Seven Wonders.

On 2007/07/07 AD, Petra has been selected among the list of the New Seven Wonders resulted from a controversial process of popular vote lasted for several months with the participation of 70 million people around the world. The list of New Seven Wonders includes: Great Wall of China, Christ the Redeemer statue in Rio de Janeiro, Coliseum in Rome, Taj Mahal in India, Incas monuments in Machu Picchu (Peru), and the ancient Maya city of Chichen-Itza in Mexico.

The city of Jerash lies in north of Amman, sometimes referred to as the Pompeii of the East. Jerash was part of the Greco-Roman Decapolis, the league of ten cities. It is one of the best preserved

(PETRA)

Roman towns outside Italy. Because Jerash has been covered by sand for centuries, its colonnaded streets, baths, theatres, plazas and arches remain in exceptional condition.

Abila (Decapolis) contains the Roman temples, Byzantine churches and early mosques lying amidst olive groves and wheat fields. Excavations indicate that the site was inhabited more than

(PETRA)

5,000 years ago, and appears to have been continually used by man since then.

Umm El-Jemmal is primarily notable for the luxurious buildings that offer a unique example of ancient civilizations. The remnants of the old black basalt stone-built houses were found in abundance along with the Roman churches, camps and castles.

The famous Rabad Castle (a twenty-minute drive to the west of the city of Jerash) and Iraq al-Amir, to the west of Amman, is a city dating back to the second century BC, where you can see the outstanding Greek style palace after refurbishment.

- **Archaeological sites:**

The most important archaeological sites in Jordan:

Petra: The homeland of the Nabatean Arabs, the city is carved into the mountains in full and represents one of the most important tourism attractions in Jordan. Petra is located just 262 km to the south of Amman.

Jerash is the city of Roman monuments, with ancient cultural heritage. It is one of the few ancient cities in the world which has kept all its monuments until today. Jerash is located 50 km to the north of Amman.

Heading to west to discover Ajloun, which is famous for its historical citadel ((Rabd Castle)). Being on the top of the citadel, you can see breathtaking scene because of its beauty and splendor.

(Jerash)

Known in ancient times as the (Gadara), Umm Qais is located in the far north of the country; it lies on a high hill near the city of Irbid. Umm Qais is a part of Roman Decapolis, the league of ten cities, overlooking the Sea of Galilee, the Golan Heights and the Yarmouk River. It is one of the most prominent tourist attractions in Jordan, and it is famous for its Greek and Roman amphitheaters and buildings.

Karak, located in the south, contains an important castle dating back to the time of Salahuddin, known as (Karak Castle). The castle was built by the Crusaders to represent a strategic point of contact between Shoubak Castle and Jerusalem, during their control over the Royal Road, which includes many castles located on the highlands overlooking it. Castle towers overlook the breath-taking landscape of the surrounding area. Salahuddin was able to storm the castle after the defeat of the Crusaders in the battle of Hittin.

(Karak Castle)

(Quseir Amra)

Jordanian desert and the southern region include desert palaces and castles which stand testament to a fascinating era in the country's rich history, including the following:

Quseir Amra, one of the rare Islamic architectural masterpieces in the heart of desert. The palace is famous for the magnificent dome, beautiful decorations and frescoes showing scenes of hunting trips and animals in the region in that era.

Qasr al-Kharanah, 65 kilometers east of Amman, is one of the most important monuments of the Umayyad and its remains are well preserved.

Qasr al-Hallabat is 25 km away from the city of Zarqa. Archaeological evidences refer to the Nabataean origin of the building. However, the available monuments date back to the Roman era, where castles were built to protect the eastern roads.

Qasr Mshatta lies near Queen Alia International Airport in Amman. It is a spacious palace characterized by arcades and arches.

Qasr at-Tuba is about 95 km southeast of Amman. It is a huge palace built of bricks hardened by heating.

Qasr al-Azraq "Blue Fortress" lies near the city of Zarqa, dating back to the Roman era. The Castle is entirely built of black basalt stone. The walls of the castle overlook Azraq oasis, which was a major stop for caravans in the past.

Karak Castle (in the city of Karak) is located on Royal way which passes through the south of Jordan. The Castle was built by the Crusaders, liberated by Salahuddin then enlarged by the Mamluks and historically linked to the Crusades.

Showbak Castle dates back to the same era. The Crusaders named it (Montreal) in the sense royal mountain.

(Showbak Castle)

(Rabad Castle)

The two castles include a lot of corridors, tunnels and fortifications towers that reflect the martial arts' style of the Middle Ages.

Rabad Castle represents the architectural style of Arab Muslims. The Castle was built by Izz al-Din Usama ibn Munqidh, one of Salahuddin's generals between 1148 to 1185 AD, with the aim of repelling the Crusader expansion and the protection of roads with Damascus and northern Syria.

Rabad Castle, located in Ajloun 75 Km north of Amman, was called by that name because of its location, as it lies down on the back of a high-rise Hill (known as Jabal 'Auf after a Bedouin tribe "Bin Auf" settled in that area during the reign of the Fatimids). The castle has another name "Salahuddin castle", being named after the Islamic leader Salahuddin (adopted as the base of his armies towards the city of Jerusalem).

- **The holy Religious sites:**

Al-Maghtas (to the east of the Jordan River) lies in Wadi Kharrar area (Bethany). Jesus the Christ, at the age of thirty, was baptized in front of the Prophet Yahya bin Zakaria, marking the revelation of God's message to humankind through this ritual.

The area includes many wells and ponds. It is believed that early Christians used it in a group ritual of baptism.

Jordanian Department of Antiquities has restored the site, which was visited by His Holiness Pope John Paul II and declared it as a place of Christian pilgrimage beside four other sites in Jordan.

(AL-Maghtas)

(His Holiness Pope John Paul II in Jordan)

Jordan is rich in religious monuments, being the land of monotheistic religions, in addition to the monuments dating back to immemorial centuries for the peoples and civilizations such as "Edom and Moab and Ammon, and Gilead, and Beria". There are shrines and mosques and tombs of the companions of the Prophet (peace be upon him); the most famous shrines of companions, namely: Abu Dhar al-Ghafari, Abu Obeida Amer bin Jarrah (Amin al-Ummah / Custodian of Ummah); in addition to the martyrs of the Battle of Mu'tah, Led by Jafar ibn Abi Talib, Zaid bin Haritha, Abdullah bin Rawahah and Al-Harith bin Omair.

Shrines and mausoleums spread over an area of Jordan from north to south. The tomb of the companion (Awimmer bin Malik Al-Khazraji Al-Ansari), also known as Abu Aldra (Levant judge), exists in the vicinity of Soum in Irbid. The tomb of the great companion (Farwah bin Omar Al-Juzami) lies in north of tafilah (South Central Jordan). He was the first Muslim martyr out of the Arabian Peninsula, killed and crucified by Roman because of his propagation of Islam.

(DANA BIOSPHERE RESERVE)

- **Nature Reserves:**

Jordan has its rich and diverse environment. The kingdom enjoys the natural wealth which combines desert and countryside, where you can see both desert and green fields. Life and living creatures, plants and animal, vary depending on this biodiversity. Nature reserves have been established to preserve the rare wildlife species and protect them from extinction.

Dana Biosphere Reserve, one of the most important Reserves, covers Tafeileh Heights and extends up to Wadi Araba reaching a total area of 308 square kilometers. Al-Shaumari Wildlife Reserve, established in 1975 AD near Azraq in the Eastern Desert, has an area of 22 square kilometers. Mujib Biosphere Reserve, which lies along the sea Dead and extends to the heights of Karak, has an area of 220 square kilometers, and it contains different types of wild animals, plants and birds. Azraq Wetland Reserve, located in Azraq oasis in the Eastern Desert, has an area of 21 square kilometers and is considered to be a passage for migratory birds between Europe, Asia and Africa.

- **Medical Tourism:**

Jordan earns up to $ 700 million per year as revenues from medical tourism. According to the World Bank, Jordan ranks first in the region and fifth in the world in this field.

Amman contains a lot of government and private hospitals, frequented by Arab patients from the Arab Gulf, Iraq, Yemen and the Maghreb countries. Lower prices and high quality treatment, which is superior to Europe and the United States, attract patients to Jordan.

Medical tourism in Amman is characterized by a distinct experience in the field of Heart Surgery as well as the application of a lot of micro-surgery with respect to the eyes, kidneys and lungs.

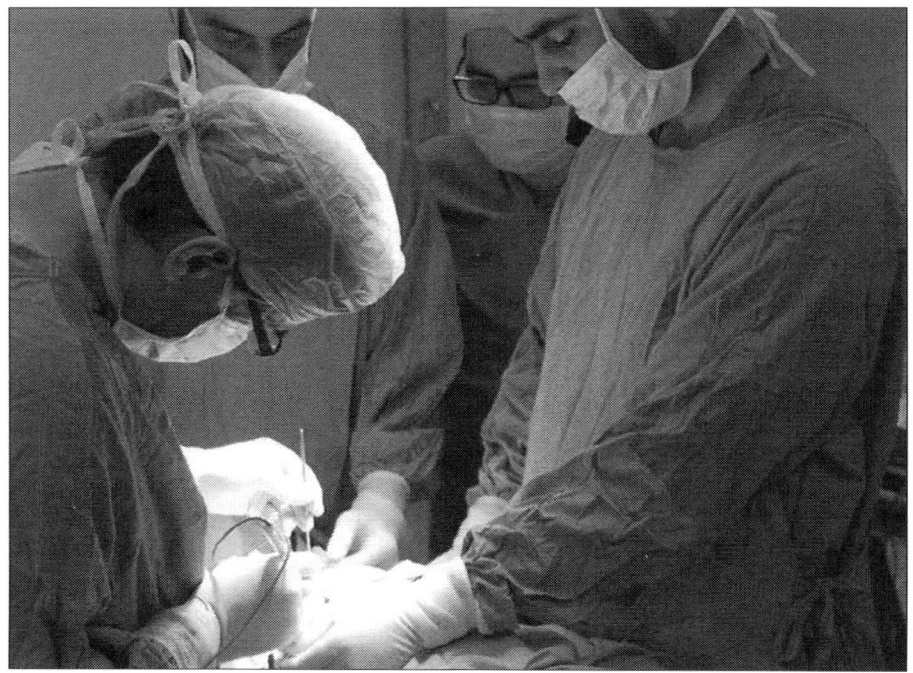

(Surgeries)

Jordan is the land in which recovery from diseases is mixed with recreation. Thanks to the great grace Allah granted to the Jordanian territory, where all elements of the natural treatment exist, like warm water rich in salt, the volcanic mud, the mild weather and picturesque nature, making it a spa frequented by a lot of people seeking recovery from various diseases.

مركز عشتار لأمراض وجراحة وتجميل الجلد والليزر

- **The most important spas, namely:**

  1- Afra Hot Springs

  2- Hamma springs

  3- Hammamat Ma'in / Ma'in Hot Springs

The warm mineral water, characterized by therapeutic properties, may be used in different manners like hydro-jet baths and showers, Jacuzzi bath, water bed and feet bath. The Dead Sea mud also has therapeutic benefits, in addition to Electrotherapy department using water and medical exercises. As well as physiotherapy service especially underwater can be offered under the supervision of

(Afra Hot Springs)

physicists specializing in this field. The inhalation of vapor rising from the mineral water treatment helps to cure respiratory diseases, especially among smokers. The hot water treatment is useful in special situations, including "chronic rheumatism, muscle spasms, back pain, blood vessels and veins diseases, varicose, skin diseases, and can refresh the whole body in general of nervous and mental fatigue, endocrine secretion and chronic sinusitis.

Hammamat Ma'in constitutes a landmark on the map of tourism in the governorate of Madaba and its suburbs. Winter is the peak season for that area because of its warm climate on the edge of the Jordan Valley between the mountains and the hot water.

(Hammamat Ma'in / Ma'in Hot Springs)

THE HASHEMITE KINGDOM OF JORDAN

CHAPTER TEN

JORDANIAN PROFESSIONAL ASSOCIATIONS

CHAPTER TEN
JORDANIAN PROFESSIONAL ASSOCIATIONS

Jordan Global and Professional associations, along the lines of the rest of the world, constitute an important part of civil society institutions; through the role they play in the service of their members and their contributions to building a prosperous and progressive society.

Professional associations are organized institutions of a group of individuals with specific professional competencies; aiming to achieve the goals and objectives defined by the association law.

The emergence of professional associations in Jordan dates back to 1950s of the last century, after the issuance of the Jordanian Constitution in 1952 AD; where professionals were allowed to form private associations.

Professional associations in Jordan possessed a prominent and important activity in 1980s and 1990s of the twentieth century for a variety of reasons, namely:

1- The accumulated experience in associations' activities.

2- Large numbers of professionals of associations.

3- Unrestricted Freedom and Democracy, evidenced by the fact of the return of parliamentary life in 1989 AD and the issuance of the Political Parties Act No. 32 of 1992 AD.

4- The strong participation of associations in the Jordanian society through the organization of conferences, seminars, lectures, festivals, exhibitions and issuance of associations' magazines.

5- Financial support provided by associations to charities in Jordan to support the Arab people in Palestine, Iraq and Sudan during the crises they have suffered.

The number of associations' members has exceeded 100,000; these associations are active in the development of the professions they represent and raise the level of professional performance of their members by organizing lectures, conferences, seminars and continuing education courses in various fields of specialization. Professional associations provide their members with important services such as low-interest loans, housing plans, health insurance, pension and some other services

Professional associations possess an effective contribution to public issues and have a firm political attitude regarding all national, Arab and Islamic interests, granting it a broad popular support. Such attitude is the same of all public bodies of associations (as the intellectual elite in society); these bodies shall elect the Executive Committee for two years.

The freezing of partisan life in Jordan since 1956 AD till its resume in 1989 AD contributed to grant Professional associations a significant role in the social and political reality similar to the role of political parties; where the associations started to support the welfare of the people of Jordan and the core issues of the nation.

The associations have a set of committees caring about such issues.

Jordan contains many associations like:

1- Jordan Medical Association

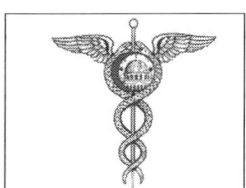

2- Jordanian Dental Association

3- Jordanian veterinary association

4- Jordanian Geologists Association

5- Jordan Press Association

6- Jordan Pharmacists Association

7- Jordan Bar Association

8- Jordan Construction Contractors Association

9- Jordan Nurses and Midwives Council

10- Jordan Engineers Association

11- Jordan Agricultural Engineers Association

12- Jordanian Artists Association

13- Jordanian Teachers Association

In general, professional associations are similar in terms of its financial resources that are formed on the whole of the following resources:

1- Association's registration and re-registration fees

2- Annual subscriptions

3- Donations and grants from the Jordanian society

4- The income and revenues resulting from investment of associations' money.

THE HASHEMITE KINGDOM OF JORDAN
FROM ABDULLAH I TO ABDULLAH II

THE HASHEMITE KINGDOM OF JORDAN

CHAPTER ELEVEN

MEDIA AND PRESS

CHAPTER ELEVEN
MEDIA AND PRESS

Information and Communications Technology (ICT) market in Jordan has witnessed significant growth, where Jordan precedes all Arab countries in the liberalization of ICT market, as it has updated %75 of laws relevant to ICT market.

The volume of revenues of ICT has doubled over the past five years due to high demand, popularity and the need for this sector among all segments of society with different cultural, social, economic and political levels.

The percentage of technical disciplines' universities graduates in Jordan is the highest among all countries in the region. Fiber optic cables were used in the beginning to build communications networks in Jordan in the late eighties; first through the Air Force projects to the establish private internal networks for military matters, then the optical fiber cables passed through several stages in the nineties and the twentieth century leading to a wide usage of fiber-optic networks in government and private authorities.

The first stage was implemented through the national fiber optic network program and the second through companies like Batelco Jordan, Zain, Ummniah companies.

National Fiber-Optic Network Program aimed at connecting Jordanian schools, universities and colleges with broadband networks and modern infrastructure in order to improve the educational process and increase the spread and use of computers and the Internet.

Statistics, released by the Telecommunications Regulatory Commission (TRC) in Jordan, indicate an increase in the number of subscribers and users of telecommunications, in addition to the increased prevalence of both fixed-line and cellular phones which led to increased investment in this sector (telecommunications

sector) as reflected positively on the national economy. ICT sector has provided many jobs for the national skilled and expert labor in this field, resulting in the rise in the general total production and gross national income earnings.

This helped to support and strengthen the audio-visual and print media, secure all possible means of providing access to information from its sources accurately and quickly, and the provision of news and information for all sectors of society.

Jordanian newspapers have a constructive and effective role in the transfer of information and events is in line with the reality of social and economic aspirations through modern media renaissance in addition to highlighting the accelerating political events and the formation of the active national character affiliated to their homeland and people.

This goes in line with preservation of what has been achieved in our pursuit towards accomplishing the aspirations of the nation through a comprehensive development vision.

This reflects the reality of the situation and the interaction between all classes of society through healthy and rapid information. So, due attention is already paid to educating the society and interacting with its direct and living daily issues and social matters in general in addition to enhancement of human dignity and rights while preserving his human and national identity and personality.

The press also reflects the interest of the nation achievements through highlighting the gains and accomplishments realized in addition to helping achieve the uncompleted aspirations.

E-press and E-media have a major and direct role in the interaction

with the events and news; in addition to the quick and civilized interaction between these means and the public regarding the transfer of accurate and correct information, showing it in a timely and proper manner. It also highlights the important events, human rights and rights of the citizens regardless of their different cultures and classes; especially with the high prevalence of these newspapers and websites because of the huge and rapid development of modern means of communication and technology.

THE HASHEMITE KINGDOM OF JORDAN

CHAPTER TWELVE

HASHEMITE STATESMEN OF JORDAN

CHAPTER TWELVE
HASHEMITE STATESMEN OF JORDAN

Led by the Hashemites, the modern Arab Awakening sought liberation and sovereignty. The firing of the first bullet, on 10 June 1916 AD, marked the start of the Great Arab Revolt, ushering in a noble and arduous march towards the establishment of an independent Arab nation after more than four centuries of alienation and dispossession under Ottoman rule.

The Arab Awakening movement was inseparable from the Arab consciousness, which was deepening and expanding with the increasing activity of the free Arabs, who organized themselves into independence-seeking organizations and societies. At the center of these various movements was Prince Faisal I, who served as a critical link between them and his father, Sharif Hussein bin Ali, who had been exiled to Istanbul in 1893 AD for his beliefs and activism, before returning to Mecca in 1908 AD to become its Emir. Sharif Hussein was sought as the leader of Arab renaissance and revolution because he embodied both religious and historical legitimacy as well as because he believed in the Arabs' rights to freedom, unity and independence since the end of the 19th century

The Hashemites derived their strong links with Arab notables from their moral and political standing; the Hashemites took the lead in

the modern history of the Arabs by virtue of their religious standing. The Hashemites, being associated to Mecca, had a clear impact in making steady and powerful progress while representing Arabs' aspirations to establish a free, independent country by the early 20th century.

The Hashemites kept their historical holy dynasty in Mecca since 8 AH / 629 AD, till the beginning of the 20th century. The Hashemites are the custodians of Islamic holy sites being associated to them; they praised or extolled it, keeping it away from political rivalries.

The Hashemites has created a legal and moral contract between them and the holy sites, which represents the Qibla of the Islamic nation's heart. The stance on Jerusalem "Al Quds Al Sharif" (the first Qibla) correlated with the constant emphasis on the adoption of their message, for which they've struggled, expressing the freedom of peoples and preserving the dignity of the nation

The Hashemites, even after the establishment of Jordan, remain the custodian of Arab and Islamic holy sites in Jerusalem "Al Quds Al Sharif" including its mosques and churches.

Hashemite Statesmen of Jordan:
His Majesty The Founding King Abdullah I Bin Al Hussein

(His Majesty King Abdullah I with Winston Churchill in 1921 AD.)

(His Majesty King Abdullah I with his two brothers, King Faisal I King of Iraq and King Ali king of Hejaz)

Hashemite Statesmen of Jordan:
His Majesty The Founding King Abdullah I Bin Al Hussein

(His Majesty King Abdullah I with King Abdul-Aziz,
the first king of Saudi Arabia (on his left).)

(His Majesty King Abdullah I with the people of Palestine in 1930 AD.)

(His Majesty King Abdullah I in front of the Church of Holy Sepulchre in Jerusalem in 1948 AD.)

(His Majesty King Abdullah I reviewing honor guards.)

Hashemite Statesmen of Jordan:
His Majesty The Founding King Abdullah I Bin Al Hussein

(His Majesty King Abdullah I performing the military salute.)

(His Majesty King Abdullah I signing the declaration of independence on May 25, 1946 AD at Raghadan Palace)

Hashemite Statesmen of Jordan:
His Majesty the late King Talal bin Abdullah

Hashemite Statesmen of Jordan:
His Majesty the late King Talal bin Abdullah

(His Majesty the late King Talal bin Abdullah on an official visit outside the Kingdom)

(His Majesty the late King Talal bin Abdullah with his son the late King Hussein)

(His Majesty the late King Talal bin Abdullah with King Abdul-Aziz Al-Saud)

(His Majesty the late King Talal bin Abdullah with his son the late King Hussein)

Hashemite Statesmen of Jordan:
His Majesty the late King Talal bin Abdullah

(His Majesty the late King Talal bin Abdullah with his father, the late King Abdullah I)

(His Majesty the late King Talal bin Abdullah with one of the officers)

Hashemite Statesmen of Jordan:
His Majesty the late King Al Hussein Bin Talal

Hashemite Statesmen of Jordan:
His Majesty the late King Al Hussein Bin Talal

His Majesty the late King Al Hussein Bin Talal, may Allah bless his soul, in the inauguration of the first parliament after the assumption of his constitutional powers in May, 1953

His Majesty the late King Al Hussein Bin Talal with the Army

His Majesty the late King Al Hussein Bin Talal, may Allah bless his soul, delivering an award to His Majesty the King Abdullah II Bin Al Hussein

His Majesty the late King Al Hussein Bin Talal with King Hassan II, Jamal Abdulnasser, Abdul Salam Arif, Habib Bourguiba

Hashemite Statesmen of Jordan:
His Majesty the late King Al Hussein Bin Talal

His Majesty the late King Al Hussein Bin Talal, may Allah bless his soul, in the company of the late Sheikh Zayed bin Sultan Al Nahyan

His Majesty the late King Al Hussein Bin Talal inspects a military unit with His Majesty the venerable King Abdullah II Bin Al Hussein

His Majesty the late King Al Hussein Bin Talal, may Allah bless his soul, in the company of His Majesty Sultan Qaboos bin Said of Oman

His Majesty the late King Al Hussein Bin Talal with former US President, Nixon

Hashemite Statesmen of Jordan:
His Majesty King Abdullah II Bin Al Hussein

His Majesty King Abdullah II Bin Al Hussein At the United Nations

His Majesty King Abdullah II Bin Al Hussein Attend one of the religious events in Jordan

Hashemite Statesmen of Jordan:
His Majesty King Abdullah II Bin Al Hussein

His Majesty King Abdullah II Bin Al Hussein meets American President, Obama

His Majesty King Abdullah II Bin Al Hussein with King Salman bin Abdul Aziz

His Majesty King Abdullah II Bin Al Hussein holds a cabinet meeting

His Majesty King Abdullah II Bin Al Hussein heads the Jordanian delegation in the Arab League Summits

Hashemite Statesmen of Jordan:
His Majesty King Abdullah II Bin Al Hussein

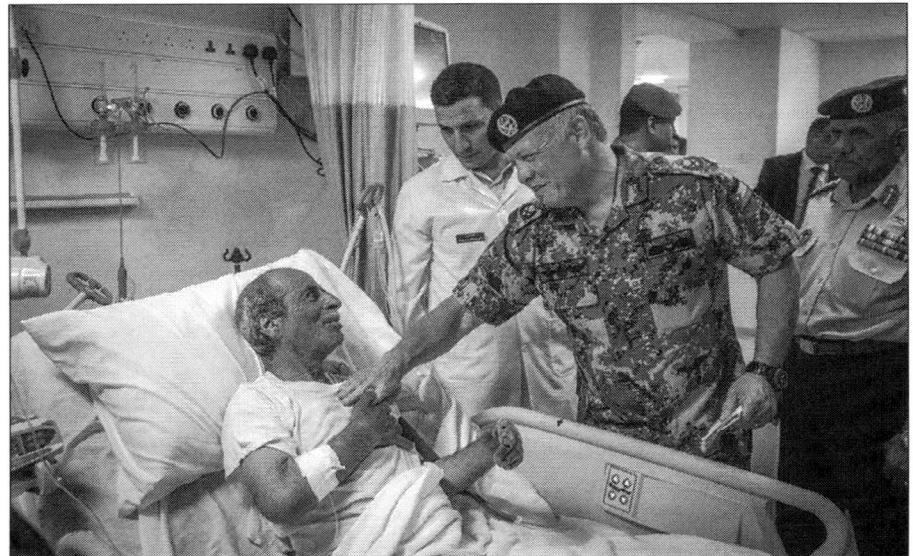

His Majesty King Abdullah II Bin Al Hussein visits a Jordanian patient

His Majesty King Abdullah II Bin Al Hussein greets his people

His Majesty King Abdullah II Bin Al Hussein opens a vital project in Jordan

His Majesty King Abdullah II inaugurates the Royal Hashemite Court's grid connected solar power plant

Hashemite Statesmen of Jordan:
His Majesty King Abdullah II Bin Al Hussein

His Majesty King Abdullah II Bin Al Hussein bestows the Speaker of the House of Representatives, Atef Tarawneh, with the Order of the Star of Jordan

His Majesty King Abdullah II in a visit to the Hashemite University

His Majesty King Abdullah II Bin Al Hussein receives the Chairperson of the National Committee of the Chinese People's Political Consultative Conference

His Majesty King Abdullah II in a visit to the Northern Military Zone

Jordan Prime Ministers under the Hashemite Rule

- **His Excellency Mr. Rashi Tali':**

He was born in Lebanon 1877. He received his education in Astana. He was elected as a representative in the Chamber of Deputies for Jabal Al Arab. He was also the county executive of Horan, Tripoli Lebanon and Latakia. He was appointed Minister of Interior and the Wali (governor) of Aleppo. He was the first prime minister in the Transjordan government.

- **His Excellency Mr. Mazhar Raslan:**

He held the post of justice, health, education advisor and a member of the National Congress in 1921. He held the position of a financial advisor in 1921. Also in 1921, he was the Prime Minister and the Financial Consultant. From 1921 to 1922, he was the Prime Minister and the Royal Consultant. From 1922 to 1923, he was the Minister of Interior. In 1923, he was the Prime Minister.

- **His Excellency Mr. Ali Rida al-Rikabi:**

After the Ottoman Turks had departed from Arab lands, he formed the first cabinet in the history of Syria. Later, during two periods, as Prime Minister in Jordan, al-Rikabi established Jordan's administrative and financial system. He held many positions and took over many responsibilities and offices, because he was a decisive administrator with a legendary honesty. He was also a part of the modern history of Syria.

- **His Excellency Mr. Hassan Abu Al-Huda:**

From 1923 to 1924, he was the Prime Minister. From 1924 to 1926, he was the Minister of Finance. In 1926, he was the Prime Minister and the Minister of Interior. From 1926 to 1929, he was the Prime Minister and Minister of His Excellency Mr. Finance. From 1929 to 1931, he was the Prime Minister.

Jordan Prime Ministers under the Hashemite Rule

- **His Excellency Mr. Abdullah Siraj:**

From 1931 to 1933, he served as Prime Minister while simultaneously holding the portfolios of Finance and the Interior Ministry, as well as the office of Chief Justice.

- **His Excellency Mr. Ibrahim Hashem:**

Hashem was born in Nablus 1866. He received his education in Astana and earned the certificate of law from Istanbul. The posts he held included Prosecutor General of Beirut, Prosecutor General of Jaffa in 1915. He was also Head of the Criminal Court and a Professor of law in Syria University. He also joined the army. In 1922, he held the portfolio of Justice, and formed the cabinet many times in 1933. In 1958, he was the Vice-President of the Arab Federation.

- **His Excellency Mr. Tawfik Abu al-Huda:**

He was born in Acre 1895. King Abdullah Bin Al Hussein granted him the honorary title of Pasha. He received his education in Acre and studied law in Astana, Beirut. He held many posts. He was an army officer in 1915. In 1920, he was an employee in Damascus. He was also the Head of Procurement in Transjordan. He was the Head of Accounting Department in the Ministry of Finance, and the Director of Land Registration Directorate. On September 28th 1938, he formed his first government.

- **His Excellency Mr. Samir al-Rifai:**

He was born in Safed 1901. He got the secondary school certificate from Safed. His higher education was in the College of Arts and Sciences and the American University of Beirut, and also joined the institutes of law. He was Director of the Prime Minister's Office in 1924, and First Assistant Secretary-General of the Government in 1927. In 1930, he was the Director of International Property and Secretary of the Prime

Jordan Prime Ministers under the Hashemite Rule

Minister in 1933.

He was the Minister of Education in 1937. In 1941, he became Minister of Interior, Education and later the Finance and Justice. In 1944, he formed the government. In 1947, he formed the government. In 1951, he was the Prime Minister and the Minister of Foreign Affairs. In 1955, he was the Prime Minister and the Minister of Foreign Affairs. In 1958, he was the Prime Minister and the Minister of Foreign Affairs.

- **His Excellency Mr. Sa'id al-Mufti:**

He was born in Amman in 1898 and studied in Damascus. From January 2nd 1924 to December 1st 1924, he was the Deputy Administrative Officer of Amman. On January 1st 1952, he was the Administrative Officer of Amman. On November 15th 1967, he was the Mayor of Amman. He was a member of the first Legislative Council on October 17th 1929 and on October 18th 1933. He was the Mayor of Amman on November 3rd 1938. On August 7th 1939, he was the Treasury Minister. From July 13th 1941 to October 14th 1944, he took over the Ministry of Transport. From October 20th 1947 to January 1st 1950, he was a member of the House of Representatives. From December 28th 1947 to July 29th 1948, he was Minister of Commerce, Industry and Supply. From September 16th 1948 to April 12th 1950, he was the Minister of Interior. From April 12th 1950 to October 11th 1950, he was the Prime Minister. He was also the Prime Minister from February 4th 1950 to October 14th

1950. From April 20th 1950 to 1951, he was a member of the House of Representatives. From July 25th 1951 to May 5th 1953, he took over three terms as the Prime Minister and the Minister of Interior. From May 2nd 1954 to May 30th 1955, he was the Prime Minister and the Minister of State. From May 6th 1956 to June 26th 1956, he was the Prime Minister.

From April 15th 1957 to April 24th 1957, he was the Prime Minister and the Minister of Interior and Agriculture. On September 5th 1962, he was appointed as a Member of the Board of Trustees of the Arab League. From March 27th 1963 to July 6th 1964, he was Deputy Prime Minister. On October 24th 1963, he was the Chairman of the Board of Trustees of the University of Jordan. On October 31st 1963, he was the Speaker of the Senate.

Orders and Honors:

He received Jordan Order of Independence of first class in addition to the Order of the Star of Jordan of first class. He also received the Iraqi Order of the Two Rivers and the Supreme Order of the Renaissance in addition to the Order of Civil Merit (Syria) and the Order of the Holy Sepulcher.

- **His Excellency Mr. Fawzi Al-Mulki:**

From 1947 to 1948, he was Minister of Transport. In 1948, he was the Minister of Foreign Affairs and Transport. From 1948 to 1949, he was the Minister of Defense. From 1949 to 1950, he was the Minister of Defense. In 1950, he was the Minister of Defense. In 1950, he was the

Jordan Prime Ministers under the Hashemite Rule

Minister of Defense. From 1953 to 1954, he was the Prime Minister and Minister of Defense. From 1955 to 1956, he was the Minister of Defense and Education. In 1956, he was Deputy Prime Minister and the Minister of Foreign Affairs and Education. In 1957, he was the Minister of Education and Public Work.

Orders and Honors:

He received the Order of the Star of Jordan of first class.

- **His Excellency Mr. Hazza' al-Majali:**

He was assassinated in his office.

He was born in 1918. He attended Al-Salt school for his secondary education 1938, and later studied Law in Damascus.

The posts he held included the Department of Land and Survey and Madaba Court of Peace. After that, he worked as a lawyer and returned to Jordan to work for the "Royal Protocol". In 1948, he was appointed as Chairman of the Greater Amman Municipality, and then served as Prime Minister from 1955/12/15 to 1955/12/20 and from 1959/5/6 to 1960/8/28.

- **His Excellency Mr. Sulayman al-Nabulsi:**

He was born in Salt 1908.

After the secondary school, he graduated from the American University of Beirut with a degree in science.

In 1932, he served as a teacher in Karak. In 1933, he worked as an employee in the Cabinet. In 1935, he was a supply monitor. In 1938, he served as the Assistant Minister of Finance, then the Secretary of the Prime Minister in 1942. Then, he served as the Minister of Finance and Economy from 1947/2/4 to 1947/12/27. He held the same post from 1950/12/4 to 1951/7/25. He served as Jordan's Ambassador to the United Kingdom from 1953 to 1954. Then, he became a Prime Minister from 1956/10/27 to 1957/4/10. From 1957/4/15 to 1957/4/24, he took over the ministries of Foreign Affairs and Transport. From 1954 to 1957, he was the Secretary-General of the Jordanian National Party. From 1963/11/1 to 1971/10/30, he was elected as a member of the House of Representatives.

Orders and Honors:

He received the Supreme Order of the Renaissance, Jordan Order of Independence, in addition to the Order of the Star of Jordan.

Jordan Prime Ministers under the Hashemite Rule

- **His Excellency Mr. Hussein Fakhri Al-Khalidi:**

He was born in 1892 in Jerusalem where he received his education. Then, he studied medicine in the American University of Beirut. He served in the Turkish Army. He was appointed as a doctor in Aleppo. In 1934, he was appointed as the Mayor of Jerusalem and then he served as the Custodian and Supervisor of the holy spots, Minister of Foreign Affairs and was elected as a member of the House of Senate. In 1955, he became Minister of Foreign Affairs and in 1957 he took over the cabinet as a Prime Minister.

- **His Excellency Mr. Bahjat Talhouni:**

He was born in Salt 1913. His scientific qualifications included the Secondary School Certificate from Salt in 1933 and the Certificate of Law from the University of Syria in 1936. He worked as a lawyer. Then, he served as a judge in 1938/11/1, the Prosecutor-General of Irbid in 1939/10/6, Judge of Salt Court of Peace in 1943/3/1, President of Karak Court of First Instance in 1943/11/15, President of Irbid Court of

First Instance in 1951/7/1,

President of Amman Court of Appeal from 1952/11/16 to 1953/5/5, Minister of Interior and of Justice from 1953/5/5 to 1953/11/5, Chief Justice from 1953/11/6 to 1954/5/2, the Hashemite Royal Court Chief from 1954/5/15 to 1960/8/29, Jordan Prime Minister from 1960/8/29 to 1962/1/28, a member of the House of Senate from 1962/12/20 to 1963/3/28, the Hashemite Royal Court Chief from 1963/3/29 to 1964/7/6, Prime Minister and the personal representative of the King from 1967/6/15 to 1967/6/17, Advisory Board member in 1967/8/1, Prime Minister and Minister of Foreign Affairs and a member of the House of Senate from 1967/4/25 to 1967/10/7, Prime Minister and Minister of Interior and of Defense from 1968/4/25 to 1968/9/10, Prime Minister and Minister of Defense from 1968/9/10 to 1968/12/26, Prime Minister from 1968/12/26 to 1969/3/24, the Hashemite Royal Court Chief from 1969/6/19 to 1969/8/12, Prime Minister from 1969/8/13 to 1970/4/19, a member of the House of Senate in 1969/9/12, Prime Minister from 1970/4/19 to 1970/6/27.

Orders and Honors:

He received Jordan Order of Independence of first class in addition to the Golden Medal of Independence from the President of Pakistan, the Bright Scarf and Order of China, the Order of the Holy Sepulcher and other Arab and Foreign orders

Jordan Prime Ministers under the Hashemite Rule

- **His Excellency Mr. Wasfi al-Tal:**

He was born in Irbid 1920. He studied philosophy in the American University of Beirut. He was assassinated when he was in an external mission outside the country.

The posts he held included a teacher in 1942; then, he joined the British military college in Palestine, and he served as a captain in the British Army during World War II. He worked in the Arab Office in Palestine in 1948, and took part in the 1948 Palestine war, fighting for the Arab armies. He joined the Syrian Army as a Captain in 1949 and in the same year he joined the Jordanian civil service as an employee in the Department of Statistics. In 1955, he served as Director of Publications. He worked in the Foreign Service from 1956 to 1957. In 1957 he became the Chief of Royal Protocol, and Charge d' affaires in Iran in 1958. He became President of the National Guidance in 1960 and the Ambassador to Baghdad in 1961. He held the position of Prime Minister from 1965 to 1967. In 1967, he became the Royal Court Chief, and from 1963 to 1971 he was member of the House of Senate. In 1970/10/29, he was the Prime Minister, Minister of Defense and a member of the Board of Trustees of the University of Jordan.

- **His Excellency Sharif. Hussein bin Nasser:**

He was born in Taif in 1906. He received his education in Hejaz and Istanbul.

From 1929 to 1948, he held many administrative posts in the Iraqi government and the Iraqi Royal Court. From 1949 to 1961, he moved to Jordan and worked in the Foreign Affairs as a Minister Plenipotentiary and Ambassador to Turkey, France and Spain. In 1961, he was the Hashemite Royal Court Chief. From 1962 to 1963, he was the Minister of the Royal Court. From 1963 to 1964, he became the Prime Minister for two terms. In 1964, he was the Minister of the Royal Court. In 1967, he was the Prime Minister and Minister of the Royal Court. In 1969, he was the Hashemite Royal Court Chief and a member of the House of Senate.

Jordan Prime Ministers under the Hashemite Rule

- **His Excellency Mr. Saad Jumaa:**

He was born in Tafila in 1916. He earned the Certificate of Law from the University of Damascus in Syria in 1947.

The posts he held included Director General of Press and Publications -1948 1949, Head of the Political Division, Ministry of Foreign Affairs 1950-1949, Secretary to the Prime Minister -1950 1954, Vice-Minister of Interior, Mayor of Amman 1958-1954, Vice-Minister of Foreign Affairs 1959-1958, Ambassador to Iran then Syria 1962-1959, Ambassador to the United States of America 1965-1962, The Chief of the Royal Hashemite Court 1965, Prime Minister and Defense Minister 1967, Member of the House of Senate 1969-1967, Ambassador at Ministry of Foreign Affairs 1969, Ambassador to the United Kingdom -1969 1970 and Advisory Board member in 1967/8/1.

Orders and Honors:

The Order of the Star of Jordan of first class, the first class Hamayouni Order (Iran), the first class order of China and the first class order of Italy.

His Initiatives:

He headed the Jordanian delegation to the Kingdom of Saudi Arabia, Yemen and Lebanon concerning the United Arab Kingdom in 1972. He visited most of the Arab and foreign countries.

- **His Excellency Mr. Abdul-Monem Rifai:**

He was born in Tyre (Sour), Lebanon in 1917. He graduated from the American University of Beirut in 1938.

The posts he held during his career include:

- School teacher in Amman (1938)

- Under the rule of His Majesty the late King Abdullah I, he was the Chief Government Secretary and the Director of Publications in 1940

- Worked at the Hashemite Royal Palace (1942–1941)

- Consul to Egypt, Lebanon and Syria (1944–1943)

- Delegation member to the British Mandate in 1946

- Consul to the United States and a United Nations Permanent Representative (1959)

- Ambassador to the United States (1957–1954)

- Ambassador to Lebanon (1958–1957)

- Ambassador to the United Kingdom (1958)

- The Chief of National Guidance (1959 - 1958)

- United Nations Permanent Representative (1959)

Jordan Prime Ministers under the Hashemite Rule

- Ambassador to Egypt and an Arab League Permanent Representative (1966)

- Minister of State for Foreign Affairs (7th October 25 – 1967th April 1968)

- Minister of Foreign Affairs (25th April 24 – 1968th March 1969)

- Prime Minister (24th March 13 – 1969th August 1969)

- Still the Prime Minister and the Minister of Culture and Information after the Cabinet reshuffle in 1969

- Member of the Senate of Jordan (30th June 1971 - 1969)

- Minister of Foreign Affairs and Deputy Prime Minister (12 August 26 - 1969 June 1970)

- Prime Minister (27 June 16 - 1970 September 1970)

- According to a Royal decree, he was nominated the Personal - Representative of the King and the Arab League Representative of Jordan.

Orders and Honors:

He received the Order of the Star of Jordan of first class and the Supreme Order of the Renaissance.

His Initiatives:

He headed the Jordanian delegation to Kuwait and Syria concerning the United Arab Kingdom in 1972.

- **His Excellency Mr. Mohammad Daoud:**

Mohammad Daoud was born in Silwan, Jerusalem in 1914. He obtained the Secondary School Certificate. In 1948, he joined the Palestinian police and later joined the Jordanian police. He was a member of the Armistice Commission from 1953 to 1958. Then, he was head of the Armistice Commission from 1958 to 1970. He was appointed Prime Minister and Minister of Foreign Affairs of the military government from 1970/9/16 to 1970/9/25.

- **His Excellency Mr. Ahmad Toukan:**

Toukan was born in 1903 in Nablus. His scientific qualifications include BSc of Engineering Sciences, American University of Beirut, 1925 and MSc of Physics, University of Oxford, 1929.

The posts in his career include:

- A professor in the Arab College of Jerusalem (1934 -1929)

- Director of Tulkarem Teacher Training Center (1935 - 1934)

Jordan Prime Ministers under the Hashemite Rule

- Minister of Education of Transjordan (1937 - 1935)

- Inspector of Science and Mathematics in the Central Department of Education of the Government of Palestine (1944 - 1937)

- Headmaster of Khadouri Agricultural High School (1947 - 1944)

- The Chief inspector of the Central Department of Education of the Government of Palestine (1948 - 1947)

- Minister of Education in the West Bank (1950 - 1946)

- Minister of Public Works and Reconstruction in 1950

- Minister of Education in 1950

- Minister of Education and of Foreign Affairs in 1951

- Head of the Jordanian delegation in the Joint Armistice Commission (1952 - 1951)

- Minister of Education from 1954 – 1953

- UNESCO Expert and UNRWA Deputy Head of Education (1961-1954)

- Education Expert at the International Bank for Reconstruction & Development (1966-1962)

- Minister of Foreign Affairs in 1967

- Minister of State and Deputy Prime Minister in 1967

- Minister of Foreign Affairs and Deputy Prime Minister (1969 – 1967)

- Deputy Prime Minister and Minister of Foreign Affairs and of

Tourism and of Antiquities in 1969

- Deputy Prime Minister and Minister of Defense (1970 - 1969)

- Deputy Prime Minister 1970

- Minister of Municipal and Rural Affairs in 1970

- Chief of the Hashemite Royal Court in 1970

- Minister of Foreign Affairs and Prime Minister in 1970

- Prime Minister and the General military ruler in 1970

- Minister of the Hashemite Royal Court (1972 - 1970)

- Member of the Board of Trustees of the University of Jordan (1972 - 1971)

- Chief of the Hashemite Royal Court in 1972

- Chairman of the Board of Trustees of the Arab League (1972)

Orders and Honors:

He received Jordan Order of Independence of first class, the Order of the Star of Jordan of first class and the Supreme Order of the Renaissance.

His Initiatives:

He visited many Arab and foreign countries. He was fluent in English and French.

Jordan Prime Ministers under the Hashemite Rule

- **His Excellency Mr. Ahmad al-Lawzi:**

He was born in Jubaiha, Amman in 1925. He studied at the Teachers Training College in Baghdad, receiving a degree in literature in 1950.

The posts he held:

- A teacher (1953-1950)

- Deputy Chief of Royal Protocol (-1953 1956)

- Chief of Royal Protocol (1961-1956)

- Chief of Ceremony in the Ministry of Foreign Affairs in 1957

- He was elected to the House of Representatives for two terms from 1961 to 1963

- Deputy Chief of the Royal Court 1963

- Minister of State for Cabinet Affairs in 1956

- Member of the House of Senate of Jordan between 1965 and 1967.

- Minister of Interior for Municipality and Rural Affairs in 1967

- Member of the House of Senate of Jordan 1971 – 1967

- Minister of Finance 1971 -1970

- Member of the House of Senate of Jordan in 1971

- Formed the Cabinet and became Minister of Defense 1972 -1971

- Prime Minister and Minister of Defense in 1973

- Member of the Board of Trustees of the Arab League (1972)

Orders and Honors:

He received the Order of the Star of Jordan of first class, Jordan Order of Independence of first class, the Supreme Order of the Renaissance and other Arab and Foreign orders.

- **His Excellency Mr. Zaid Samir Al-Rifai:**

He was born in 1936. He received his primary education in Al-Mutran School in Amman, and his secondary education was in Victoria College in Cairo. He got a degree in Political Science from Harvard University and a Master of Law and international relations from Columbia University.

The posts he held:

- An employee in the Ministry of Foreign Affairs

- Worked in the Embassies of Jordan in Cairo, Beirut, the United Nations and London

- He held many positions in the Hashemite Royal Court: in 1964 he began his career in the Royal Court serving as the Chief of Royal Protocol, Secretary-General of the Royal Court and the private

Jordan Prime Ministers under the Hashemite Rule

Secretary of His Majesty the King, and Chief of the Hashemite Royal Court

- Jordan's Ambassador to the UK in 1971

- He returned from the UK to be the Political Adviser to His Majesty the King.

- He formed his first government in 1973 and held the ministries of Foreign Affairs and of Defense in addition to the Cabinet.

- He was elected a member of the House of Senate for many terms

- He was the President of the House of Senate in 1997.

- **His Excellency Mr. Mudar Badran:**

Badran was born in Jerash, in 1934. He studied Law at the Damascus University and graduated in 1956. Then, he earned the certificate of Finance & Economics Diploma at the Damascus University in 1956.

The posts he held:

- Badran started his career as a Justice Advisor in the Jordanian Armed Force in 1957.

- Prosecutor-General of the Armed Forces Treasury in 1962

- Later, he served as the Assistant Director of secret service for

Foreign Affairs in 1965

- Director of secret service in 1968

- After retiring from the military service as a General, he served as the Secretary-General of the Hashemite Royal Court in 1970 and later the Chief Secretary-General of the Hashemite Royal Court

- His Majesty the King's Advisor for National Security Affairs

- A member of the Executive Commission of the National Arab Federation

- Chairman of the Executive Office of the occupied territory affairs in 1972

- Minister of Education from 1973 to 1974

- Chief of the Hashemite Royal Court (1976 - 1975)

- Prime Minister and Minister of Foreign Affairs and of Defense from 1976 to 1979

- A member of the House of Senate

- Prime Minister and Minister of Defense from 1980 to 1984

- Chief of the Hashemite Royal Court in 1989

- Prime Minister and Minister of Defense from 1989 to 1991

- A member of the House of Senate

- Chairman of the Royal Commission for the construction of Yarmouk University

- Chairman of the Royal Commission for the construction of the

Jordan Prime Ministers under the Hashemite Rule

University of Science and Technology

- Chairman of the Royal Commission for the construction of the Hashemite University

- Chairman of the Board of Trustees of the Hashemite University

Orders and Honors:

He received Jordan Order of Independence of fourth class in addition to the Order of the Renaissance of third class. He also received the Order of the Star of Jordan of first class and the Supreme Order of the Renaissance.

- **His Excellency Sharif. Abdulhamid Sharaf:**

He was born in 1939. He earned the certificate of Philosophy from the American University of Beirut in 1959.

He had the Master Degree of International Law from the same university in 1962.

The posts he held:

- Chairman of the Ministry of Foreign Affairs Department for Arab Affairs and Palestine in 1962

- Radio and television director in 1963

- Director of the International Organizations Department at the

Foreign Ministry in 1964

- Assistant Chief of the Hashemite Royal Court

- Minister of Culture and Information in 1965

- Ambassador to Washington in 1967

- Jordan's Representative at the United Nations in 1972

- Chief of the Hashemite Royal Court in 1976

- Prime Minister in 1979

- **His Excellency Dr. Kassim al-Rimawi:**

He was born in Beit Rima in 1918.

He got the Master Degree from Columbia University in New York in 1954. He earned the PhD degree in Economics and Education from the same university in 1956. In the same university, he worked as a Professor of Administrative Sciences and Social Affairs. He also got the Diploma of Law from London College.

The posts he held:

- Minister of Agriculture and Construction in 1962

- Minister of Agriculture from 1962 to 1963

Jordan Prime Ministers under the Hashemite Rule

- Minister of Interior for Municipality and Rural Affairs 1966 – 1965

- Minister of Interior for Municipality and Rural Affairs 1967 -1966

- Minister of Interior for Municipality and Rural Affairs and of Agriculture in 1970

- Minister of Agriculture from 1979 to 1980

- Prime Minister and Minister of Defense in 1980

- A member of Jordan House of Representatives for Ramallah

His earlier posts included:

- Accountant in British Mandate Palestine government (1963 - 1944)

- Secretary of the Holy Jihad in 1947

- Observer and Representative of Palestine to the United Nations and Ass. Professor in Columbia University (1957 - 1952)

- General Manager of Jordan Phosphate Mines Company in 1957

- Served as an Expert in the Ministry of Economy and Statistics in 1961

Orders and Honors:

He was granted the International Scientific Award from Columbia University and the Order of the Star of Jordan of first class.

- **His Excellency Mr. Ahmad Obeidat:**

The posts he held included:

- Minister of Interior 1984 – 1980
- Prime Minister and Minister of Defense 1985 – 1984

Orders and Honors:

He was granted the Order of the Star of Jordan of first class.

- **His Royal Highness Prince Zaid bin Shaker:**

He was born in September 1934. He studied at Victoria College in Alexandria, Egypt. He graduated from the Royal Military Academy Sandhurst in 1955. He also graduated from Leavenworth College in 1963.

The posts he held:

- The companion of His Majesty King Al Hussein bin Talal from 1955 to 1957.

- The assistant military attaché at the Embassy of Jordan in London

Jordan Prime Ministers under the Hashemite Rule

from 1957 to 1958

- A tank commander

- Promoted to colonel and the commander of the Royal Tank Corps

- Brigadier general and commander of a tank division.

- Assistant Chief of staff for the armed services (1970)

- Chief of staff (1972)

- Lieutenant General 1974

- Field Marshal, Chief of the Hashemite Royal Court and the King's Advisor for then Arab Army Affairs (1987)

- Prime Minister and Minister of Defense (1989)

- Chief of the Hashemite Royal Court 1989

- Prime Minister and Minister of Defense 1991

- Chief of the Hashemite Royal Court 1993 1989

- Prime Minister and Minister of Defense 1996

- His Hashemite Majesty King Al Hussein granted him the title of Prince 1996

Orders and Honors:

- He received many Arab and foreign orders; the most important of them are;

- Order of the Star of Jordan of first class

- The Supreme Order of the Renaissance

- The Order of the Renaissance of first class

- **His Excellency Mr. Taher al-Masri:**

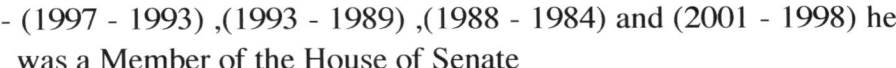

He was born in Nablus in 1942. He studied at An-Najah National University in Nablus. He earned the Bachelor of Business Administration from the University of North Texas in 1965.

The posts he held:

- Served in the Central Bank of Jordan 1973 – 1965
- A member of the House of Representatives 1974 – 1973
- (1997 - 1993) ,(1993 - 1989) ,(1988 - 1984) and (2001 - 1998) he was a Member of the House of Senate
- State Minister for the Occupied Territory Affairs 1974 – 1973
- An Ambassador at the Ministry of Foreign Affairs 1984 – 1975
- Ambassador to Spain 1978 – 1975
- Ambassador to France 1983 – 1978
- Jordan's Permanent Representative in the UNESCO 1983 – 1978
- Jordan's Non-resident Representative in Belgium 1980 – 1979
- Jordan's Representative in European Common Market 1980 – 1978
- Jordan's Representative in the UK 1984 – 1983
- Ministry of Foreign Affairs 1988 – 1984
- Deputy Prime Minister and State Minister for Economic Affairs 1991 & 1989
- Head of the House of Representatives Committee for Foreign

Jordan Prime Ministers under the Hashemite Rule

Affairs 1991 – 1989

- Prime Minister and Minister of Defense (1993 - 1992) & (1991)
- Speaker of the House of Representatives (1994 - 1993)
- Commissioner for Civil Society Affairs at the Arab League in Cairo (2002)

Orders and Honors:

- The Supreme Order of the Renaissance (Jordan)
- The Order of the Renaissance of first class (Jordan)
- Order of the Star of Jordan of first class (Jordan)
- The Order of Isabella the Catholic (Spain)
- Order of Civil Merit (Spain)
- National Order of Merit, the rank of officer (France)
- National Order of the Legion of Honor, the rank of knight (France)
- National Order of the Legion of Honor, the rank of grand officer (France)
- The British Empire Medal
- Order of Merit of the Federal Republic of Germany
- Order of the Cross, of first class
- Knights Grand Cross with Collar of the Order of Merit of the Italian Republic
- The National Order of the Cedar
- The Decoration of Honor for Services to the Republic of Austria
- Order of Diplomatic Service Merit (Korea)

Other Activities:

- Member and secretary of the Royal Commission for the formulation of the National Charter in 1990
- Chairman of the Board of Trustees of the University of Science and

Technology since 1998 till now

- Member of the Euro-Mediterranean Anna Lindh Foundation's Advisory Council for Dialogue of Civilizations since 2004
- Chairman of the Board of Haya Cultural Center since 1992 till now
- Chairman of the administrative board of the National Assembly of freedom and democratic approach (1997 - 1993)
- President of the administrative board of the Association protect Jerusalem 2001 – 1996 & since 2003 till now
- Chairman of the administrative board of the Jordanian Spanish Friendship Association since 1998 till now

- **His Excellency Dr. Abdelsalam al-Majali:**

Majali was born in Al Karak in 1925. He received his medical degree from Syrian University in 1949. He also got a diploma of Laryngology and Otology from the Royal College of Physicians in London in 1953. He was awarded by a fellowship of the American College of Surgeons in 1960. He was awarded an honorary doctorate from the University of Ankara.

The posts he held:

- A general practitioner in the Arab Legion (1950 - 1494)

Jordan Prime Ministers under the Hashemite Rule

- ENT specialist in the main hospital of the Arab Legion 1960- 1953

- Commander of the main military hospital

- ENT Consultant

- Director of the Royal medical services

- ENT Consultant for the Jordanian Armed Forces

- Minister of Health 1969

- Minister of Health 1970

- Minister of Health and Minister of State for Cabinet Affairs 1971 – 1970

- Professor of Medicine in the University of Jordan in 1971

- Minister of Education and Minister of State for Prime Ministerial Affairs 1979 – 1976

- President of the University of Jordan 1989 – 1980

- Head of the Jordanian delegation in the Arab-Israeli peace negotiations 1991

- Prime Minister and Minister of Foreign Affairs and of Defense 1995 – 1993

- Prime Minister and Minister of Defense 1998 – 1997

- **His Excellency
  Mr. Abdul Karim al-Kabariti:**

He was born in Amman in 1949. He received his bachelor's degree in business and finance from the United States of America, and studied geology for three years in the American University of Beirut.

The posts he held included:

- Worked for many companies

- Established an exchange office

- An financial consultant in New York

- A member of the eleventh Jordanian House of Representatives in 1989

- Minister of Tourism and of Antiquities (1991 - 1989)

- Minister of Labor 1993 – 1991

- A member of the twelfth Jordanian House of Representatives in 1993

- Minister of Foreign Affairs 1996 – 1995

- Prime Minister and Minister of Foreign Affairs and of Defense (1997 - 1996)

Jordan Prime Ministers under the Hashemite Rule

- ## His Excellency Dr. Fayez Tarawneh:

Tarawneh was born in Amman in 1949. He received a bachelor's degree in economy from the University of Jordan in 1971. He also got a Master's degree (1974) and a PhD (1980) in economics, both from the University of Southern California.

The posts he held:

- Assistant Chief of Royal protocol (1980 - 1971)

- Economic Secretary of the Prime Minister (1984 - 1980)

- Economic Advisor of the Prime Minister (1988 - 1984)

- Ambassador to the USA (1997 - 1993)

- Chief of the Royal Hashemite Court 1998

- Chairman of the Board of Trustees of Al Hussein bin Talal University 1999

- A member of the Jordanian delegation, which was in charge of peace negotiations with Israel 1994 - 1991

- Headed the Jordanian delegation, as he was in charge of peace negotiations with Israel in 1994 - 1993

- A member of the Arab Thought Forum

- A Member of the International Affairs Association

- A member of the 18th House of Senate

- A member of the 19th House of Senate

- A member of the 20th House of Senate
- A member of the 21st House of Senate
- A member of the 22nd House of Senate
- A member of the 23rd House of Senate
- A member of the 24th House of Senate
- A member of the 25th House of Senate
- Chairman of the Board of Trustees of Al Al-Bayt University 2010 – 2009
- United Arab Investors Company

His ministerial posts included:

- Minister of Trade, Industry and Supply in 1988
- Minister of Trade, Industry 1989 – 1988
- Minister of Foreign Affairs 1998 – 1997
- Prime Minister and Minister of Defense 1999 – 1998
- Prime Minister and Minister of Defense in 2012

Orders and Honors:

- Jordan Order of Independence of first class
- Jordan Order of Independence of second class
- The Order of Renaissance
- The Special Order of Al Hussein

Jordan Prime Ministers under the Hashemite Rule

- **His Excellency Mr. Abdulraouf Al-Rawabdeh:**

He was born in Al-Sarih, Irbid in 1939. He got the Bachelor of Pharmacy from the American University of Beirut (Grade Excellent) in 1962.

His ministerial posts included:

- Minister of Transport 1977 – 1976

- Minister of Transport and of Health 1978 – 1977

- Minister of Health 1979 – 1978

- Minister of Public Works and Housing 1991 – 1989

- Minister of Education and Minister of State for Cabinet Affairs in 1995 – 1994

- Deputy Prime Minister and Minister of Education 1996 – 1995

- Prime Minister and Minister of Defense 2000 – 1999

Legislative Offices:

- A Member of the 1st, 2nd, 3rd National Advisory Council 1983 – 1978

- Deputy Chairman of the National Advisory Council 1983 – 1982

- A Member of the 11th Jordanian House of Representatives 1993 – 1989

- A Member of the 12th Jordanian House of Representatives

- A Member of the 13th Jordanian House of Representatives

- A Member of the 19th Jordanian House of Senates
- The First Deputy Chairman of the House of Senates
- A Member of the 14th Jordanian House of Representatives
- A Member of the 15th Jordanian House of Representatives
- A Member of the 23th Jordanian House of Senates
- The Second Deputy Chairman of the House of Senates
- A Member of the 24th Jordanian House of Senates
- The First Deputy Chairman of the House of Senates
- A Member of the 25th Jordanian House of Senates
- The First Deputy Chairman of the House of Senates

The Local posts:
- The Mayor of Amman 1986 – 1983
- Chairman of the Capital Construction Organization and the Mayor of the Great Municipality of Amman 1989 – 1987

Administrative Posts:
- Pharmacies Inspector
- Head of Pharmacy Department of the Ministry of Health
- Director of Pharmacy and Supplies Department
- Director of Planning and External Relations at the Ministry of Health Department
- Director of Yarmouk University Department of Administration and Services
- Deputy Chairman of the Board of Trustees of the University of

Jordan Prime Ministers under the Hashemite Rule

Science and Technology

The Private Sector Posts:

- Chairman of the Board of Trustees of the Jordanian Community College
- Chairman of Board of Directors of Jordan Phosphate Company
- Vice Chairman of the Fertilizers Company
- Chairman of the board of directors at Zaytuna College
- Member of the board of directors in Al-Aqsa Schools
- Chairman of the Board of Trustees of Jadara University for Graduate Studies

His initiatives and activities:

- Secretary-General of the Awakening Party
- Deputy Secretary-General and Head of the Politics Department of the Constitutional National Party
- Pharmacists Syndicate Member
- A Lecturer in Faculty of Nursing
- A Member of the Faculty Council of the Faculty of Medicine, the University of Jordan
- A Lecturer in Faculty of Pharmacy in the University of Jordan
- A Member of the Faculty Council of the Faculty of Nursing, the University of Jordan
- Chairman of the Society of Friends of the Faculty of Pharmacy, the University of Jordan
- Member of the Curricula and Textbooks Committee

- Chairman of the Al-Sarih Sports and Social Club
- President of the Jordan Football Association
- A Member of the Jordanian Olympic Committee
- A Member of the Jordanian Association for Environmental Pollution Control
- President of the Jordanian-Polish Friendship Association
- Member of the board of the Jordan University Hospital
- Member of Jordan Society for the Conservation of Nature
- Chairman of the Board of Trustees of King Abdullah II of Jordan Award for Innovation

His Publications:

- Al-Wajeez in pharmacology, three editions
- Pharmacology for Assistant pharmacist, four editions
- Bacteriology for Assistant pharmacist
- Physiology for Assistant pharmacist
- Democracy between Theory and Practice
- Parliamentary Elections between Theory and Practice
- Education and Future (Jordanian Perspective)
- Dictionary of Jordanian Tribes

Orders:

- The Order of the Star of Jordan of first class in 1976
- Medal of Honor, rank of higher officer of the Italian Republic in 1982

Jordan Prime Ministers under the Hashemite Rule

- Order of Merit of the Federal Republic of Germany 1984
- Silver Medal of Honor of the Republic of Austria 1987
- The Premier Order of Education 1997
- Order of the Renaissance of first class 1999
- The Order of Isabella the Catholic, the rank of the Great Cross (Spain) 1999
- The Royal Norwegian Order of the superiority of the Class 2000
- French National Order of Merit of the First Class 2000

- ### His Excellency Mr. Ali Abu Al-Ragheb:

He was born in Amman in 1946. He obtained his BSc in Civil Engineering in 1967 from the University of Tennessee in the United States in 1967.

Legislative Offices:

- Member in the Great Municipality of Amman
- Member of Businessmen Association Board
- Member of the 13th House of Representatives
- Chairman of the Financial and Economic Committee in the 13th House of Representatives

- Member of Energy and Fortune Committee in the 13th House of Representatives
- Minister of Commerce, Industry and Supply 1991
- Minister of Energy and Mineral Resources 1993- 1991
- Minister of Commerce and of Industry 1996 1995
- Minister of Commerce and of Industry 1997- 1996
- Prime Minister and Minister of Defense 2002 -2000
- Prime Minister and Minister of Defense 2003- 2002
- Prime Minister and Minister of Defense 2003

Local Government Posts:

- Project Manager in the Ministry of Municipal, Rural and Environmental Affairs
- The Great Municipality of Amman Engineering Manager
- Partner and Managing Director of National Engineering and Contracting Co
- Contractors Chief
- Member of the Economic Advisory Council
- Chairman of the Royal Commission in charge of the establishment of the Special Economic Zone in Aqaba

Orders:

- The Order of the Star of Jordan of first class
- The Order of Renaissance of first class

Jordan Prime Ministers under the Hashemite Rule

- **His Excellency Mr. Faisal Al-Fayez:**

He was born in Amman on April 22nd 1952. He was educated at the College De La Salle (1970) and then went on to Cardiff University, United Kingdom where he received a degree in Political Science in 1978. In 1981, he did a master's degree in international relations in Boston University in Brussels.

Career Experience:

- Consul at the Embassy of Jordan in Brussels 1983 - 1979

- The Legal, Economic and Protocol Departments of the Ministry of Foreign Affairs 1986 – 1983

- Assistant Chief of Royal Protocol at the Royal Court 1995 - 1986

- Deputy Chief of Royal Protocol at the Royal Court 1999 - 1995

- Chief of Royal Protocol at the Royal Court 2003 – 1999

- Minister of the Royal Hashemite Court 2003

- Prime Minister and Minister of Defense 2005- 2003

Orders:

- 1987: Order of Order of Independence of first class

- 1995: Order of Independence of second class

- 2000: Order of the Star of Jordan of fourth class

- **His Excellency Dr. Adnan Badran:**

Badran was born in Jerash on December 15th 1935. He received his Bachelor of Science from Oklahoma State University and Ph.D. degree from Michigan State University, the United States in 1963.

Career Experience:

- Prime Minister and Minister of Defense 2005/4/12

- President of Philadelphia University 2005 – 1998

- Deputy Director-General of UNESCO, Paris 1998 – 1993

- Assistant Director-General of UNESCO, Paris 1993 – 1990

- Minister of Education 1990 – 1989

- Minister of Agriculture 1989

- Secretary General of the Higher Council for Science and Technology 1987 – 1986

- President and founder of Yarmouk University and the University of Science and Technology 1986 – 1976

- A Professor of Biology in both Universities

- A Professor of Molecular Biology and Physiology in the University of Jordan 1976 – 1974

- Dean of the Faculty of Science, the University of Jordan 1976- 1971

- Associate Professor in the Faculty of Science, the University of Jordan 1970 – 1966

Jordan Prime Ministers under the Hashemite Rule

- Principal researcher at the Boston Center for Research, the USA 1966 – 1963

- Assistant researcher at the University of Michigan 1963- 1963

Fellowships:

- Secretary General and member of the Academy of Sciences for the Third World since 1991

- Fellow of the American Society of Biological Sciences

- Fellow of the American Society of Plant Physiology 1963

- Member of the Board of Trustees of the following universities:

- Yarmouk University 1985- 1976

- University of Jordan 1985 – 1976

- Mutah University 1988 – 1978

- Philadelphia University 2000 – 1990

- Girls University 1998 – 1992

- Member of the Executive Board of the International Union of Science and Biology 1988 – 1985

- President of the Union of international universities heads for the Middle East 1986- 1980

- Member of the Executive Board of the International Federation of universities 1986 1978

- Member of the International Council for Science and the Commission of Science for developing countries, Paris 1994 – 1990

- Fellow at the European Academy of Sciences and Arts and the Arts since 1997

- Associate Chief of the Encyclopedia of Life since 1997

- Chairman of the Jordanian National Commission for UNESCO and Vice President of the UNESCO General Conference, Paris 1989

- Vice President of the International Union of Biological Sciences, Paris 1980 - 1975

- Vice President of the Royal Society for Nature Protection, Jordan 1980 - 1970

- Fellow of the American National Academy of Sciences committee to support research in the developing countries (1983 - 1980)

- Member of the Executive Committee of Oceanography at UNESCO 1984

- Fellow of Arab Thought Forum and the Council of International Affairs, Jordan since 1979

- Aspen Forum, Colorado 1980

Honorary Awards:

Badran received an honorary doctorate and a number of decorations and medals from a number of universities and governmental organizations.

His works and publications:

He wrote 15 books about science and ecology. He also published over 70 researches about the physiology of Plant enzymes related to breathing cycle and metabolism in scientific journals and periodicals. He also published studies about higher education and the strategies of science and technology in the Arab World.

Jordan Prime Ministers under the Hashemite Rule

- His basic initiatives and activities:

- Supervising Master and Doctorate theses in science

- A principal investigator in the field of enzymes in plant oxidative stress and enzymes venting that led to recording four international inventions outputs which are still valid

- Building since curricula, especially Life Sciences in collaboration with UNESCO and ALECSO

- Producing books and learning material

- Establishing two universities in the North of Jordan that include humanitarian, social, scientific, engineering and medical specialties

- Establishing the Marine Sciences Center in Aqaba

- Establishing strategies for the development of higher education, science and technology for the coming generation

Orders:

- Order of Independence of first class

- **His Excellency Dr. Marouf al-Bakhit:**

He was born in Mahis, Balqa. His qualifications included bachelor's degree in General Management and Political Science from University of Jordan. He also earned a Master's in Public Administration from the University of Southern California, and a PhD in strategy studies from King's College, London.

The posts he held include:

- Prime Minister and Minister of Defense 2011

- Prime Minister and Minister of Defense 2007- 2005

- Chief of the National Security and the Vice Director of the King's Office on November 16th 2005

- Jordan's Ambassador to Israel 2005

- Jordan's Ambassador to Turkey 2002

- Member and secretary of the Supreme Steering Committee and the General Coordinator for the peace process in the Middle East, 1999

- Professor of political science in Mutah University from 1997 to 1999

- Retired from the Armed Forces in 1999 as Major General

- From 1990 to 1991, he held many posts, including: vice-president of Mutah University for military affairs

- Director of development and studies

Jordan Prime Ministers under the Hashemite Rule

- Purchasing manager
- Personnel manager in the Headquarters of the Jordanian Armed Forces
- Attended many courses in the Command and Staff College
- Jordan's representative in the Arms Control and Regional Security Talks within the multilateral work groups that have been launched from Madrid
- Joined the Jordanian Armed Forces in 1964

Orders:

- He holds fourteen Jordanian decorations and honors

- **His Excellency Mr. Nader Al-Dahabi:**

He was born in Amman, Jordan in 1946.

Career Experience:

- Prime Minister and Minister of Defense 2011 - 2007
- Chief Commissioner of the Aqaba Special Economic Zone Authority (ASEZA) 2007 – 2004
- Minister of Transport, of Tourism and of Antiquities 2004 – 2003
- Minister of Transport 2003 – 2001
- CEO of Royal Jordanian Airlines from 1994 to 2001
- Assistant Commander of the Royal Jordanian Air Force for logistics from 1992 to 1994

Scientific Qualifications:

- Msc. in Public Administration from the Auburn University (Alabama, USA) in 1987

- MSc in aeronautical engineering from Cranfield Institute of Technology in the United Kingdom 1982

- BSc. in aeronautical engineering from the Hellenic Air Force Academy in 1969

- High School from Al Hussein College in Amman in 1964

Memberships and activities:

- Chairman of the Board of Trustees of Tafila Technical University 2007 – 2005

- Member of Education Council 2007 – 2005

- Chairman of Aqaba Port Corporation 2007 – 2004

- Chairman of Aqaba Railway Corporation 2004 – 2001

- Chairman of Board of Directors of Hejaz Railway Company 2004 – 2001

- Chairman of the Board of Royal Jordanian Falcons 2001 – 1994

- Chairman of the Board of Trustees of the Royal Jordanian Air Academy 2001 – 1994

- Member of the Supreme Committee of the Jerash Festival 2001- 1994

- Member of the Supreme Committee of Tourism 2001 – 1994

- Member of the International Air Transport Association (IATA) board of governors from 1998-1995

Jordan Prime Ministers under the Hashemite Rule

- President of International Air Transport Association (IATA) 1997 – 996
- Chairman of the Arab Air Carriers Organization from 1995-1994

Orders:

- Order of Renaissance of first class
- Order of the Star of Jordan
- Order of Independence of second class
- Order of Merit of second class

Languages:

- English and Greek

- **His Excellency Mr. Samir al-Rifai:**

He was born in Amman in 1966

Scientific Qualifications:

Rifai received his bachelor's degree in Middle East Studies in Harvard University in the USA, and obtained his master's degree in International Relations from Cambridge University in the UK.

The posts he held:

- Prime Minister of the Royal Hashemite Kingdom

- Secretary General of the Royal Hashemite Court 1999 1998
- Minister of the Royal Hashemite Court
- The adviser to the King in 2005
- Chief executive officer and founder of Jordan Dubai Capital
- Chairman of the board of directors of Jordan Dubai energy investments and Infrastructure.
- Chairman of the board of directors of Jordan Dubai Capital, the investment arm of Jordan Dubai Capital, in the field of financial investments
- Chairman of the board of directors 'Jordan Dubai Islamic Bank
- Chairman of the Investment Promotion Committee at the Royal Court
- Chairman of the Preparatory Committee of the Amman Message
- Member of a committee to pursue interfaith dialogue
- Member of the Higher Steering Committee for the peace process
- Board member of King Abdullah II Award for Excellence Performance and Transparency in the public sector

Orders:

- Order of the Star of Jordan of first class
- Order of Independence of first class

Jordan Prime Ministers under the Hashemite Rule

- **His Excellency Mr. Awn Al-Khasawneh:**

Prime Minister and Minister of Defense

He was born in Amman in 1950.

Scientific Qualifications:

He received his university education at Cambridge in England, where he attained a bachelor's degree in history and law and a master's degree in international law with honors.

Career Experiences:

- Prime Minister and Minister of Defense 2011 / 10 /4.

- Joined the Jordanian ministry of foreign affairs as a member of Jordan's permanent delegation to the United Nations

- Represented Jordan in 19 sessions of the legal committee of the United Nations Association

- Rapporteur of the Legal Committee in 1976 and participating in many international treaties that include:

- Anti-hostage-taking treaty

- Vienna Convention on the Law of Treaties between States in international conventions

- Vienna Convention on countries inheritance in the archives, courts and records

- Rome treaty to combat hostile action to international navigation

- Director of the Legal Department of the Ministry of Foreign Affairs
- Advisor to His Royal Highness Prince Prince Al-Hassan bin Talal
- Advisor to His Majesty King Al Hussein bin Talal and Chief of the Royal Hashemite Court in 1998 – 1996
- Elected as an expert and a member of the Committee on Prevention of Discrimination and Protection of Minorities
- Re-elected to this post for three terms from 1982 to 1993
- Elected as Chairman of the same Committee in 1993
- Appointed by the same Committee as a Special Rapporteur on the forcible transfer of population. He put a three-fold report that has been translated into the languages of the United Nations and is considered one of the most important references in this field.
- Supervised the Presidential and legislative elections in Guatemala
- Elected by the United Nations Association as a member of the International Law Commission in 1986, which is the highest committee responsible for the development of law in the United Nations
- Participated in the creation of many international agreements in the last quarter of the last century that include:
- Code of Crimes against Peace and Security of Mankind
- Articles related to the international liability
- Law of international rivers and watercourses and other
- Re-elected as a member in the committee for three terms till 2000
- Elected in a secret ballot by the UN and the Security Council as a

judge in the International Court of Justice

- Re-elected as a judge in the International Court of Justice in 2009 for nine years

- Elected by the Court judges as a Vice-president

- Participated in 40 international issues His separate or dissenting opinions are studied in most of the advanced universities of the world such as:

- The issue of Bosnia and Herzegovina (the issue of genocide) in which he gave a contrary opinion to the majority

- The issue of the border dispute between Qatar and Bahrain

- Issue of the advisory opinion on the construction of Israeli West Bank barrier

- The issue of Kosovo's independence

- The issue of the war between Georgia and Russia and others

Scientific and academic activities:

- Delivered lectures in many lofty universities including (Oxford, Cambridge, London, Brunel, Sorbonne and Geneva) as well as universities in Brazil, Costa Rica, Zanzibar and India

- Chairman of the Islamic and international law in the International Law Federation

- Since 2005, he is working on an inclusive record of all the treaties signed by the Islamic states since the dawn of history till now.

- An arbitrator in the case of Abyei between Sudan's government and the Liberation Army of South Sudan

- He had a contrary opinion to the majority and his opinion is taught in many important universities.

Orders:

- Order of Independence of first class in 1993
- Order of the Star of Jordan of first class in 1996
- The Supreme Order of Renaissance of first class in 1996
- Légion d'Honneur, Grand Officier (1997) (France)

- **His Excellency Dr. Abdullah Ensour:**

- Born in Salt, January 1939, 20

Scientific Qualifications:

- Ph.D. in planning at Sorbonne University
- Master's degree in institutions management, at the University of Michigan in the United States
- bachelor's degree in statistics from the American University of Beirut
- high school from Slat Secondary School

Senatorial Posts:

- A member of the House of Representatives in 1993, 1989 and 2010 as:
- Chairman of the Finance and Economic Committee

Jordan Prime Ministers under the Hashemite Rule

- Member of the Foreign Affairs Committee
- Member of the Committee on Education and Higher Education
- A member of the House of Senate in 1997 and 2009 as:
- Member of the Finance Committee
- Member of the Foreign Affairs Committee

Ministerial Positions:
- Minister of Planning
- Minister of Education
- Minister of Industry and Trade
- Minister of Higher Education
- Minister of Administrative Development
- Media Minister
- Deputy Prime Minister 2016 – 2013

Experiences and Memberships, Current and Previous Councils:
- Director General of the Budget Department
- The Ministry of Finance Secretary General
- Director General of the Income Tax Department
- Governor of Jordan at the World Bank
- Deputy Governor of Jordan at the International Monetary Fund
- Jordan's permanent delegate to UNESCO
- Chairman of the Jordanian-French Business Club Management
- Member of the Royal Commission National Agenda

- The official spokesman and a member of the Royal Commission for "Jordan First"
- Chairman of the Higher Education Council
- Chairman of the Board of Trustees of the Private Jordanian University of Zaytouna
- Vice Chairman of the Board of Trustees of the University of Science and Technology.
- Vice Chairman of the Board of Trustees of the Balqa Applied University.
- Vice Chairman of the Board of Trustees of the Hashemite University.
- Member of the Board of Trustees of the University of Jordan.
- Member of the Board of Rights in the University of Jordan.
- Administrative and Financial Director of the Royal Scientific Society.
- Teacher, inspector and director in the Ministry of Education
- Member of the National Commission for Development Planning.
- Chairman of the Supreme Council for the fight against illiteracy.
- Chairman of the Cement Company.
- Vice Chairman of the phosphate company.
- Vice Chairman of the Iraqi Jordanian Land Transport Company.
- Member of the Board of Management of Bank of Jordan.
- Member of the Council of Arab African International Bank.
- Member of the Council of Arab Company for Investment Management.

Jordan Prime Ministers under the Hashemite Rule

- Member of the Board of Directors of Aqaba Railway.
- Member of the Board of Royal Jordanian Management.
- Member of the Board of Jordan Investment Corporation management.
- Member of the Board of Management the authority of the port of Aqaba.
- Member of the Board of Jordan Enterprise Manager for the development of economic projects.
- Board Member of the Noor Al Hussein Foundation.
- Board Member of the Queen Alia Fund Management.
- Chairman of the newspaper Voice of the People (Sawt Al Sha'b).
- Chairman of the Board of Directors Haya Cultural Center.
- Chairman of the graduates of French universities Club.
- Member of the Board graduates of American universities Club.

Orders:
- Order of Independence of first class
- Order of the Star of Jordan of first class
- The Supreme Order of Renaissance of first class
- Légion d'Honneur, Grand Officier (France)
- Education Jordanian Medal – Excellent

- **His Excellency Mr. Hani Al-Mulki:**

He was born in Amman in 1950.

Scientific Qualifications:

- bachelor's degree in production engineering in Egypt in 1974

- Master's degrees in Systems Engineering from the USA in 1977

- Doctoral degrees in Systems Engineering from the USA in 1979

His most important posts:

- Chief Commissioner of the Aqaba Special Economic Zone Authority in 2014

- Member of the House of Senate 2014- 2013

- Minister of Industry and Trade 2014- 2013

- Jordan's Ambassador to Cairo 2011 – 2008

- Member of the House of Senate 2007 – 2006

- Advisor to the King 2006 - 2005

- Minister of Foreign Affairs 2005 – 2004

- Jordan's Ambassador to Cairo 2004 – 2002

- Permanent representative in the Arab League 2004 – 2002

- Executive Vice President of the Higher Council for Science and Technology 2002 – 1999

- Minister of Industry and Trade 1997

Jordan Prime Ministers under the Hashemite Rule

- Minister of Supply 1998 – 1997
- Minister of Water and Irrigation 1999 – 1998
- Minister of Energy and Mineral Resources 1999 – 1998
- Chairman of the Royal Scientific Society 1997 – 1989
- Secretary-General of the Higher Council for Science and Technology 1997 – 1993
- Chairman of the negotiation committee which produced the Israel-Jordan peace treaty between Jordan and Israel from 1996 – 1994
- Executive Director of the Islamic Academy of Sciences (OIS) 1989 – 1987
- Director of Renewable Energy Department - the Royal Scientific Society 1987 – 1984

Orders and Honors:

- Order of Independence of first class - Jordanian
- Order of the Star of Jordan of first class
- Cordon of power of the outstanding class – Denmark
- Order of leadership- Swiss
- Order of Grand Officer- French
- The retention order- Dutch

THE JORDANIAN TRIBES: THEIR ROLE IN THE ESTABLISHMENT OF JORDAN AND THEIR CURRENT ROLE

The clearest description of the moral value of the family or tribe in Jordan is that it represents the impassable societal scope that a person should never surpass, rebel against or violate its rules and values by committing a behavioral or moral infringement. Thus, the members of the tribe should retain its history, reputation and good image. This is why the tribe is a deterring factor for its members not to deviate from its authentic and inherited customs and traditions.

It is necessary to tackle or remind of one of the outputs of this social entity, namely the Foundation for Relief and Reconciliation which incarnates the true model of a patriotic foundation that is keen on preserving the moral system of Jordan that is characterized with love, intimacy, tolerance and reform. It achieves this through its role represented in reconciling between people, stopping the torrent of blood and settling conflicts between them, in order to retain the social fabric and the good relationship between the members of the larger Jordanian Community.

It is worthy to refer to the contributions of the Jordanian tribe to keep the national security by interfering in problems and conflicts in their cradle; before they fall in the hands of police or the judiciary power. They also coordinate and cooperate with these entities to allow a chance for peacemakers and good people to treat these problems amiably.

In more than one occasion, King Abdullah praised the role played by tribes and their contribution to retaining the values of tolerance and solidarity. This guarantees the consistency of the Jordanian social system as a main pillar in the formation of society. As a symbol of belonging, patriotism and noble values, tribes support the official and security institutions to achieve a state of stability and security in our society.

This highlights the importance of tackling the role of tribes in facing societal violence focusing on the preventive aspect of this topic. It is clear that the role played by tribes begins concurrently with the social problems; thus taking a curative form. Instead, the tribes of Jordan address these issues in a preventive or protective way by holding systematic meetings for reinforcing the preventive factors through the early detection of the negative behavioral aspects, creating a knowledge-based societal environment and the consistent communication between their members in the presence of the Sheikhs, elders and dignitaries to exchange opinions and speak about the different issues that concern the tribe as well as society. This keeps the person under the influence of these meetings that reflect the true nature of the tribal institution as a home of noble vales.

Moreover, the communication and exchange of meetings and visits between the administrative officers, security officials, university

presidents and school headmasters in the governorates, counties and the different corners of the country on one hand with the tribe leaders and dignitaries on the other hand strengthen the relationship and reinforces the interactive atmosphere between these parties in terms of the communication with local society and public interest. This includes the treatment of societal violence in the context of the social liability. A special attention must be paid to the choice of people. The people chosen must be effective with an influential presence in the advisory councils and committees to be formed so that they can be employed in the treatment of the local society problems.

This leads us to speak about the importance of maximizing the role and value of these tribal symbols. These people should represent the link with the local community in the relevant issues,

identifying their priorities, demands and developmental and service needs. This makes these people influential and effective between their kin in the tribe. People will look at these people respectfully and gratefully as the best and most proper people who represent and express their interests. This adds another dimension in the process of activating the moral aspect of the tribe and employing it in maintaining the social fabric.

Jordanian tribes are asked to cooperate to create a code of conduct or a moral charter that encourages people to institutionalize the role of the tribe in the context of group work in order to maintain the values of tolerance, societal solidarity as a firewall for the Jordanian moral system against the irresponsible behavioral violations represented in societal violence.

The tribes are also asked not to blindly follow or support the troublemakers among their offspring. They should let them fall in the hands of justice according to the followed systems, laws and legislations. This is in accordance with what His Majesty said in the 26th graduation ceremony of Mutah University officers. He said that our tribal culture and structure doesn't approve violence. He said that we are all of tribal origins; either in the desert, village, cities or camps. This is the source of our national strength and unity and an important reason of our societal security and stability.

The family or tribe has never been a source of chaos, violence or violation of laws as it may be thought by those who do not know the true meaning of the tribe and the nature of the tribal society.

THE HASHEMITE KINGDOM OF JORDAN

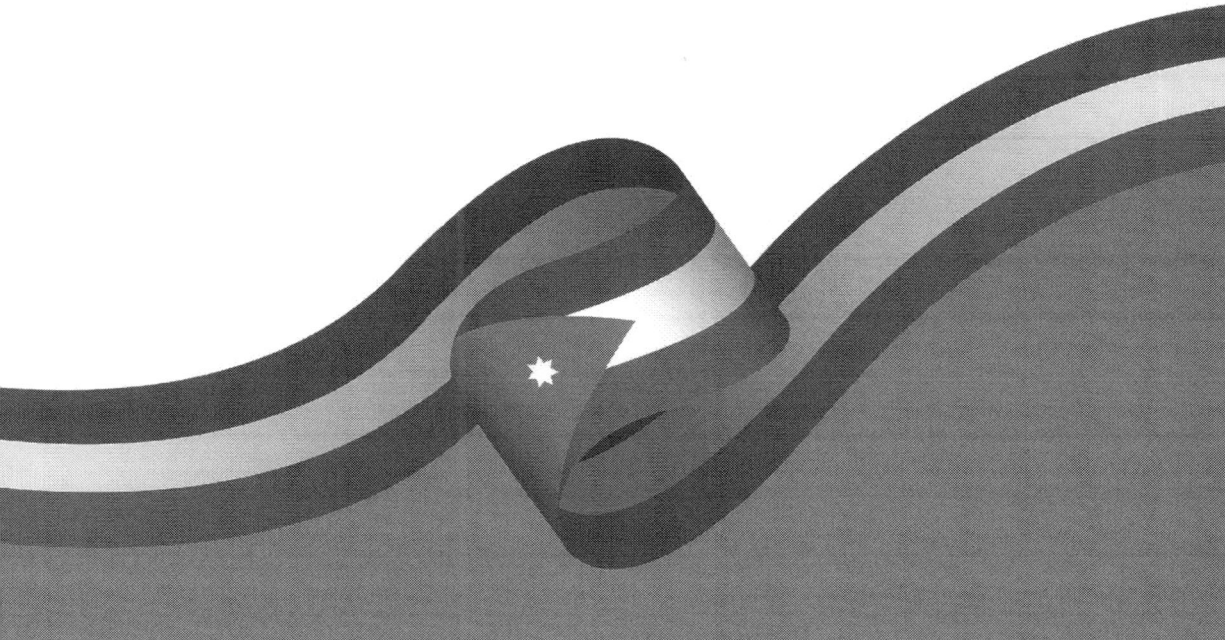

CHAPTER THIRTEEN

ADMINISTRATIVE DIVISIONS OF JORDAN AND THE DEVELOPMENT OF THE CAPITAL, AMMAN

CHAPTER THIRTEEN
ADMINISTRATIVE DIVISIONS OF JORDAN AND THE DEVELOPMENT OF THE CAPITAL, AMMAN

Jordan is administratively subdivided into 12 governorates. The governorates consist of counties and districts.

The administrative governor (the governor) takes over the affairs of the governorate. The county-executive (mutasarif) is responsible for the executive branch of a district. The Mukhtar (chosen person) is responsible for a clan or neighborhood; as announced by the Minister of Interior in the Official Gazette. Some members of the tribe or residents in the neighborhood are appointed with him to help in his mission. Cities and towns are divided into blocks and tribal units.

The Jordanian state has gone through many administrative divisions that date back to the Transjordan era. Since then, these administrative divisions have passed many stages as follows.

- **Administrative divisions in the Transjordan:**

This stage was branched off two sub-stages. The first sub-stage was from 1927 -1921.

Transjordan consisted of three provinces: Salt, Ajloun and Karak. Each province consisted of administrative districts, directorates. The province was administrated by a county-executive (mutasarif) and the administrative district was administrated by a district administrator.

In 1923, the previous subdivision was modified and Transjordan consisted of six provinces: Amman, Karak, Madaba, Salt, Jerash and Irbid. The division titles "province" and "nahia" were replaced with "magistracy", and the division titles "county", "district" and "nahia" were abolished.

In 1927, the administrative division had been in accordance

with different-level magistracies as follows:

First-level magistracies in: Irbid, Salt, Karak and Ma'an

Second-level magistracies in: Jabal Ajloun (Mount Ajloun), Jerash, Madaba, Amman, Tafila and Aqaba

Third-level magistracies in: Al-Koura, Bani Kinana, Ramtha, Bakura, Umm Qais, Tall Al-Arba'in, Giza, Theban, Wadi Seer, Al-Zarqa, Ghor Safi and Shobak.

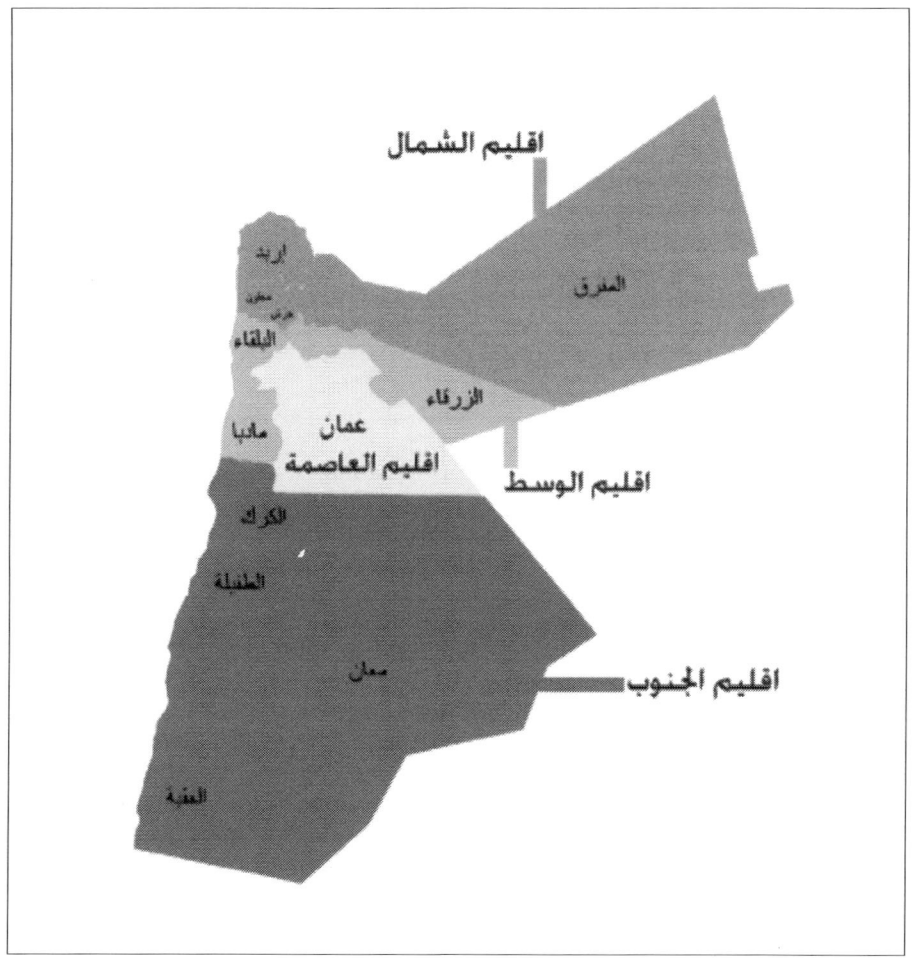

Amman

From 1928 to 1946, the Transjordan was divided into four counties:

1. **Ajloun County:** its sector is Irbid. This county comprised 221 villages and three districts: Irbid, Ajloun and Jerash, and was followed by further nahias: Ramtha, Koura, and Bani Kinana.

2. **Balqa County:** its sector is Salt. This county comprised 83 villages and three districts: Amman, Salt, and Madaba.

3. **Karak County:** its sector is Karak. This county comprised 93 villages and tribes spread over the districts of Karak, Tafila, Iraq Nahia and Ghor Al-Mazra'a (Al-Mazar Nahia).

4. **Ma'an County:** its sector is Ma'an. This county comprised 38 villages and tribes spread over the districts of Ma'an, Aqaba, Shobak nahias and Wadi Musa.

In 2000, the kingdom was divided in accordance with the Regulation of Administrative Divisions No. 46. This division included three regions, 12 governorates, containing 51 counties, and 38 districts as follows:

1: **North Region:** it contains four governorates as follows: Irbid, Ajloun, Jerash and Mafraq, and includes 16 counties and 14 districts.

2: **Central Region:** it contains four governorates as follows: Amman, Al-Zarqa, Balqa and Madaba, and includes 19 counties and 15 districts.

3: **South Region:** it contains four governorates as follows: Karak, Ma'an, Tafila, and Aqaba, and includes 16 counties and 9 districts.

- **Amman, the Capital, and its Development:**

Amman is the capital of Jordan and the administrative centre of the Amman Governorate. It is the largest and most populous city of Jordan. Its population with the population of the neighboring suburbs (the Greater Municipality of Amman) exceeded 4 million people living on an area of 1,680 square kilometers, according to the Jordan General Population and Housing Census by the Department of Statistics from November 30th to December 10th 2015.

The city is located at the center of the Hashemite Kingdom of Jordan on the 31st north circle of latitude and the 35th east line of longitude in a hilly area. Being established in the valleys between mountains, the city narrowed its population and they had to widen across the peaks until Amman spanned over 20 hills.

Amman is the commercial and administrative center as well as the economic and educational heart of Jordan. It is a source of attraction for Arab communities thanks to its distinctive location and modern architecture. It is also an annual destination for tourists from Western Europe, North America, Japan, Australia, the neighboring Arab countries, especially Arab-Gulf families who visit it for its touristic attractions in general and its therapeutic medical tourism in particular.

Amman

Amman at night

Amman is granted a strategic location in Sham (the Levant) and the Middle East. This location controls the national economy and activates about %90 of the national investments.

The history of Amman goes back to 7000 BC; this makes it one of the world's oldest populated cities up to date. Amman is an ancient city built on the ruins of "Rabbath Ammon" that was later known as "Philadelphia". The Ammonites took the city as their capital and called it "Amman" from "Rabbath Ammon".

The city was built on seven hills, and it was seemingly then center of the region then as well as one of the four capitals of Sham (the Levant) and one of the ancient Sham (Levant) cities that became the capital of the Transjordan whose name changed into the Hashemite Kingdom of Jordan, after it gained its independence in 1946.

Modern Amman embraces a varied collection of population from different origins and from different areas. Some of them came from close Jordanian cities; some came from Palestine, Caucasus, Syria or Iraq.

Recently, the Greater Municipality of Amman achieved a notable development; the city expanded unprecedentedly and its inclusive plan won global awards that include: the World Leadership Award in Town Planning Category and the Prestigious "City of the Year – Asia Pacific" Award.

Amman consists of 27 geographically-distributed districts; each one of them has its integral staff. They are administrated by the Council of the Greater Municipality of Amman consisting of 68 members and 14 commissions headed by the Mayor.

Amman won international recognition as one of the best Middle East cities in terms of economy, environment, labor market, and the social and cultural features.

Amman spans over a number of hills (jibal) 750 meters above the sea level and the average height of its hills (jibal) is 918 meters.

Aqaba is 360 km south of Amman; Irbid is approximately 80 km north and the Jordan River is 45 km west.

Jerusalem is 80 km west of Amman; Damascus is 180 km north; Baghdad is 800 km east and Mecca is 1225 south.

The city dates back to 7000 BC, and it has witnessed many civilizations as suggested by the archaeological sites all over the city. The Roman Theatre is one of the remains of the Roman era; Jabal Al-Qalaa (Amman Citadel) with its various patterns of archaeology speaks of the Ammonite, Greek, Romania, Byzantine and Umayyad civilizations; Rujm Al-Malfouf refers to the pre-history period the worshipers of nature and its elements such as the sun, the moon and stars.

The Hittites and Hyksos came to Amman followed by the Ancient Titans, then Bani Ammon tribes, the Ammonites, who called the city its name "Rabbath Ammon" or "Rabbath" which means the capital or the king's court. With the passage of time, the word "Rabbath" has been dropped and the name became "Ammon". The Umayyads gave the city its current name "Amman".

In the beginning, Ammon did not stand up to the Assyrians, but they continued their struggle against the Babylonians leading to an economic deterioration. Under Nebuchadnezzar, the Babylonians continued their attacks on the south of the Assyrian Empire and controlled it. The Ammonites joined the Arameans against the Assyrians in the early 9th century BC. The Assyrians occupied the Ammonite Kingdom, and the Assyrian King Sennacherib granted the Ammonites their autonomy. Thanks to the Assyrian domination which established security, the Ammonites could control the routes of commercial convoys.

By 612 BC, the Babylonians had inherited the Assyrians' properties in Asia. Then, in 590 BC, the King of Egypt invaded some of the Sham (the Levant) parts including Palestine and the East of Jordan. Later in 586 BC, Nebuchadnezzar, the Babylonian King then, enslaved the people of Jerusalem and returned the area to his tenure.

In 539 BC, the Persian Cyrus could destroy the Babylonian Empire and established the Persian Empire. He occupied Palestine and Jordan and entered Amman which was under the rule of the Persian Empire during that t period. The Persian granted Amman its autonomy during (332 -540 BC), but the Greeks terminated the Persian rule and the Greek Empire era started.

Under the rule of the Ptolemaic Greeks who dominated the entire region, Rabbath Ammon became Philadelphia (the brotherly love) by Ptolemy II, according to Philadelphus. Ptolemy II also made Jabal Al-Qalaa (Amman Citadel) a location of temples following the

Acropolis of Athens. The village of Iraq Al-Amir was named after the palace of King Tobias known as Iraq Al-Amir.

Amman was divided into two states -Nabatean and Seleucid- until the Roman King "Herod" in 30 BC occupied it, marking the beginning of the Roman and Byzantine Eras until the mid7-th century.

A Street in Amman

The Roman Theatre

- **The Islamic Era:**

This era is marked by the Islamic conquest of Sham (the Levant) after the Islamic conquest and victory in Amman under the leadership of Yazid bin Abi Sufyan who put an end to the Ghassanids who were dominating Balqa region of which Amman was a part.

- **The Umayyad Era:**

Under their reign, the Umayyads built a great palace on top of Jabal Al-Qalaa (Amman Citadel). Amman acted as their administrative and coinage center where the Prince lived and the garrisons watched the commercial convoys' routes and guarded the pilgrimage route as well as the water sources such as Birkat Zizia and Al-Qastal.

- **The Abbasid Era:**

When the Abbasids came in power, Amman (administrative center) witnessed fights that destroyed walls and forts in an internal military confrontation. Historians refer that the Abbasids barricaded themselves in Amman when the Umayyads revolted to claim their caliphate under the rule of Caliph Al-Ma'mun Bin Al-Rashid.

Jabal Al-Qalaa (Amman Citadel)

- **The Fatimid Era:**

In the Fatimid Era, Amman was noted to be the center of power. Towards the end of their era, in the late 11th century AD, the volume of external pressure increased concurrently with the Crusades. In 1184 AD, Salahuddin Al-Ayyubi went through Amman on his way to Karak. Since then, it became a part of the Ayyubid state. During the Mamluk Era (1516 -1258), Amman experienced stability and prosperity of its markets in the season of pilgrimage, but it went in oblivion and negligence till the end of the 19th century AD.

- **The Ottoman Era:**

In the Ottoman Era, the Grand Vizier, Kamil Pasha, proposed a suggestion to the Sublime Porte to annex Amman to the adjustment of the administrative divisions of Syria. But his suggestion did not come to life, although it signified the importance of Amman at that time. Hence, the city suffered from clear negligence and its stature had fallen back on behalf of other closer cities like Salt. However, the Hejaz Railway established by Ottomans which passed Amman was one of the undeniable positive efforts of the Ottomans; it effectively contributed to the city's renaissance and the end of its long hibernation in the end of the Ottoman Era during the tenure of Sultan Abdul-Hamid II.

THE HASHEMITE KINGDOM OF JORDAN

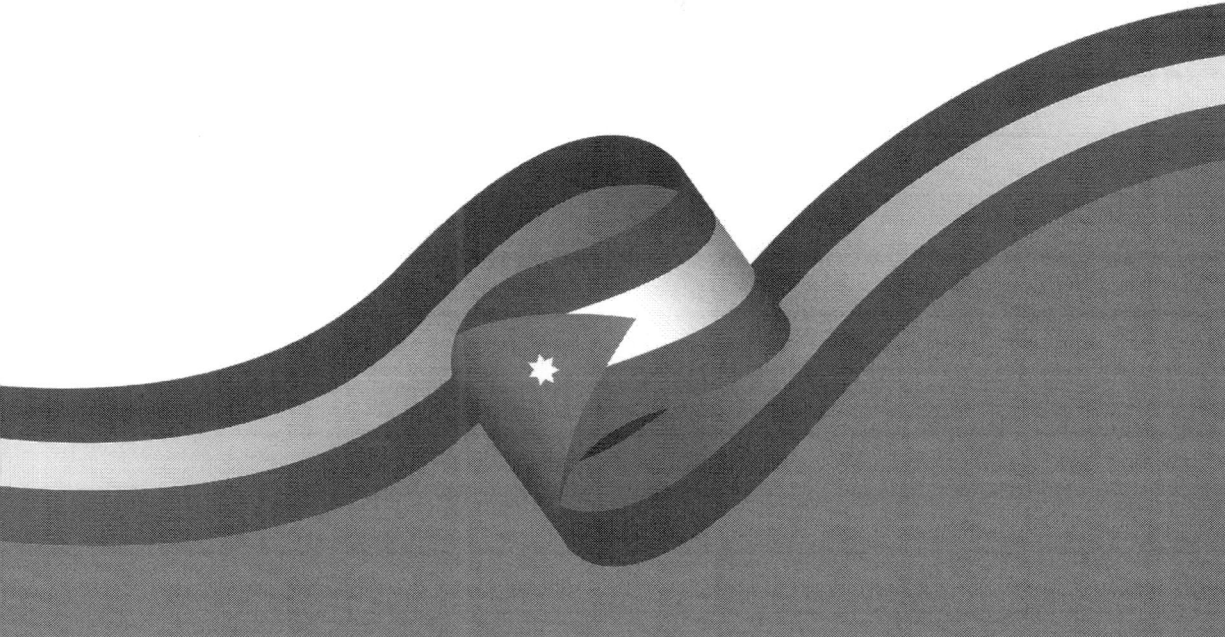

CHAPTER FOURTEEN

EDUCATION AND UNIVERSITIES

CHAPTER FOURTEEN
EDUCATION AND UNIVERSITIES

Education
The education system of the Hashemite Kingdom of Jordan has been improved consistently since the mid1900-s. The role played by a good education system has been significant in the development of Jordan from a predominantly agrarian to an industrialized nation. Jordan's education system ranks number one in the Arab World and is considered one of the finest education systems in the developing world countries.

Nature journal reported Jordan having the highest number of researchers in research and development per million people among all the 57 countries that are members of the Organization of Islamic Cooperation (OIC). In Jordan, there are 2,000 researchers per million people, while the average among the members of the OIC is 500 researchers per million people. This signifies that the number of researchers per Jordanian people is higher than its counterpart in Italy and Greece, and is closer to its peer in the UK and Ireland.

The gross primary enrollment in basic education rate reached %97 in 2000, while the illiteracy rate reached %90 to be one of the highest rates in the Middle East and North Africa. At the same time, Jordan ensures a high level of gender parity; the gender parity index for gross female enrollment ratio in primary and secondary education reached %50 in 1991.

Jordan is taking serious steps towards the knowledge-based economy; therefore, it adopted modern curricula and methods of knowledge based economy education (creative thinking, critical thinking, student-centered education and etc.)

A due help has been given to students and teachers to realize the difference

between the knowledge-based education and the traditional teaching system based on memorization and initiation. The outputs

Prof. Azmi Mahafza
(The current president)

Prof. Ekhleif Tarawneh

Prof. Adel Altweisi

Prof. Khalid AlKaraki

of public education have been shown for all subjects and grades, and many vocational fields have achieved medium results. Teachers have been given a training program to develop the basic skills of information technology and computer. Moreover, they have been trained and granted certificates of the

Prof. AbdulRaheem AlHunaiti

Prof. Abdullah AlMousa

International Computer Driving License (ICDL) and World Links. Actually, %80 of teachers began to adopt modern teaching methods that comply with the knowledge based economy education.

Jordanian students have witnessed a notable improvement in the international standards of the scientific and mathematical courses. The international and regional rank has made a steady pace from 2003 to 2007 representing an unequaled achievement in most of the countries of the world.

Jordan also aspires to allow a developed and motivating educational environment by establishing environmentally-distinctive educational facilities and the use of computer information and technology inside the classrooms in order to reinforce the educational experience of

Prof.
Walid Maani

Prof.
Fawzi Gharaibeh

Prof.
Mahmoud Samrah

Prof.
Ishaq AlFarhan

Prof.
AbdulSalam AlMajali

Prof.
Abdulkareem Khalefah

Prof.
Naser Aldeen AlAsad

students. About %70 of basic and secondary students have an access to the electronic education portals, and %84 of schools connect to the internet through Jordan Telecom and Jordan National Broadband Network.

- **Higher Education:**

Access to higher education is open to holders of the General Secondary Education Certificate who can then choose between private Community Colleges, public Community Colleges or universities (public and private). The credit-hour system, which entitles students to select courses according to a study plan, is implemented at universities.

This system also allows the student to flexibly choose the number of hours and the morning or evening permanency.

There are ten public universities; most of them are associated with universities in the United States and the UK. There are also 17 private universities that are recognized on the Arab countries level, in addition to some foreign universities such as the American University and the German Jordanian University.

• **The Public universities of Jordan:**

1- The University of Jordan

2- Yarmouk University

3- Mutah University

4- Jordan University of Science & Technology

5- The Hashemite University

6- Al albayt University

7- AL-Balqa Applied University

8- Al Hussein Bin Talal University

9- Tafila Technical University

10- German Jordanian University

11- The World Islamic Sciences and Education University

- **The private universities and educational institutions of Jordan include:**

1- Amman Arab University

2- Applied Science University

3- Philadelphia University

4- Isra University

5- Petra University

6- Al-Zaytoonah University of Jordan

7- Jerash University

8- Irbid National University

9- Zarqa University

10- Princess Sumaya University for Technology

11- Amman Arab University

12- Middle East University

13- Jadara University

14- American University of Madaba

15- Ajloun National University

16- Jordan Applied University College of Hospitality and Tourism Education

17- Jordan Academy of Music

18- University of Finance and Banking

19- Arab Open University / Jordan Branch

20- Faculty of Educational Sciences and Arts /UNRWA

The universities of Jordan attract Arab and non-Arab foreign students every year.

University stages and degrees include:

- **Associate degree (diploma):** it is obtained from community colleges. It is a two-year study after the secondary school.

- **Stage I Bachelor's Degrees:** normally take four years. In Pharmacy and Engineering, studies last for five years. In Medicine, they last for six years.

- **Stage II Master's Degrees:** it ranges from one to two years. There are other postgraduate degrees equivalent to the master's degree in some Jordanian universities like the Magisterstudium in the German Jordanian University, the DEA's degree in the Universities which follow the French system and the MBA for the students who have significant work experience.

- **Stage III Doctorate Degrees:** A Doctorate Degree is awarded after three to five years of further study. Its areas are so limited such as Islamic sharia and Arabic language.

THE HASHEMITE KINGDOM OF JORDAN

CHAPTER FIFTEEN

THE ARAB SPRING AND ITS INFLUENCE ON JORDAN

CHAPTER FIFTEEN
THE ARAB SPRING AND ITS INFLUENCE ON JORDAN

> Undoubtedly, the Arab Spring had an influence on Jordan. But fortunately, the nature of the Jordanian citizen and the Hashemite Leadership made its influence a peaceful one. This is one of the positive aspects of the Arab Spring on Jordan.

Jordan's response to the Arab Spring resulted in creating a national agenda and drawing a roadmap for reform. The reforms achieved in Jordan since the beginning of the reformist activism throughout one and a half years can be summarized in three stages:

The first stage: it is represented in the establishment of a national dialogue committee as an important station during the outbreak of the Arab Spring that contributed to calming the Jordanian street down. This committee had a public and official cover that included all the political, intellectual and social spectrums of society.

The second stage of reform: the great constitutional amendments represented a massive quantum leap that resulted in the abolition of some restrictions imposed by the 1952 Constitution that seized the political and parliamentary work,

the formation of an Independent Elections Commission, and achieving judicial independence.

The third stage: it is represented in the liberties laws, establishing Teachers' Association and a number of corruption issues referred to the judiciary.

The reflections of the Arab Spring on Jordan were positive. They have been represented in the mature public activism whose results include the constitutional amendments, Elections Law and fighting corruption.

In Jordan, we lived the experience of the Arab Spring. Despite the demonstrations and sit-ins, no single drop of blood has been shed.

The economic conditions undergone by Jordan are the biggest challenge for the administration due to the shortage of resources.

The Arab Spring has negative as well as positive impact that benefited the citizens and officials of Jordan. Governments should be attentive to them and treat the economic problems and favoritism. They should also activate accountability, censorship and corruption control. They also have to reduce unemployment; rationalize manpower in all areas of government work, and face the emerging repercussions by national dialogue between all parties.

The Arab Spring can be said to be a historical entitlement that all Arabs experienced in varying proportions. It also had a positive effect on Jordan thanks to the elevated sense of the Hashemite leadership and the awareness of the Jordanian people and their confident vision in this concern.

GLIMPSES OF THE MARCH OF THE HASHEMITE KINGDOM OF JORDAN WRITTEN BY AN ELITE OF BRITISH PARLIAMENTARIANS

"The United Kingdom and the Hashemite Kingdom of Jordan have a long standing relationship that has existed since the time of the founder of the kingdom, King Abdullah I of Jordan.

The kingdom's evolution is a remarkable phenomenon in our era, because it is one of the few Middle-Eastern countries that has undergone such a rapid development in this short time.

This book paints a detailed and fascinating picture of the kingdom's modern history, and is essential reading for all those who wish to understand the true nature of the reality of contemporary in Jordan."

- **Stephen Kinnock**

    Member of Parliament for Aberavon

"There has never been a more troubled time than the present for the people of the middle east and there has never been a greater need for a comprehensive and authoritative book that describes the modern Hashemite Kingdom of Jordan. Fortunately we now have such a book and in Mohamed Al-Tawara we have an author who combines facts with an elegance of style – even in translation from the original Arabic.

Many know the beauties and history of ancient Jordan but few can claim to understand or appreciate the nation from the time of King Abdullah I to the present day.

There is now no longer an excuse as this book will answer your questions but also pose others for the future.

Thoroughly recommended for any student of the region and for anyone who has experienced the mystery, history and wonder of this extraordinary and unique land."

- **Stephen Pound**

    Member of Parliament for Ealing North

"The UK has a long history of friendship with Jordan. In an uncertain world with unprecedented challenges in the Middle East, it is more important than ever to nurture and deepen those bonds of friendship and cooperation. At a personal level I also know that when you visit Jordan, it is an experience you never forget and that you come away with an affection for the country, its heritage and its people that never leaves you. I would urge anyone who has not been to Jordan to visit and to taste the magic for yourself."

- **Richard Burden**

    Member of Parliament for Birmingham Northfield

- *That's what some members of the British Parliament said about the Hashemite Kingdom of Jordan and His Majesty King Abdullah II Bin Al-Hussein*

CONCLUSION

In this book, we addressed the political, economic, scientific, historical, touristic as well as other information concerning the Hashemite Kingdom of Jordan. However, this is not sufficient for this period of the history of Jordan since its inception as a political system since the reign of His Majesty the late King Abdullah I to His Majesty King Abdullah II Bin Al Hussein , may Allah prolong his life. This period is difficult to be narrated in one book; the achievements are great; the challenges are heavy and the journey is extended: the journey that has put Jordan as a key player on the global, international and regional world's map.

This mission endured by the Hashemites, this Message incepted by King Abdullah I and ably reached King Abdullah II Bin Al Hussein is a lantern of civilization and progress built on the hands of men true to what they promised Allah, who enjoyed the highest levels of transparency and truthfulness with their people which exchanged their love with love and sacrifice.

Each Jordanian should raise his head in respect and recognition for these people who raised the Jordanians' heads high in the sky, eased all the difficulties in the paths of the future and lightened the dark horizons of Jordanians so that they can proceed confidently in their journey.

Blessed is the King!
Worthy of people's love,
How lucky are Jordanians
For this success above!

- The Author

REFERENCE

- Official Website of His Majesty King Abdullah II bin Al Hussein

- Official Website of Her Majesty Queen Rania Al-Abdullah

- Official Website of His Royal Highness Crown Prince Al Hussein Bin Abdullah II

- Cabinet of the Hashemite Kingdom of Jordan

- Royal Jordanian Airlines Website

- Jordan Ministry of Education Website

- The Official Site of the Jordanian e-Government

- Jordan Ministry of Foreign Affairs and Expatriates- the Kingdom Map

- Wikipedia, the free encyclopedia- The Hashemite Kingdom of Jordan

- History of the Hashemite Kingdom of Jordan- Jordan Chechen

- Constitution of Jordan – Wikipedia

- Ministry of Social Development- Hashemite Kingdom of Jordan

- Documentaries of the history of the Hashemite Kingdom of Jordan

- Documentaries of the policies of the Hashemite Kingdom of Jordan

- Website of the International Council for Human Rights, Arbitration, Politics and Strategic Studies

- Alrai Newspaper Website

- Addustour Newspaper Website

- Alghad Newspaper Website

- Jordan News Agency (Petra) Website

- Website of Jordan Phosphate Mines Co JPMC

- Website of Arab Potash Company

- The Constitutional Court of Jordan Website

- The Judicial Council of Jordan Website

- Jordan House of Representatives Website

- Jordan House of Senate Website

TABLE OF CONTENTS

Topic	Page
Dedication to His Majesty	9
Dedication	11
Introduction	13
Acknowledgements	17
Preface	19
Introduction	23
Jordan's National Unity From King Abdullah I, the Founder To King Abdullah II, the Reinforce	32
Jordan: A Fascinating Success and Notable Development Since the Establishment and Independence till the Present Day	39
Chapter One : The Hashemites and the Building of the New State	55
Chapter Two: His Majesty King Abdullah II and his Family	77
Chapter three: Facts about Jordan	173
Chapter Four: An Overview of Jordanian Politics	193
Chapter Five: Parliamentary Life and Political Parties in Jordan	207
Chapter Six: Jordanian Authorities	219
Chapter Seven: Foreign and Arab Relations	253
Chapter Eight: Components of the Society Demographics of Jordan	269
Chapter Nine: Jordan's Economy and Its Branches	285
Chapter Ten: Jordanian Professional Associations	343
Chapter Eleven: Media and Press	351
Chapter Twelve: Hashemite Statesmen of Jordan	357
Chapter Thirteen: Administrative Divisions of Jordan and the Development of the Capital, Amman	445
Chapter Fourteen: Education and Universities	459
Chapter Fifteen: The Arab Spring and its Influence on Jordan	469
Glimpses Written by an elite of British parliamentarians	473
Conclusion	476
References	478
Table of Contents	480

Langvara Translation Company

Printed in Great Britain
by Amazon